Energy and Transportation in the Atlantic Basin

Paul Isbell and Eloy Álvarez Pelegry
Editors

Center for Transatlantic Relations
The Paul H. Nitze School of Advanced International Studies
Johns Hopkins University

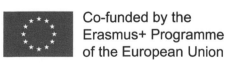

Co-funded by the
Erasmus+ Programme
of the European Union

Paul Isbell and Eloy Álvarez Pelegry, eds., *Energy and Transportation in the Atlantic Basin*

Distributed and available via Brookings Institution Press
https://www.brookings.edu/press/

Center for Transatlantic Relations
The Paul H. Nitze School of Advanced International Studies
The Johns Hopkins University
1717 Massachusetts Ave., NW, 8th Floor
Washington, DC 20036
Tel: (202) 663-5880
Fax: (202) 663-5879
Email: transatlantic@jhu.edu
http://transatlantic.sais-jhu.edu

ISBN 13: 978-1-947661-01-1

Cover Photograph: AKaiser, shutterstock.com

Contents

Preface

We are pleased to present the book *Energy and Transportation in the Atlantic Basin: Implications for the European Union and Other Atlantic Actors*, a collaboration among member institutions of the Jean Monnet Network on Atlantic Studies and the first tangible output of the Network's research efforts.

The Jean Monnet Network on Atlantic Studies is an initiative across the four Atlantic continents by 10 leading centers — many with Jean Monnet professors and in countries identified by the EU as key strategic partners — aimed at the interdisciplinary exploration of three pan-Atlantic themes of particular relevance to the EU: energy, commercial interactions, and challenges to human security.

The objective of the project is to create and develop a pan-Atlantic research network, to contribute to a nascent epistemic community in New Atlantic Studies and to offer strategic perspectives for the design of energy, trade and security policies in the countries of the Atlantic world. The Jean Monnet Project is also supported and co-funded by the Erasmus+ Program of the European Union.

The institutions involved in the Network consortium are each vibrant centers of EU-related studies in their respective regions. Most have collaborated — recently as part of the FP 7 project Atlantic Future — on themes related to Atlantic issues and the role of the EU as a key actor in this space.

Fundação Getulio Vargas, through its International Intelligence Unit, based in Rio de Janeiro, leads the consortium; its members are:

- Fundação Getulio Vargas (FGV), Brazil
- Johns Hopkins University SAIS (the Center for Transatlantic Relations, CTR), United States
- University of Pretoria, South Africa
- Universidade Nova de Lisboa (IPRI: Instituto Português de Relações Internacionais), Portugal
- CIDE (Centro de Investigación y Docencia Económicas), Mexico
- Roskilde University, Denmark

- Orkestra-Basque Institute for Competitiveness, University of Deusto, Spain
- CIDOB (Barcelona Centre for International Affairs), Spain
- Universidad Autónoma de Madrid, Spain
- OCP Policy Centre (OCP Foundation), Morocco

The Center for Transatlantic Relations of Johns Hopkins University SAIS led the first year's agenda on energy, and placed the focus on the nexus between energy and transportation. On July 20–21, 2017, the Jean Monnet Network´s first research conference (Energy and Transportation in the Atlantic Basin) took place at the John Hopkins University's Paul H. Nitze School of Advanced International Studies (SAIS) in Washington, D.C. Together with work leading up to and following it, the conference catalyzed the research and insights that have produced the book in hand.

We wish to show our appreciation to the European Commission, that provided the funding which has made this research and related book publication possible. We are especially grateful to the team at the leading institution, in Rio de Janeiro, and to all partners in the Network who have participated in the energy cycle, as well as the outside collaborators who have contributed to the conference and the book.

It is our hope that the present work will successfully propel this Jean Monnet Project into its next annual cycle, dealing with trade. In addition, that the Network will position its members individually and together as a go-to resource on the contemporary role of the EU in the wider Atlantic space, advancing the comparative knowledge of integration processes in Europe and other Atlantic regions.

Daniel S. Hamilton
Johns Hopkins University SAIS

Renato G. Flôres Jr.
International Intelligence Unit
Fundação Getulio Vargas

Introduction

Paul Isbell and Eloy Álvarez Pelegry

The purpose of this book is to stimulate the activity and effectiveness of the Jean Monnet Network on Atlantic Studies, to explore the current state and future directions of the nexus between energy and transportation in the wider Atlantic world, and to identify the implications for the European Union and other Atlantic actors.

The book draws on the collaboration, research and analysis of a number of colleagues from around the Atlantic Basin. They come from both the member institutions of the Network and beyond. Most have worked previously on issues pertinent to Atlantic energy, and have collaborated with the EU's *Atlantic Future* project, or with the Center for Transatlantic Relations' *Atlantic Basin Initiative*, or with one of the other wider Atlantic projects that have been undertaken in recent years by a number of public, private and academic entities around the Atlantic and now also contribute to what has become a budding epistemic and policy community in the New Atlantic— the wider Atlantic or the Atlantic Basin. The authors also come from a range of professions (academics, think tank analysts, development specialists, public and private sector practitioners) and they have made diverse types of contributions to the Jean Monnet Network project's research and analyses (chapters include academic, analytical, policy, and exploratory strategic pieces).

The book attempts to draw an initial, analytical Atlantic map of the nexus between energy and transportation—and of their potential co-transformations—highlighting the strategic terrains of the maritime realm, ongoing economic globalization and global value chains, multi-sector technological transformation, climate change, development and governance. The book also builds upon (and modifies) insights from previous work undertaken within the context of the Atlantic Future project and the Atlantic Basin Initiative.

In Chapter One, R. Andreas Kraemer lays out the current contexts, trends and outlooks in energy and transportation across the wider Atlantic and on each of the Atlantic continents, and concludes that energy and transportation are now engaged in an interdependent process of co-transformation which is moving principally in the direction of more renewable energy in the energy matrix and more electrification in general, but particularly in transportation.

In Chapter Two, Martin Lowery and Michael Leitman analyze three nascent trends and potential lines of action—the democratization of energy, the dynamic grid, and the broader electrification of the economy—which together could contribute to an economically beneficial and emissions-reducing transformation of the energy and transportation sectors of the Atlantic Basin. They propose an alternative business model, the energy cooperative, as a potential vehicle for contributing to the transformation.

Part Two is dedicated to energy and land transportation in the Atlantic Basin. In Chapter Three, Eloy Álvarez Pelegry, Jaime Menéndez Sánchez, and Macarena Larrea Basterra present empirical data on the recent evolution of alternative vehicles and fuels in European passenger transportation (focusing on electric and gas vehicles) and they analyze their future trends. On the basis of their original study of passenger mobility in the Basque country, they conclude that electric vehicles and hybrids (with some contribution from gas vehicles) represent the overall best options for decarbonizing the European passenger transportation sector.

In Chapter Four, Lisa Viscidi and Rebecca O'Connor present the panorama for energy and transportation in Latin America and the Caribbean (LAC), placing the focus on passenger and public transportation. They highlight the potential for more vehicle fuel efficiency, quality and emissions standards to reduce greenhouse gas GHG and air pollutant emissions in LAC, as well as the need to maintain investment in public and urban transportation, and to encourage electric vehicle penetration, if the region is not to experience more than a doubling of transport emissions by 2050.

In Chapter Five, Roger Gorham analyzes the expanding carbon footprint of African transportation and reviews the broad policy options available to African decision-makers and other relevant actors, along with the many of the barriers to their successful application. He identifies a number of potential modal shifts (reform of the private informal bus sector, more public urban transportation, improvements to last-mile connectivity through use of ICT applications and sharing platforms, a potential shift of freight from road to rail) along with smart motorization policy to reduce the fleet's average age, as policy areas with decarbonization potential in the short to middle run.

Part Three is dedicated to energy and transportation in the maritime realm of the Atlantic Basin. In Chapter Six, Jordi Bacaria and Natalia Soler-Huici bring our discussion of Atlantic energy and transportation, and of their decarbonization nexus, into the maritime realm. They trace the history of the expansion of the shipping industry, and of maritime GHG and air pollutant emissions, and analyze their various drivers (including the declines in shipping costs, containerization of manufactured goods trade, increases in shipping volume and vessel size, improvements in ship design and efficiency, the ongoing development of global value chains, among others). They evaluate the history of the regulation of maritime emissions by the International Maritime Organization, balanced against projected trends in maritime emissions growth, and propose Atlantic Basin cooperation, led by the European Union, to reduce maritime emissions at a faster rate in the Atlantic.

In Chapter Seven, João Fonseca Ribeiro focuses on the strategic potential of port-cities as policy fulcrums for the decarbonization of energy and transportation in the Atlantic Basin, and not only in the maritime realm. He maps out the various integrated sustainable growth strategies of both the EU and the African Union in energy, transportation, infrastructure, maritime affairs and climate change, emphasizing the importance of such strategy and policy integration, and highlighting their impact upon, and the integrated role they envision for, port-cities. After analyzing current trends affecting port-cities, and offering a vision of the strategic and policy paths port-cities might pursue, he proposes pan-Atlantic cooperation—again possibly spearheaded by Europe—among Atlantic Basin port-cities for the greening of maritime energy, transportation, and climate change infrastructures.

The Shifting Atlantic Energy Renaissance: From Unconventional And Offshore Oil To Low Carbon Energy

Only a few years ago, as the last oil price cycle enjoyed its peak—a plateau of $95–$110 per barrel that lasted from 2010 to 2014—an Atlantic energy renaissance took shape in the form of a boom in unconventional and offshore oil and gas. During that time, the shale revolution of North America was paralleled and accompanied by a unique new Atlantic oil ring that was also emerging in the deep offshore, particularly in the Southern Atlantic (if largely unnoticed by many American and European observers).

It was noted at the time that, as a result of such a sudden and clear preeminence taking root on the frontiers of what had traditionally been known as difficult or expensive hydrocarbons—and not just in the U.S. or the Hemisphere of the Americas, but also across the wider Atlantic space—the center of gravity for global energy supply had begun to shift out of the Great Crescent (comprised of the Middle East, Central Asia and Russia) and into the Atlantic Basin (Europe, Africa, Latin America and the Caribbean, North America and the maritime realm of the Atlantic Ocean). At the same time, the center of gravity for global energy demand was shifting from the Northern Atlantic to Eurasia—but particularly East Asia.[1.]

After long decades during which many Westerners (or Atlantics) felt compromised in economic, geopolitical, and security terms by their oil import dependency, the wider Atlantic region, taken as a whole, had rapidly become energy autonomous. Indeed, large parts of the basin—especially North America and the Southern Atlantic—appeared on the verge of becoming important exporters at the margin to the oil-import dependent East, the oil demand of which was now beginning to outstrip the capacity of the Middle East to supply it, at least as long as the Atlantic world remained oil import dependent in net terms.

Putting aside, for the moment, the various possible interpretations, then and now, of the geopolitical significance of an Atlantic energy renaissance—against the backdrop of the Pivot to Asia and the belief in an Asian or Pacific Century—the debate over the usefulness of energy as a geopolitical lever or over significance of the weighting of the energy variable within the equation of geopolitical power, the important issue to note with respect to energy and transportation is that any such Atlantic energy renaissance had been based on a technological revival of fossil fuels, and sustained by a relatively high oil price. As a result, the energy horizon of Atlantic Basin that emerged during the period of the last oil price peak was one centered around (and implicitly assuming) continued and sustained fossil fuel relevance, if not centrality.

As an extension of this horizon, the predominant view of the future of Atlantic transportation assumed the maintenance of the status quo's traditional fossil-liquids-based transportation system, and its infrastructure base and marketing networks around the world. This fossil-liquids transport system serves internal combustion engine vehicles, run on liquid derivatives of fossil fuels (mainly gasoline and diesel), principally on roads (and to a much lesser extent rail), along with the equivalent fossil-liquid-powered ships and jet planes in the maritime and aviation spheres and their respective infrastructures (ports and airports).

---

1. See Paul Isbell, "An Introduction to the Future of Energy in the Atlantic Basin," in Paul Isbell and Eloy Alvarez Pelegry (eds.), *The Future of Energy in the Atlantic Basin* (Washington, D.C., Center for Transatlantic Relations, JHU SAIS, 2015).

In part this was because, at that time, feasible alternatives to the current fossil-liquids transportation system did not emerge clearly. The fuel switching options available to transport were generally constrained to fossil fuels—compressed natural gas (CNG), liquefied natural gas (LNG) and liquid petroleum gases. The only other obvious liquid alternative to gasoline or diesel are biofuels. While they are compatible in certain percentages with the current liquids-based transportation infrastructure, biofuels are only economically viable and environmentally suitable in certain countries of the Southern Atlantic (like Brazil and some Atlantic African countries) and Southeast Asia, and even then, not as a comprehensive alternative capable of fully displacing fossil fuels in transportation.

The most comprehensive alternative—electrification, if in conjunction with LNG, and possibly renewable energies (RE)-generated synfuels including biogas—would require a large-scale transformation of the underlying infrastructure configuration: the transportation and manufacturing and fossil liquids industries and infrastructures would need to be transformed or displaced by the progressive and widespread electrification of the transportation sector and supported by significant RE penetration in the generation mix.

Until recently, this has always been viewed as too far away in the future to be seriously considered, particularly given the growing perception of fossil abundance that came with the first phase of the Atlantic energy renaissance. During the last high oil price cycle, the power over mind-sets, across continents, countries and classes, of the long-standing centrality of the fossil fuel industry, epitomized and symbolized by the automobile and the truck, remained intact and largely dominant. Renewable energies, already showing enormous promise and basically begging for rollout support and capacity investment, were still considered too expensive and too unreliable by enough people in many places. What passed for a common sense, real world consensus still provided support for the fossil-dominated energy reality of the global map. Meanwhile, the ships of the maritime realm, even more so than the planes and jets of the airspace, remained largely at the margins of the consciousness of a land-centered, continentally-focused global public.

But the horizon for the Atlantic energy renaissance, and the future of transportation, have both rapidly and radically shifted since the great oil price collapse of 2014-2016 (which established the current price plateau of around $45 to $55 a barrel). Much of the deep offshore oil of the Atlantic Basin was suddenly pushed back beyond the horizon by prices below $50 (most Atlantic offshore oil required an oil price of at least $70-$80 to be economical to produce). Even the shale sector experienced significant consolidation and a slowing of production. However, despite the lower prices, renewable energy continued to boom. As costs continued to fall, decarbonization of the power sector proceeded apace. In the wake of the Paris Agreement, attention has turned to the next major sector in line: transportation.

For the first time in the history of fossil energy, the return of a sustainable upward cycle in oil price has been put into serious doubt. The last upward cycle of the oil price (roughly from 2004 to 2014) not only began to kill off demand and to overstimulate production of more high-cost oil and gas (i.e., in the offshore), it also provided support to renewable energy which, together with scattered if growing state facilitation and backing, and ongoing RE and battery cost declines, has been minimally sufficient for the sector to become established and to begin to challenge the growth of fossil fuels. Not only did oil demand fall in cyclical terms; it also began to structurally disappear. With the passing of just a decade, attention has shifted from the controversy over peak oil (a projected imminent peak in global supply) to a discussion over the timing of the arrival of peak demand.

Today the Atlantic energy renaissance has transformed from a story about emerging Atlantic Basin dominance in fossil fuel supply (and its geopolitical implications) to one about the growing realities and potentials of renewable energy, alternative fuels and electrification in transportation, dynamic grid transformation, and the emergence of new business market and regulatory models, along with the establishment and exchange of Atlantic best practices. This book explores the nature of this shift in the Atlantic energy renaissance and its intersection with Atlantic transportation, the bastion of oil. The incumbency of oil in transportation is far more central and structurally influential than the market power and infrastructural hold of any of the fossil fuels in any other sector, making its transformation the key climate change challenge.

Transportation As the Key to the Low Carbon Transition

During the last decade, as a nascent low carbon economy began to take shape around the world, the bulk of decarbonization efforts have concentrated on renewable energy rollout within the electricity sector. As a result, and considering projected policy, technology and cost trends foreseen within the Paris Agreement, the prospects for decarbonizing the world's power sectors by mid-century are, depending on the scenario considered, now relatively optimistic. Nevertheless, without a corresponding decarbonization effort in the multi-modal and multiply-segmented global transportation sector, defending the 2-degree guardrail of the Paris Agreement is probably out of reach.

As the group of eight multilateral development banks (MDBs) maintained in a joint statement on the eve of the Paris accord: "Actions to reduce greenhouse gas emissions and stabilize warming at 2 degrees Celsius will fall short if they do not include the transport sector." Near complete decarbonization of transportation will almost certainly be necessary to achieve the even more ambitious target of 1.5 degrees C.

The transportation sector burns nearly two-thirds of the oil consumed each day around the world and represents 27 percent of all energy used globally. As a result, transportation now accounts for one-quarter of all energy-related CO_2 emissions and over 15 percent of *total global* GHG emissions (including F-gases and emissions from the land sectors). Furthermore, transportation is growing more quickly—around 2 percent a year—than all other energy demand sectors. As a result, the transport sector is the fastest growing source of GHG emissions, with a projected 70 percent increase by 2050.

As the second largest total GHG source after the power sector (31 percent), transportation is basically on par with the emissions produced by the land sectors—collectively known as AFOLU emissions (agriculture, 10.5 percent of total global GHG gases in 2015, and forestry and land-use, 6 percent). This makes transportation the new central arena in the decarbonization of the world's energy economy. Such an emissions profile also clearly implies that forest protection and the restoration of degraded lands are also key strategic supports to the global decarbonization effort on the land side of the GHG equation. In addition, beyond the transportation and land-use sectors, the next major strategic area of action will be the development of blue ecosystems services as the sustainability lever for the growth of the blue (or ocean) economy. Indeed, energy and transportation, agriculture, forestry and land-use, and the broader maritime realm are all positioned for major co-transformation.

Overlapping Energy, Transportation, and ICT Co-Transformations

The transformations now underway in energy, transportation and information and communications technology (ICT) (including smart phones, social media, automation, internet of things, etc) have long developed along largely separate tracks with different rhythms and patterns. Nevertheless, there has been mutual interaction among different pairs of this trilogy of sectors. Energy and transportation infrastructure have reinforced each other for a century and continue to mutual depend on each other (see R. Andreas Kraemer, Chapter One). The ICT revolutions have fed transportation volume and shaped its structural and modal evolution both on land and at sea. Global transportation, in turn, is being transformed in a structural fashion by both the ongoing push of economic globalization and the shifting development of global value chains—both of which are stimulated by ICT advances— and by the nearly-universal global consensus that the sector must be decarbonized (see Jordi Bacaria and Natalia Soler-Huici, Chapter Six).

In their current transformative stages, however, these revolutions are beginning to integrate with each other at their common intersection. The synergistic result is a growing movement in the direction of (1) an increasingly electrified world of (2) increasingly distributed low carbon energy production, incorporating (3) prosumer economic participation in generation and the provision of storage (and other ancillary) services to the grid, and (4) integrated by ICT applications and related technological advances for effecting efficient market transactions and technical clearings in (5) an increasingly interactive and electricity based energy and transportation system.

Because of the numerous potential synergies presented by the overlapping of these global transformations, their current intersection appears to structurally favor renewable energies, electricity, and electrification of transportation more than any other energy, energy carrier, or transport infrastructure. As a result, these co-transformations are also contributing to further transform both the automobile industry and the multimodal transportation network, enabling deeper electric vehicle (EV) and electricity penetration, in both freight and passenger transportation, in both the maritime and terrestrial transportation realms (see R. Andreas Kraemer, Chapter One).

This is not to say that the future of energy and transportation is to be electric, only that a large part of the land-based (and some of the maritime) systems easily could be. As the authors of this volume either explicitly acknowledge or implicitly accept, a largely (if not completely) electrified world probably would not be the worst of possible futures, at least not in the wider Atlantic. Nevertheless, there is also a range of other approaches, independent of electrification, which offer the potential to reduce emissions in the transportation sector.

Transportation Contexts and Trends in the Atlantic Basin

Transportation is a segmented sector supporting and binding national, continental, and global economies. The sector is split by function between passenger and freight transportation, and is segmented by mode of transport: (1) road; (2) rail; (3) ship; and (4) air. Although both passengers and freight can conceivably move by all transportation modes, certain types of transport demand are more dominant within certain modes than others. For example, 60 percent of global transport demand is passenger transportation, which is growing at a rate of 1.5 percent annually on average, and such growth is projected to continue 2040. Most of this transportation demand is still focused on roads. This is particularly true of Europe, where the road segment accounted for 82.5 percent of the total EU passenger transport in 2012 (see Eloy Álvarez Pelegry, et al, Chapter Three). The same is basically as true for Latin America and Africa, where private demand for light-vehicle passenger vehicle travel are poised to boom—unless such projected future demand is shifted successfully to public transportation which uses higher capacity road and rail vehicles. The global vehicle fleet numbers approximately 1.2 billion today, around 95 percent are light-duty passenger cars. That number is expected to hit 2 billion by 2035. Clearly, efficient and low-carbon transformation of road passenger light duty vehicle traffic is a key priority on all the Atlantic continents.

However, freight and cargo transportation are also significant and growing, particularly in the Southern Atlantic. Freight traffic can be divided into bulk/dry goods (including solid energy, like coal), liquid energy (like oil and LNG) and container traffic (principally manufactured goods, and which can easily travel on different modes). Freight transport in non-OECD will grow by 30 percent from 2015 to 2040. More than half of the growth of the world's freight transportation energy use will come from non-OECD countries. Freight traffic is still predominantly undertaken by heavy-duty road vehicles (i.e., trucks), at least on land, but maritime cargo has also increased significantly in recent decades and continues to do so (see Jordi Bacaria et al, Chapter Six). On the other hand, rail transport could take on a greater role, as part of a mode shift to cut transportation costs and overall freight transport emissions, if only in certain regions under particular circumstances (see Roger Gorham, Chapter Five; and João Fonseca Ribeiro, Chapter Seven).

The four land-based energy and transportations systems of the Atlantic world have each been configured within the respective possibilities created, and limits imposed, by the concrete geographies and specific economic and technological histories of their corresponding continental spheres. As such, they are quite distinct from each other, and relatively independent and autonomous (see R. Andreas Kraemer, Chapter One). Yet they have all been shaped and are increasingly linked by the maritime energy and transportation space of the Atlantic Basin (see Jordi Bacaria and Natalia Soler-Huici, Chapter Six, and João Fonseca Ribeiro, Chapter Seven).

Northern Atlantic land-based transportation sectors are relatively mature: in the U.S. and Europe, where fuel economy and vehicle emissions standards have had a long and relatively effective history, oil demand and emissions have levelled, and efficiency has risen. Indeed, in Europe and the U.S., the growing if nascent (and not completely exclusive) trend, in large part stimulated by these very vehicle and fuel standards, is toward electric vehicles in passenger mobility and LNG in road-based (i.e., heavy-duty vehicles) and maritime freight transport (see Álvarez Pelegry et al, Chapter Three and Fonseca Ribeiro, Chapter Seven). Although EVs still only comprise about 1 percent of the light-duty vehicle fleet in the Northern Atlantic and Asian economies, the EV market is poised at an inflection point, propelled forward by the rapid development of new influencing factors.

Collapsing renewable energy prices and lower battery costs are driving the energy and transportation co-transformations. Renewable electricity generation has fallen more than 50 percent in the last decade and a similar reduction is forecast for the next ten years. The story is the same with respect to the costs of battery storage: McKinsey projects that battery prices will fall from $383/kWh in 2015 to $197/kWh in 2020, to $163/kWh in 2025, and to as low as $150/kWh in 2030 (see Álvarez Pelegry et al, Chapter Three). The home solar complexes (solar roof panels—even elegant tiles— together with electric vehicles and home battery and charging facilities) now being promoted by Tesla (and highlighted by R. Andreas Kraemer in Chapter One) represent a key infrastructure nexus that can drive the electrification of the passenger transportation sector, particularly in the U.S. and Europe.

In Europe, integrated policies are in place to promote alternative transportation fuels and the strategic expansion of broader continental transportation infrastructures (along with the specific infrastructures for electric and compressed natural gas vehicles, and LNG facilities for cargo transport included in the TEN-T EU transportation corridor and infrastructure strategy), thus removing one of the principal barriers to the rapid expansion of EVs and electrification of transport more broadly. The EU's integrated energy, transport and climate strategies also incorporate the broader maritime realm, and maritime transport in particular, as well as the crucial land/sea-energy/transportation interfaces of the port-cities, in an overarching climate and green growth strategy to meet the objectives of Europe's 20-20-20 program and the Paris Agreement (see Álvarez Pelegry et al, Chapter Three and Fonseca Ribeiro, Chapter Seven).

In North America, the principal transportation policies focus on fuel efficiency standards (including a mandatory target of 36mpg by 2025, along with the only existing targets in the world for heavy freight vehicles). Furthermore, gas continues to displace coal in the generation mix and renewable energies (REs) now dominate new capacity additions. States and cities have become the principal promotors and facilitators of the uptake of REs in the generation mix, and even of public transportation. Electrification of transportation is also proceeding apace, increasingly in a sustainable self-generating way, as costs of both renewables and batteries continue to fall, and as new EV models penetrate the market (see R. Andreas Kraemer, Chapter One; and Eloy Álvarez Pelegry et al, Chapter Three).

Meanwhile, in the Southern Atlantic of Latin America and Africa, much of the land-based transportation demand which accompanies economic development—which the U.S. and Europe have already experienced—has not yet taken place. But without a change in energy, transportation and other related policies and practices, a massive increase in transport demand is on its way in the Southern Atlantic, along with the significant increase in all types of emissions (GHGs and air pollutants like NOx and SOx) that will come with it. Furthermore, in both of these continents, fuel efficiency, quality and emissions standards are either weak or non-existent, and they are undermined by significant imports of second-hand vehicles from the advanced economies which are older, dirtier and less efficient (see Lisa Viscidi and Rebecca O'Connor, Chapter Four; and Roger Gorham, Chapter Five)

In Latin America and the Caribbean region, where urbanization rates are high (85 percent) and growing, much passenger transportation already takes place via public transportation networks. More than one-third of all Latin Americans rely on the use of public transportation on a daily basis, but in many cities this number is higher than 50 percent (Bogota, Medellin, Lima and Quito) and in some cases, like Mexico City and Panama City, more than two-thirds (see Lisa Viscidi and Rebecca O'Connor, Chapter Four). However, with continued economic growth the private transportation fleet is mushrooming as the middle class continues to expand (and as last-mile connectivity continues to be a challenge for public transportation), driving demand for light-duty vehicles. The region has the fastest growing motorization rate in the world, around 4.5 percent a year. Motorization has nearly doubled from 2000—from 100 vehicles per 1000 inhabitants to 170. The LAC regional fleet is expected to triple to more than 200mn vehicles in 2050, according to business as usual projections.

Meanwhile Africa generates only 3 percent of global CO_2 emissions and only 4 percent of transport-related CO_2 emissions. This is low by global standards but still a concern for the future given that the intensity of transport-related CO_2 emissions relative to economic output is high; therefore, as African economies continue to grow, transport emissions will rise faster in Africa than in other world regions (see Roger Gorham, Chapter Five). Also, the proportion of CO_2 emissions than come from transport is higher than in most other regions. Transport emissions are growing faster than any other source of emissions in Africa. The current and expected dynamics of transport emissions in LAC is similar to those of Africa, if somewhat less acute.

This situation is the result, on the one hand, of a still high level of energy poverty—most people in Africa (65 percent to 75 percent) do not have access to electricity or clean cooking fuels, let alone to private vehicle transportation—and, on the other hand, to the current predominance of the informal private bus sector in the passenger transportation sphere. Anywhere from 36 percent to 100 percent (with a median of 86 percent across a group of 20 African cities) of all road-based passenger transport was carried by paratransit vehicles, mainly minivans and small buses (see Roger Gorham, Chapter Five). This dominant mode share is characterized by market weakness and informalities, along with an aging, inefficient and dirty fleet, making it a challenge to effectively reform even as it holds much potential for improving economic efficiency and last-mile connectivity with public transportation, and reducing emissions. Compounding such barriers and problems are the previously mentioned realities that Africa (and to a lesser extent LAC) is a technology taker in the energy and transportation sectors, and that vehicle inefficiencies and emissions leak from the Northern Atlantic into Africa in the form of poorly regulated second-hand vehicle imports.

In the realm of freight transportation infrastructure, and of multi-modal linkages between land and maritime transport, Africa has attempted to follow Europe's lead, in its own way, to map out a transportation corridor and infrastructure strategy (both terrestrial and maritime), consistent with long term development goals, the post-Millennium goals and the decarbonization of transport. This integrated continental strategy is manifested in the African

Union's Agenda 2063, the 2050 Africa's Integrated Maritime Strategy, and the Program for Infrastructure Development in Africa (PIDA). Nearly $30 billion is being invested by the multilaterals, regional instruments and other donor countries, within this strategic framework, in ten major transport corridors and in port expansion projects in more than 10 Africa countries (see Fonseca Ribeiro, Chapter Seven). But in Africa trade and customs restrictions rival the lack of transport infrastructures as the major barrier to more intra-African trade.

Policy Approaches to the Decarbonization of Atlantic Transportation

Given these distinct states of economic and transportation development across the wider Atlantic space, it is useful to view the different Atlantic continents and maritime sphere through the lens of the EASI framework (developed by the Africa Transport Policy Program; see Roger Gorham, Chapter Five). This analytical framework provides for a policy-based decomposition of the sources of CO_2 growth and consists of four layers, or angles, of approach — (1) Enable; (2) Avoid; (3) Shift; and (4) Improve — that may be utilized for increasing the efficiency, and reducing the emissions, of the transportation sector in each continental sphere of the Atlantic Basin.

The Enable component is grounded in the quality and resilience of the institutions of governance, regulation, and policy. This is the foundational realm of the state (and its various subnational instances) which can contribute to (or undermine) the transformation of transportation and its decarbonization. It determines the ability of governments and governance systems to organize themselves in a manner than can generate CO_2 emissions savings via the other methods of approach (i.e., to avoid future transport demand, to shift transport demand from one mode to another, and to improve the vehicles, and fuels/modes of propulsion, involved in each mode). Broadly speaking, the Enable component is stronger in the Northern than in the Southern Atlantic; and it is also relatively more effective in Latin America than in Africa.

The Avoid approach engages land-use, urban and transportation planning in order to avoid future individual passenger demand altogether. Generally speaking, this can be achieved through the design and development of dense, compact multi-use urban environments capable of relying on high volumes of public transport, mass transit and non-motorized transportation (e.g., bicyles and walking). The Avoid approach is most suitable in European urban settings (and to a lesser extent North America), but this is tougher to achieve in the dynamic, highly unregulated demographic and economic patterns (and imperfect markets) of Africa where cities tend to sprawl in a way that fails to capitalize upon the positive aggregating economic effects that cities in the North have generally produced (See Roger Gorham, Chapter Five) LAC falls somewhere between the Northern Atlantic and Africa with respect to the short-term viability of such an Avoid approach.

The Shift approach incorporates the realm of multi-modal transportation infrastructure, policy, and reform. In the area of passenger mobility this typically involves a shift of passenger traffic from lower occupancy private light duty vehicles (the road passenger transport mode) to the higher occupancy vehicles of public transportation and mass transit, (including bus rapid transit, metros and light rail). With respect to freight transport, this could also involve shifting cargo traffic from truck transportation on roads to railroad transport. This is generally more feasible as an approach in the Northern Atlantic, where infrastructure exists and capital for its further development is more available, markets are less imperfect, regulatory regimes are more established, and a history of urban planning is more entrenched. However, the Shift approach is also already well-developed in LAC and could be applied in Africa with appropriate financing, planning, attention to emerging technologies, smart regulation, and targeted market intervention (see Roger Gorham, Chapter Five).

Finally, the Improve approach focuses on improving the quality of transportation vehicles (cars, trucks and ships, for example) and/or their fuels. This can be achieved through appropriate policy and regulatory standards which mandate higher fuel efficiency and quality, and lower emissions. The response of the energy and automotive sectors in the face of obligatory standards could stimulate the production and marketing of lower emissions vehicles and fuels, and even, perhaps, the electrification of transportation.

Such Improve techniques are now more than evident in the more mature energy and transport economies of the Northern Atlantic continents. In part this is because the less mature transportation systems in the Southern Atlantic are technology takers (as Kraemer points out in Chapter One) and as such are dependent on the technological improvements in vehicles and fuels developed elsewhere. But they are also often dependent on these same foreign markets, typically in the Northern Atlantic or Asia, for their supplies of vehicles and fuels as well. Therefore, the Southern Atlantic paradoxical serves as a sink accumulating the leakage from more advanced economies of typically older, less efficient and higher-emitting vehicles which, once retired from the markets of Europe and North America by technological improvements and increasingly stringent vehicle and fuel standards, leak into the Southern Atlantic, where they are sold as cheaper secondhand vehicles, far more accessible to the middle classes, and the masses aspiring to middle class status in Africa's cities, which are growing at the fastest rates in the world (see Roger Gorham, Chapter Five).

Despite the structural barriers that face the Southern Atlantic with respect to energy and transportation transformation, including the leakage of second-hand vehicles from the Northern Atlantic and Asia, weaker regulatory regimes and enforcement, and the role of the informal market, some interesting opportunities present themselves at this juncture, particularly to Africa but also to Latin America. These opportunities take the form of technological and organizational leapfrogging and can be clearly grasped from the developing context of two other technological and policy realms impacting upon the energy-transportation nexus in the Atlantic Basin: (1) the changing nature and potentials of the dynamic electric grid, particularly with respect to energy and transportation, and the various new business, market, system and regulatory models that are emerging to shape and engage such a modernized and transformed grid; and (2) the maritime realm of energy and transportation, and the port-cities which serve as the geographic, strategic and policy interfaces of land and sea transportation, the key enablers of global value chains, and the environmental stewards of the blue economy.

The Changing Nature and Potentials of the Electric Grid

The electric grid was once the specialized and relatively stable terrain of engineers, public utilities, and regulators. For most of the last century, the grid in its various national and regional forms remained highly centralized, handling one-way flows of electricity (traditionally generated from coal, nuclear, hydro and oil, but with time also gas, and more recently REs) from central power stations, through the transmission networks and distribution systems, to the end-user. The most interesting aspect of the traditional centralized grid model was the long-running attempt to resolve its ongoing and changing regulatory challenges, and to maintain fair and stable balance between producers and consumers.

However, possibilities for a more dynamic grid are emerging. Multiple new horizons have been opened up by new and interlocking technological developments in energy, transportation and ICT and related sectors, many of which enable demand side measures (DSM) to efficiently manage two-way flows of energy and data, on much more flexible and linked grids (including microgrids), and with much more effective storage capacity, a higher amount of distributed energy generation, less need for investment in (and management of) transmission systems, higher overall efficiency and quality, and increasingly lower energy and transportation emissions (see Lowery and Leitman, Chapter Two),

There is potential for major grid modernization and transformation all across the wider Atlantic space, and in many parts of the Southern Atlantic this presents itself in the form of enormous leapfrog potential with respect to both the utility-centric, centralized grid model and to continued use of fossil fuels in transport and their accompanying infrastructures.

In Northern Atlantic, this would imply upgrading and modernizing an already mature and complex grid to accommodate a changing, increasingly low carbon energy mix. In LAC, where there is nearly universal access, the challenge is to adapt the existing grids to harness additional low emitting technologies so that further economic development and increased per capital electricity consumption does not result in significant increases in GHGs. In Africa, where electricity access is still highly limited, grids are not fully deployed in rural areas, and where national grids do exist, they tend to function poorly, and their reach is limited. Distributed RE-powered microgrids (possibly administered through ESCOS, energy services companies, or through energy cooperatives) could facilitate a leapfrogging of an entire infrastructural stage in development. A largely non-grid reality could evolve into microgrids and then into a network of microgrids.

Within this context of potential grid transformation, new models of energy generation and distribution have begun to emerge in the Atlantic Basin, primarily in the Northern Atlantic, but they also hold much promise for the South.

First, there has been the development of distributed energy resource systems (DERs) which are characterized by small scale generation and a closer positioning to the centers of demand. When connected to other grids DERs provide for significant resilience and demand-side management possibilities which reduce the need for transmission line planning and investment, and the political opposition that often comes with it.

The efficiency of both connected grids and microgrids will depend on managing two-way flows of data and power. An agile fractal grid would be able to isolate sections of a distribution system for protection purposes and to provide a reliably continuous flow of power from DERs when central station power is not available. Such an integration of the potentials of DERs and microgrids leads to a more resilient grid, which overlaps with climate change adaptation priorities. Grid resiliency would be even further enhanced by the progressive electrification of transport. Distributed energies, particularly renewables, microgrids, and ICT-supported platform, sharing and prosumer market and business models in energy, transportation and related sectors, along with further development of EVs, could drive such grid modernization.

Second, there is also the growing energy cooperative movement. Energy cooperatives are strongest and most widespread in North America and Europe, but they are expanding in Latin America and show much promise for Africa (see Lowery and Leitman, Chapter Two). Energy cooperatives in North America have grown out of the older commons model of rural electrification that was born in the 1930s and later spread. Cooperatives are now abetted by ICT and other related technologies. Some analysts see the convergence of these multiple technological and market trends as giving rise to a new energy commons in an increasingly zero-marginal cost society. Under such a perspective, cooperatives could become an alternative organizing principle and business model for the modernized and transformed dynamic grid, with the potential to stimulate renewables and transport electrification, and to facilitate technological leapfrogging, particularly in Africa (see Lowery and Leitman, Chapter Two; and João Fonseca Ribeiro, Chapter Seven).

The energy cooperative model—in which consumers of energy are also potentially owner/ producers as well as providers of energy storage and other ancillary services to the grid—overlays particularly well with the emerging trend toward distributed energy (as in community solar development) and the introduction of more flexible microgrids within and beyond the reach of national electricity grids. The cooperative model also dovetails very well with the more overarching trends generated by the mutual co-transformations of energy, transportation, ICT and related technological realms mentioned earlier: including the democratization and prosumerization of energy; the electrification and multi-modalization of transportation; and innovative ways of engaging the dynamic grid (see Lowery and Leitman, Chapter Two).

The cost and emissions synergies generated by the overlapping co-transformations in energy and transportation, in the broad ICT and technological realm, and in manufacturing and trade, are creating an interlocking set of policy and economic incentives pressing toward the prosumerization and democratization of energy production, the development of microgrids powered by distributed renewable energies (sometimes in combination with gas, hydro, or diesel), and the progressive electrification of transportation and the broader economy. This dynamic grid modernization and transformation would stimulate new market, business, system and regulatory models for the energy and transportation sectors capable of generating economic efficiency and emission reduction gains.

Any such transformative modernization of conventional centralized electricity grids would also force a redefinition of the function and role of what have traditionally been known as utilities. With the prosumerization of energy generation, use and trade, utilities could become distribution system operators (DSOs) and provide only grid management services, allowing and facilitating consumers to choose among multiple wholesale power and energy service suppliers. Alternatively, utilities could become more consumer-centric, offering or facilitating the same innovative energy services, in competition with other third-party providers (i.e., ESCOs).

The Maritime Energy and Transportation Realm in the Atlantic Basin

The Atlantic maritime realm is partially obscured by long-term terrestrial blinders that produce a widespread distorting mental map effect known as sea blindness—a generalized relative lack of consciousness of the sea and the realities and developments of the maritime realm. The Atlantic is no different than the other ocean basin regions in this regard.

One result of this blind spot in our policy and regulatory perspectives is that the Atlantic Ocean is in danger of becoming a potential sink for the leakage of air-borne emissions like GHGs and air pollutants from the continental reach of land-focused national and regional legislative and regulatory jurisdictions. This leakage is similar in effect to the earlier-mentioned leakage of second-hand (older, less-efficient, dirtier and higher emitting) vehicles from the Northern Atlantic into the Southern Atlantic vehicle sink. In this regard, the seas and oceans remain a vulnerable sink for pollution and emissions leakages from land-based regulatory regimes (see Jordi Bacaria and Natalia Soler-Huici, Chapter Six; and Fonseca Ribeiro, Chapter Seven).

While the land-based emissions regime is firmly under control of the UNFCCC process and the Paris Agreement, the maritime emissions regime has been delegated to the International Maritime Organization. This intergovernmental global organization has proceeded more slowly than land-based national policy and regulatory jurisdictions with respect to regulation of maritime air pollutants (which negatively affect the air quality of port-cities and coastal hinterlands), but especially of maritime GHG emissions (which affect the entire world by undermining the progress and effectiveness of land-based emissions reductions efforts framed by the UNFCCC and the Paris Agreement). (See Fonseca Ribeiro, Chapter Seven)

The maritime realm has undergone enormous transformation and growth in the last century, driven in large part by the globalization of the economy, the expansion of international trade, the boom in maritime transport and, more recently, the deepening and constantly shifting development of so-called global value chains. These trends, in turn, have been fed by a reduction in maritime transport costs, brought on by the continued increase in the size of ships, improvements in ship design and efficiency, and the containerization of much of merchandise trade in manufactured goods. All of this has contributed to an explosion in maritime trade and transport (see Jordi Bacaria and Natalia Soler-Huici, Chapter Six). Although the Atlantic Basin currently transports less maritime cargo than the other major ocean basins, much future maritime transport demand is poised come from Southern Atlantic economies.

In the second phase of post-Cold War (or post-Wall) globalization, global value chains have become interdependent with trade and transportation volumes, patterns, routes and modal systems. The more fragmented production is distributed throughout a geographically disperse value chain, the more intermediate goods comprise that value chain and, therefore, the more container transportation will be required. Expanding, deepening and shifting global value chains (GVCs) will continue to exert a trend toward increasing VKT (or vehicle kilometers traveled) of freight transportation as gross domestic product (GDP) rises. This has given rise to a paradox of carbon-efficient maritime transport: although maritime transportation is the least carbon-polluting transportation mode by unit of cargo transported, the overall increase in maritime transport demand—driven by falling costs and the development of global value chains based on multiplying types of intermediate goods—ends up pushing up overall maritime emissions, and at faster rates. Globalization, through global value chains and expanded trade and transportation, generates the externality of increasing the aggregate emissions from the maritime realm which is still only insufficiently regulated (see Jordi Bacaria and Natalia Soler-Huici, Chapter Six).

This challenge is compounded by the fact that the decarbonizing options available for maritime transport energy are less obvious and less diverse than those available for land-based transportation. Currently, LNG is the leading maritime fuel alternative to the use of bunker fuels (fuel oil) given that some gas infrastructure already exists, LNG is also relatively abundant and offers some air pollution and emissions reduction gains (see Joao Fonseca Ribeiro, Chapter Seven).

But as a result of deepening global value chains, an increasingly important mutual dependency has developed between terrestrial and maritime (and even air) transportation systems. The transport of merchandise trade in one of these systems often depends on, or conditions, the transport volumes and types in the other. International trade depends on the efficient functioning of both. Therefore, progressive movement toward renewable energy and the electrification of land transportation can facilitate and stimulate the progressive greening of maritime transportation through the provision of clean energy to ships while at shore in port (and even on approaches and departures).

In this emerging context of heightening mutual relevance and dependency between the terrestrial and maritime trade and transportation systems the role of the port-city takes on new salience. Port-cities serve as the geographic and modal interfaces for terrestrial and maritime transport, and as such become the strategic fulcrum and the integrated policy and regulatory platforms for the energy, transportation, ICT, manufacturing, trade and climate change co-transformations (see João Fonseca Ribeiro, Chapter Seven).

The port-city is an appropriate and effective level of governance for stemming regulatory leakages of emissions from the land into the sea, and it can act a lever for reducing both terrestrial and maritime emissions. As the natural nodes of influence over the blue growth of the Atlantic Ocean, port-cities can also serve as the economic and technological platforms for the sustainable development and governance of the blue (or ocean) economy.

But maritime transport and port-cities are increasingly subject to transformative pressures — including the trend toward deep water ports (as ship size continues to rise) and the ongoing deepening and shifting of GVCs (which intensifies competition between ports). The result can often be an antiquated and decaying port-city. Even when a port relocates, a port-city mismatch in policy and planning can lead to a long-term decline of the urban area around the old port and a lack of economic and regulatory integration between the new port and the city.

Cities are already increasingly acting as strategy and policy protagonists in the effort to reduce GHG emissions and air pollutants. They are increasingly interacting with each other in cooperative networks, sharing best practices, lessons learned and even new applicable models. There is room for coastal cities, and for Atlantic port-cities in particular, to further engage such efforts at transnational cooperation.

The potential synergistic effects on overall efficiency, emissions and growth stemming from a transformation of port-cities would be large, given their unique capacity to guide and implement integrated continental, regional and national strategies in overlapping energy, transportation, climate and maritime policy terrains. Strategically aligned and renovated, green port-cities could serve as catalysts for a progressive (if partial) greening of the maritime realm, as facilitators of improved multi-modal transportation systems linking ports with continental hinterlands, and as integrated policy agents and regulators for smart green and blue growth.

Part I

Innovative Perspectives on Energy and Transportation in the Atlantic Basin

Chapter One

The Co-Transformation of Energy and Transport: Outlook for the Wider Atlantic

R. Andreas Kraemer

The world is undergoing rapid transformations in several sectors. Chief and prominent among them is the energy sector, but there is also a new and welcome dynamism in transport. These transformations must succeed—and development towards sustainability be accelerated—for the planet to provide an acceptable environment for future generations. The Atlantic Lifestyle has driven human civilization to crash into planetary boundaries,[1] with Earth Overshoot Day coming earlier every year.[2]

Energy transformation (*Energiewende* as it is called in Germany)[3] is well established as a concept in our minds: it is a fundamental shift away from dangerous, dirty and expensive fossil energies and nuclear power towards energy efficiency and renewable energy supply with storage of various forms deployed and linked in smart energy management systems. It is happening now, sustaining itself economically; it has become self-accelerating and self-replicating. It is now a global phenomenon that began in the Atlantic.[4]

This chapter is based on a presentation given at the Jean Monnet Network on Atlantic Studies conference, "Energy and Transportation in the Atlantic Basin: Implications for the European Union and Other Atlantic Actors," held at Johns Hopkins University SAIS in Washington, D.C. on July 20, 2017.

1. Katriona McGlade, Lucy O. Smith, R. Andreas Kraemer and Elisabeth Tedsen, "Human Environmental Dynamics and Responses in the Atlantic Space," in Jordi Bacaria and Laia Tarragona (eds.), *Atlantic Future. Shaping a New Hemisphere for the 21st century: Africa, Europe and the Americas* (Barcelona: CIDOB, 2016), pp. 69-85.

2. See http://www.overshootday.org/newsroom/past-earth-overshoot-days/.

3. R. Andreas Kraemer, "Twins of 1713: Energy Security and Sustainability in Germany," in Robert Looney (ed.), *Handbook of Transitions to Energy and Climate Security* (Abingdon, UK, and New York, NY: Routledge, 2016), pp. 413-429.

4. Paul Isbell, *Energy and the Atlantic: The Shifting Energy Landscape of the Atlantic Basin.* (Washington DC: German Marshall Fund of the United States, 2012); Christoph Stefes and R. Andreas Kraemer, *Outlook for the Fossil Fuel and Renewable Energy Industries in the Wider Atlantic Space*, Atlantic Future Business Brief (Barcelona: CIDOB, 2015); R. Andreas Kraemer and Christoph Stefes, (2016). "The Changing Energy Landscape in the Atlantic Space," in Jordi Bacaria and Laia Tarragona (eds.), *Atlantic Future*, op. cit., pp. 87-102; IRENA, *Renewable Energy Statistics* (Abu Dhabi: International Renewable Energy Agency (IRENA), 2017); IRENA, *REthinking Energy 2017—Accelerating the Global Energy Transformation* (Abu Dhabi: IRENA, 2017).

In contrast, the idea of a transport transformation is still relatively new, often belittled, and generally not very well understood. It is often reduced to telling positive or negative stories about Tesla, and guessing about the future evolution of its stock market valuation. There is no agreement yet about the desirability, direction and speed of this transformation, or even whether it is heading for electric mobility or a transport system based on renewably-produced hydrogen or other alkanes (or their derivatives) in fuel cells. Even energy-efficient Diesel engines have their apologists.

There are very different and often contradictory visions about the future of transport systems around the Atlantic: the U.S. has Tesla with its clear focus on electric mobility, Brazil has alcohol as a bio-fuel derived from sugar cane, and Germany has efficient diesel engines that might run cleanly on biogenic fuels or synthetic fuels derived from renewable electricity. These are examples both of current technologies and of possible future evolutions of the transport sector.

This chapter starts from the assumption that a transport transformation is underway, that it exhibits a strong trend towards electric mobility, and that the energy transformation and the transport transformation are interlocking and mutually supportive. It is further assumed that there is an evolving co-transformation of the two systems—the most important infrastructure systems that underpin our industrialized and urbanized civilization with their generally unsustainable production, trade, consumption and wastage patterns.

The history of the world's dominant energy systems and most of its transport modes is Atlantic: all the old and dying energy industries are Atlantic in their origin and are still dominated by economic actors, regulatory philosophies and business models that have their origin and their history in the countries of the Atlantic. The same is true for the currently dominant transport technologies, even if innovation seems to be shifting somewhat to the Pacific, notably to China and Japan. The worldwide demand for energy, as well as transport, is driven by the wasteful Atlantic Lifestyle and its adoption outside its region of origin.

The transformations of these two key industries and infrastructure systems is potentially disruptive not only for the businesses involved, which may find themselves with stranded assets, eroding balance sheets, plummeting market capitalization, and eventual bankruptcies. The transformations will also induce significant changes in resource trade, government revenue and expenditure and thus the fiscal and ultimately political stability of some countries. The wider economic implications of the end of the fossil age and the energy transformation,[5] along with the geopolitics of the shift towards renewable energies, have been the subject of reflection for over 40 years[6] but are not yet well understood.[7] The geopolitical consequences of a transport transformation are yet to be assessed.

The dynamics of the past are known; evaluations of the status quo and trends are subject to debate; and assessments of possible, probable, desirable or undesirable future evolutions of the energy and transport systems are controversial. The changes are fundamental and at least potentially disruptive, which creates hopes and fears, sometimes strong. This is fuel for an emotional energy in the discussion, in the public, among experts, investors, and policy-makers.

This chapter starts by assessing, separately, the outlook for the energy and transport sectors before exploring the combined effect and potential synergies of a co-transformation. The economic and geopolitical implications are discussed as a basis for further reflection on the trade and security policy implications in the Jean Monet Network on Atlantic Studies.

It should be noted that the current transformations are not the first. There have been previous transformations of energy systems[8] as well as transport systems, and especially the energy used in transport systems. However, the current transformation is unique as it is the first that is truly global: it is driven as much by changes in (globally available) technologies as by a motivation to fight global climate change. It was therefore also in part induced or promoted by public policy. The current transformation is focused on electricity as a relatively modern energy carrier and driven also by the digital disruption that allows for gains in dynamic efficiency of the energy system.

---

5. R. Andreas Kraemer, *Green Shift to Sustainability: Co-Benefits and Impacts of Energy Transformation,* CIGI Policy Brief 109, (Waterloo, ON: Centre for International Governance Innovation (CIGI), 2017).

6. Amory B. Lovins, (1976). "Energy Strategy: The Road Not Taken," *Foreign Affairs* (October 1976). Available as a reprint (with an introduction) at www.rmi.org/Knowledge-Center/Library/E77–01_EnergyStrategyRoadNotTaken; Amory B. Lovins, "A Farewell to Fossil Fuels. Answering the Energy Challenge," *Foreign Affairs, 91*(2), 2012, pp. 134-146.

7. For example, see Meghan O'Sullivan, Indra Overland and David Sandalow, *The Geopolitics of Renewable Energy* (New York, NY, and Cambridge, MA: Columbia University, and Harvard University, 2017).

8. The history of energy transformations in Germany is sketched in Kraemer, 2016, op. cit.

Energy Transformation in the Atlantic

There can be arguments about the energy transformation's speed, its cost and benefits, its regional and distributive effects, and other issues, such as the outlook for using fossil methane gas—euphemistically called natural gas by some—as a bridge fuel until 100% renewable energy supply is achieved.[9]

Financial analysts agree that the shift towards green energy is now economically self-sustaining, self-accelerating, and self-replicating, such is the preponderance of (permanent) benefits over (temporary) drawbacks stemming from the energy transformation. Even detractors, such as those pushing for clean coal or carbon capture and storage (CCS), implicitly acknowledge the generally accepted understanding of the current great energy transformation with their rear-guard action to slow it down.

Priorities differ among countries and regions, but there are solutions for everyone, from the transformation of the old, well entrenched and overdeveloped energy systems mainly in the North of the Atlantic Space to the underserved, poor regions in the Atlantic South, notably Africa, where off-grid power is growing faster than any grid expansion could be imagined.

Transport—shipping, aviation, road and rail transport—was ignored in the early reflections on Atlanticism starting in 2010.[10] In contrast, energy was prominent among early discussions and publications, at a time when fossil energy trade was even more dominant than it is today and the outlook for the development of new fossil resources was positive for instance in Brazil, West Africa, and Angola, and fracking was becoming more widespread in the U.S. In the early years, the general themes were observed, along with anticipated changes in the fossil commodity trade patterns and the effects of such changes on economic and political interdependencies.

---

9. For a cautionary assessment, see H. McJeon, J. Edmonds, N. Bauer, L. Clarke, B. Fisher, B. P. Flannery, J. Hilaire, V. Krey, G. Marangoni, R. Mi, K. Riahi, H. Rogner and M. Tavoni, "Limited Impact on Decadal-scale Climate Change from Increased Use of Natural Gas," *Nature 514* (7523), 2014, pp. 482-485.

10. See the early and still defining publications on Atlanticism by Ian O. Lesser, (2010). *Southern Atlanticism: Geopolitics and Strategy for the other Half of the Atlantic Rim* (Washington DC, German Marshall Fund of the United States, 2010) pp 12ff; and Mark Aspinwall, (2011). *The Atlantic Geopolitical Space: Common Opportunities and Challenges—Synthesis Report of a Conference Jointly Organised by DG Research and Innovation and BEPA, European Commission, and Held on 1 July 2011* (Luxembourg, Publications Office of the European Union, 2011) pp. 11-14.

Later analyses changed the focus, in part because of the changing economic outlook for the fossil energy industries,[11] but also in part to reflect the policy dynamics behind climate protection and the expansion of renewable energy.[12]

Looking at the status of energy systems on the four continents around the Atlantic, the following general observations can be made:

- Energy systems in the North (North America and Europe) are well developed, in some cases overdeveloped, with significant overcapacities. At the same time, energy systems in the South are still underdeveloped, either because there is no access to modern energy (as in Africa) or because the systems are not able to provide the energy services likely to be demanded in fast-growing economies (South America). Generally, the Western Atlantic or the American hemisphere is better developed than the Eastern Atlantic. In fact, much of Africa is made up of outliers within the energy system's development for their simple lack of energy infrastructure.

- Since industrialization, all of the energy systems around the Atlantic have developed a high—and dangerous—dependency on fossil energy, with the exception of those parts of Africa that have no modern energy systems to speak of. The dependence on fossil energy is strong even in areas with high levels of renewable energy, such as parts of Canada, Brazil or some Member States of the European Union, because of the need for liquid, fossil-based fuels in the current transport systems.

- All of the energy systems also maintain a share of traditional energy sources, from dung and firewood to hydropower and wind-mills, and all of them also have a mixture of modern renewable energies, such as solar power and wind power turbines. The shares of traditional and modern renewable energy differ among the countries and continents, as do their combined shares within overall energy systems.[13]

- Nuclear power retains a foothold in the North (where all of the nuclear weapons states are located), while it is waning in the South of the Atlantic (where there are no nuclear weapons states). In fact, conflict over nuclear weapons controlled by North Atlantic states being present

---

11. See Paul Isbell, "The Shifting Flows of Global Energy and Trade: Implications for Latin America," in Felix Dane (ed): *The Politics of World Security* (Rio de Janeiro, Konrad Adenauer Stiftung (KAS), 2015); and Paul Isbell, "Modern Renewable Energy: Approaching the Tipping Point?" in Vicente Lopez-Ibor (ed.): *Green Law* (forthcoming), 2017, pp. 215-237.

12. R. Andreas Kraemer and Christoph Stefes , 2012, op. cit.

13. See Paul Isbell, "Modern Renewable Energy", op. cit.

in or passing through the South Atlantic is one of the recurring conflicts that define Northern vs. Southern geopolitical and security preferences.

- Each of the continents around the Atlantic also has some specificities:

    - South America has especially strong corporatist traditions in the energy and utility industry, which makes sector transformation particularly challenging. Brazil has developed a technology and value chain from sugar-cane to alcohol as a transport fuel, which is characterized by high energy conversion efficiency compared to other biofuels. The technology is exported, and the value chains replicated in Africa where similar conditions favor sugar cane production.

    - With hydrological fracturing of oil and gas fields (fracking), North America (and here mainly the U.S.) has a unique energy technology development that is not being replicated quickly and easily elsewhere. This is for reasons that are beyond the scope of this chapter. However, the fracking revolution, as a regional Atlantic phenomenon, continues to influence the trajectory of U.S. energy policy and emissions: it drives down coal and nuclear power, but also slows the growth of renewable energy, notably wind power.

    - Europe—and the European Union (EU) at its heart—has the most advanced, comprehensive and ambitious policies for climate protection and energy transformation. The frameworks established by policy and law, at the EU level and in the Member States, address many different technology options but particularly those which generally drive down carbon emissions when compared with fossil energy, along with the share of nuclear power, and promote renewable energy supply as well as energy efficiency.

    - Africa has perhaps the most varied energy economy environment of the continents around the Atlantic. There are energy superpowers, including South Africa (coal), Nigeria (oil), Algeria (gas) and Morocco (renewables). But there are also many countries and regions with extreme energy poverty. Interestingly, it is those underserved regions that may now be the most dynamic in adopting distributed renewable energy in off-grid solutions, and innovating business models around them.

The trends and outlooks on the four continents around the Atlantic can be summarized in a similar way. Overall, they are relatively similar. Because of technology changes and economic forces, there is likely to be a convergence of end points or landing zones of the current energy transformations. Table 1 offers a cursory summary of status, trends and outlook around the Atlantic.

Table 1. Overview of Energy Status, Trends and Outlook around the Atlantic

North America

Status: Very high energy consumption. Largely grid-supplied, weak interconnections, many distribution lines over-ground and vulnerable, mid-level supply security; high levels of renewable energy (including wood for heating); the region is an innovator and technology supplier with the power (by business but also government) to direct technology development and make informed technology choices

Trend: Nuclear down, coal out, oil declining, fossil methane gas holding up (for a while), renewables up, especially solar and onshore wind; driven by states and municipalities; grid defection in some areas; growth of smart-energy applications and business models

Outlook: Accelerating green power shift, with rear-guard action by powerful coal lobby and nuclear military-industrial complex, persistence of fracking for oil and gas; disruption by technical, material and business model innovation in a conservative political environment

South America

Status: Mid-level energy consumption (with great variation). Mix of grid-supplied areas and off-grid or micro-grids, weak interconnections, many distributions lines over-ground, mid- and low levels of supply security; partly caught up in unreformed corporatism (and collateral corruption, e.g. Brazil, Mexico); Venezuela as first petro-state in collapse; the region has a weak innovation system (with Brazil being a possible exception) and is generally a technology follower with the power to chose

Trend: No entry or growth for nuclear; persistence of fossil structures in corporatist utilities, but autonomous electrification in unserved or underserved areas based on renewables (mainly solar); persistence of sugar-cane-to-alcohol in car engines in Brazil

Outlook: Falling cost of renewables will shift private investment their way, including LVDC systems; potential for conflict with incumbent utilities (and the unions behind them); utility-scale renewables may accelerate in some areas

Europe

Status: High energy consumption. Largely grid-supplied, mainly strong interconnections, most distribution lines underground, mid-to-high supply security; high and rising levels of renewables, with variations; the region is an innovator and technology supplier with largely governmental power to direct technology development and make informed technology choices

Trend: Nuclear down, and out everywhere except France, Russia and UK as nuclear weapons states; coal out, oil and fossil methane gas declining (maybe except in Russia); renewables up, especially onshore and off-shore wind, along with solar; even more interconnections, including with North Africa, growth of renewable technologies

Outlook: Continuing green power shift, spreading to the East and South-East, rear-guard action by retrograde regimes in some countries (e.g. Poland, potentially Germany prolonging the life of lignite coal), disruption is partly policy induced

Africa

Status: Low energy consumption. Large areas unserved, weak or non-existent interconnections, mostly no distribution lines, no supply security; the region can innovate in business models but is a technology taker without the power to choose in all other respects; political power often trumps economic sense

Trend: Patchy growth of utility-scale renewable energy in some countries (e.g. Morocco) but futile focus on coal in others (e.g. South Africa); some interest in nuclear driven by corruption (e.g. South Africa)

Outlook: No entry or growth of nuclear; stagnation in areas already served by grids, due to political and economic power of incumbent utilities and associated interests; first access to modern energy accelerating in areas not served by a grid, based on increasingly inexpensive, smart low-voltage direct-current energy systems; potential conflict over energy supply visions (e.g. Tanzania, where kerosene lobby fights solar power)

Source: own elaboration.

Transport Transformation in the Atlantic

All the modern forms of transport—automobiles, trains, modern ships, and aircraft—are equally of Atlantic origin and still dominated by businesses that have their origin and headquarters in the Atlantic Basin. The names of the relevant inventors are all European or of European origin, with North America being a main driver of developments in the past 100–150 years. James Watt's steam engine comes to mind, and the British engineers that first built a transport infrastructure based on coal and for coal. Rail transport is still associated with coal engines in many minds even if current technologies are electric or hybrid.

The names tell the story: MacAdam for asphalt or tar on the road, Goodyear for tires, Otto and Diesel as the dominant engine types, Ford for the production mode—Fordism—that is still at the heart of the automobile industry, even if the Toyota model of co-location of suppliers and just-in-time delivery has been superimposed in a large part on the mobility industry. This industry focuses on putting few people at a time into cars that run on fossil oil derivatives and roll on galvanized fossil oil over gelled fossil tar on the ground. That industry is now in decline—at least with respect to drive-train technologies—and is likely to erode faster than most people anticipate.

The automobile industry is on the cusp of a radical transformation which will be based on electrification, with pure electric vehicles dominating the passenger transportation matrix, along with some hybrid vehicles. Self-charging at home will increasingly become structurally dominant for private individual mobility, including commuting. This trend is starting in the Northern Atlantic (notably Norway and California—on the outer edge of the Atlantic and bordering on the Pacific) but will spread fast in the North and then from the North to the South Atlantic. The costs of the key components are coming down fast: electric motors, batteries and super-capacitators as well as light-weight materials for the car structure and body are getting cheaper faster than the amortization of the existing car fleet. Technological and economic disruption are beginning to work together and reinforce one another.

In parallel, there is a separate but also reinforcing dynamic of change in the transport sector associated with the platform and sharing economy. New, internet-enabled platforms like Uber or car sharing apps empower owners and users of cars as well as intermediaries, aggregators and transport service providers to innovate new approaches to satisfying mobility needs. Vehicle mileage is higher, with fewer cars needed for each unit of transport demand. We are beginning to witness a digital disruption of the current transport systems with an efficiency gain of potentially enormous proportions.

Autonomous driving and other cross-functionalities with internet and cyberspace will increasingly favor electric cars. Here Tesla shows the way not just with its electric drive-train but with the (remote) updates of car operating systems that allow additional functionalities to be added to cars after delivery at very low cost and without the need for visits to car workshops or dealerships. The mobility innovation system is shifting from engineering to programming, and the innovation cycle is become ever shorter as a result.

This development is about to be economically self-sustaining. In some situations, the total cost of ownership (TCO) even of an expensive Tesla Model S is already below that of similarly-sized cars with combustion engines. The cost advantage of electric mobility will become clearer with each generation of electric vehicles. Indeed, this is the major future cost assumption underpinning the study of Basque and European passenger car mobility that forms the foundation of Chapter Three of this book and the basis for its conclusion that the best alternative for replacing gasoline and Diesel cars in Europe would be the battery electric vehicle, in combination with conventional hybrid vehicles.

As in the case of energy transformation, the shift from combustion to electric engines will soon be self-accelerating, and the enabling policy frameworks will be adopted in ever more countries. No country will want or be able to stop the spread of electric vehicles as a superior and soon dominant technology configuration.

For each class, future vehicles will be simpler and much cheaper to build, with simple design, fewer parts, especially fewer moving parts. Without gear-boxes and clutches, and much simpler transmission of motor energy to the wheels, the cars will be lighter, simpler, and more versatile. With engine servicing intervals of 100,000 miles or 150,000 km for electric motors, without motor oil and spark-plugs to change, and with the most short-lived part perhaps being the wiper blades, there will be a significant reduction in the volume and value of after-sale services. This will release many qualified technicians to perform more important and valuable tasks.

Public and commercial freight transport is on a similar trajectory. New fuels, and drive or propulsion technologies, are also increasingly available for railroads, ships and aircraft. Some of these are still based on liquid fuels (like LNG or LPGs), but the quantities likely to be required for uses where electricity is not a viable option can be supplied from biological sources or synthesized using abundant and cheap renewable electricity in power-to-gas and power-to-liquid applications.

This all started in the far western reaches of the Atlantic world, notably in California, which, although on the Pacific coast is economically and culturally part of the Atlantic and even epitomizes the Atlantic Lifestyle. The iconic leader is Tesla, and while the founder Elon Musk hails from South Africa, the innovation style of the company is typical of the U.S. Pacific Coast. In fact, the company is a disrupting force not only in transport but also in solar power concepts, products and business models as well as storage and smart home development. Most innovation is undertaken by new entrants, and disruption of the incumbents is itself a defining trait of the Atlantic innovation system, notably in North America.

Atlantic leadership in transport innovation may be lost to Asia-Pacific (mainly China, but also Japan, South Korea and Taiwan). The leader in hybrid drive-train technology is Toyota, with other automakers belatedly catching up. The concept cars developed by the company are an indication that Toyota may also be able to lead in the next generation of electric cars, with small motors in each wheel and similar car concepts that can be highly efficient, very light, and easy to manufacture. The leader in market penetration and total numbers is China, where on-the-road operational experience is speeding up innovation.

The traditional U.S. motor industry, epitomized by Detroit, may try to match the innovation and dynamism of the Pacific Coast innovation system. The Chevy Volt and the admission by Cummins, the U.S. technology leader in diesel and gas engines, that their old engines may be phased out by 2040 to be replaced by electric and hybrid systems are signs that not all is lost in the world of the fossil-energy combustion engine, and that some leading companies are likely to invent their way into the electric mobility future.[14]

On the European side of the North Atlantic, the challenge of technological change and disruption is now understood, and yet the question is open if any of the European producers can catch up with the innovators in the North-West Atlantic and the Pacific. A recent phenomenon in Germany—the home of Diesel, Otto, and Wankel—is that car and truck manufacturers find that both their key suppliers and their largest customers are beginning to compete

14. Joann Muller, "Cummins Beats Tesla to the Punch, Unveiling Heavy Duty Electric Truck," in *Forbes*, August 29, 2017. https://www.forbes.com/sites/joannmuller/2017/08/29/take-that-tesla-diesel-engine-giant-cummins-unveils-heavy-duty-truck-powered-by-electricity/.

with them. The barriers to entry into the car-making business seem to have fallen to the point that no single company is now safe from being disrupted to the core.

The exception may be BMW with early and continuous investments in electric mobility, including the development of new car designs using modern materials, and clear market positioning: their i3 and i8 models are like concept cars that escaped from bays in the research and development unit and found their way onto the road. They make a strong statement that BMW has the capacity and the will to design the electric and hybrid cars of the future.

When it comes to future rail transport systems, Europe is still the technology leader. Again, the industry is Atlantic in origin, with Siemens, Alstom and ABB being leaders in Europe and Bombardier in North America.

In this process of technological and economic disruption, much of Latin America and all of Africa is a technology taker; they are dependent on the products and drive-train (or jet engine) technologies developed elsewhere. They will be forced to follow where the technology leaders take them. The battle over innovation and future dominance of the transport sector is fought among California, Southern Germany (with Stuttgart and Munich) in the Atlantic and China and Japan in the Pacific.

Energy & Transport Co-Transformation and Resource Implications

Economic forces are on the side of these parallel and mutually reinforcing transformations of the energy and transport systems around the Atlantic. Still, fossil subsidies, although declining in recent years, continue to be arrayed against them and uphold the fossil (and nuclear) energy system, and provide for continuing support for fossil-based combustion engines.

The energy and transportation transformations are mutually reinforcing. More electric vehicles connected to the grid for charging also means more storage capacity on balance, allowing the grid to incorporate progressively higher levels of electricity from fluctuating renewable sources more readily and reliably. On the other hand, a higher penetration rate of renewable energies in the generation mix will lead to a smaller carbon footprint from the transport sector. Given that new systems will provide a range of services far beyond that possible under the old fossil energy system, this co-transformation will extend to buildings (including the use of solar roof tiles and other smart home possibilities).

Both transformations have strong environmental and social value propositions. They stem from the imperative to protect the Earth's climate systems—an imperative that gains political urgency with every natural disaster that is connected to the overheating of the planet from the burning of fossil fuels. The increase in hurricanes and typhoon activity in recent years is beginning to make the stakes clearer to many who previously preferred to ignore the threat. While the economics are already driving the co-transformation of the energy and transportation systems, the question remains if the transformation will be quick enough to help avoid the worst consequences of what could already be run-away climate change. Small island states and many coastal and low-river communities are already being faced with existential crises.

Innovations in policy frameworks and international policy coordination may well be required, especially around the Atlantic.[15] Chief among those would be a coordinated push to stop, perhaps by 2020, all subsidies as well as tax and other privileges for the fossil energy industry. Concerning nuclear energy, the abolition of international agreements that protect the builders, owners, operators, and regulators of nuclear power plants from liability for damages in other countries might be put on the agenda.

Because of excessive air pollution in cities, there is pressure to removed two-stroke and Diesel engines, which might be done through "cash for clunkers" programs that reward drivers that buy electric vehicles and scrap their old and dirty fossil-energy driven ones. Cities may well find that banning dirty engines during episodes of high air pollution is the only way to ensure that pollution stays within legal limits. The more cities resort to banning Diesels, the faster the change-over in the car fleet is likely to be. In addition, cities can help the transformation of the energy and the transport system by establishing the necessary infrastructure for charging electric vehicles, and keeping parked vehicles connected to the grid so that they can provide power grid stabilization services. Existing infrastructure for street lighting can be used for the purpose at a fraction of the cost of building an additional new infrastructure of vehicle charging stations.

The resource sectors will change in response to the co-transformation of energy and transport. Demand for oil, steel and welding is weakening, and

---

15. R. Andreas Kraemer and Camilla Bausch, "Koordinierte Weltinnenpolitik: Zusammendenken im atlantischen Raum," in Wolfgang Ischinger and Dirk Messner (eds), *Deutschlands Neue Verantwortung*. (Econ, 2017) pp. 286-287; English as "Joining up in the Wider Atlantic," *IASS Blog* http://blog.iass-potsdam.de/2017/03/joining-wider-atlantic/.

will continue to do so, but demand for carbon fibers and plastics (including adhesives) will rise. Overall, fossil and ferrous metal industries will lose out to companies that supply a wider selection of elements in the Mendeleev periodic table. Current patterns of mining and metals trade will give way to a wider range of elements: demand for non-ferrous metals, metalloids and rare earth elements will continue to rise; demand for trade in ferrous metals, on the other hand, will remain flat or even decline.

The energy and transportation co-transformation will lead to shifts in trade flows and volumes. Trade in chemical energy in the form of energy commodities for one-off consumption will be displaced by trade in durable equipment for the continuous long-term harvesting of ubiquitous, free environmental flows.

There will be impacts on maritime transport. The current fleet of oil (and LNG) tankers can be retired, and the terminal infrastructure for handling fossil energies can be dismantled, freeing up space in port areas. Shipment of durable energy equipment will be largely in containers, but may require specialized transport infrastructure in some cases, e.g. the long blades for off-shore wind turbines. The minerals and other raw materials that will be in higher demand, are likely to be processed close to the mines, especially if cheap renewable energy is available in the region. Not so much of those raw materials will be transported in bulk maritime transport, but the partly refined intermediate products are most likely to be traded internationally, reducing the volume while increasing the value of shipments.

Overall, this co-transformation will be accompanied by a decline in the trade of fossil energy commodities, in both value and volume. At the same time, the revenues of petro-states will collapse, as new business opportunities simply will not compensate for the decline and loss of trade in fossil energy commodities. In the Atlantic, Venezuela provides an example of the dynamics that shape a society and a country when the resource curse is lifted and a regime can no longer count on oil revenue to stay in power. On the other hand, the total cost and capital needs for energy and transportation will fall, while the services provided expand and the related environmental and social values will rise.

Discussion and Outlook: Geopolitical Implications

The geopolitical implications of the co-transformation of the energy and transport systems are not yet fully understood. The implications for the shrinking and dying industries are clear enough: there will be capital write-offs, bankruptcies and job losses in the fossil and nuclear industries as well as among combustion-engine makers. The implications are less clear for the manufacturers of cars, trucks, buses, trams, trains, ships and aircraft. Some of them may be out-innovated and disappear, while others may thrive.

The anticipated shifts may be so dynamic that they result in social and political disruption. In fact, there are already discernible links and commonalities in North America and Europe, among populist advocates of economic nationalism, nativism and protectionism, and climate-change denial. On both continents, there are strong attachments to fossil fuels and defense of the Diesel engine, epitomized by "rolling coal," the eco-terrorist practice of smoking the environment by producing massive black-carbon plumes from the exhausts of Diesel-engine trucks. The contrasting attitudes may lead to conflicts over trade, regulation, state-aid and competition, and other areas.

The distributional effects of the necessary — and therefore welcomed, but also economically beneficial and ultimately unstoppable — co-transformation of the energy and transport sectors in each country are already proving difficult to manage. The economic and political power of the incumbent industries is strong, as is their hold over the identities and cultural values of key constituencies. There will be larger distributional effects to come among countries and continents around the Atlantic, but also beyond.

Many resource extracting and exporting countries are afflicted by the resource curse when conflicts over resource control and its economic benefits result in ever more corruption and repression, and ultimately in an oppressive autocratic regime. When the resource curse is lifted, the regime does not go away voluntarily to allow for a peaceful transition to a more liberal order, as the example of Venezuela shows. Nevertheless, the lifting of the resource curse should be good in the medium to longer term.

Chapter Two

Electrification, Collaboration, and Cooperation: Managing the Future of Energy and Transportation Systems in the Atlantic Basin

Martin Lowery and Michael Leitman[1]

The countries that comprise the Atlantic Basin[2] are facing major challenges regarding energy and transportation. There are many factors affecting the Atlantic Basin's future, such as mass migration from rural to urban areas and the resultant impact on transportation, water, food, and energy security; reconsideration of central station electric generation as the only reliable means of energy production; environmental impact of fossil fuels; accelerated adoption of renewable energy technologies; emergence of electric vehicles as a plausible alternative for multiple transportation modes; evolving expectations of consumers for greater control of their lives; and income disparity and its impact on the quality of life of low-to-moderate income people.

Concerns are also emerging about the need for greater resiliency in transportation, water, food, and energy systems in the face of both increasing demand and severe weather events. As characterized by UN-Water, "The water-food-energy nexus is central to sustainable development. Demand for all three is increasing, driven by a rising global population, rapid urbanization, changing diets and economic growth."[3]

In addition, the discovery of significant amounts of recoverable terrestrial and offshore reserves of oil and natural gas is setting the stage for the Atlantic

---

1. The authors wish to acknowledge contributions to this chapter from colleagues Jim Spiers, Paul Breakman, Keith Dennis, Jan Ahlen, Dan Waddle, and Michael Peck. The views expressed herein are those of the authors and do not necessarily reflect the views of the National Rural Electric Cooperative Association or its members.

2. This paper follows the Atlantic Basin framework as described by Paul Isbell: "In this projection, the Atlantic Basin includes Africa, Latin America and the Caribbean, North America, and Europe, incorporating these four Atlantic continents in their entirety, along with their ocean and islands." Paul Isbell, "An Introduction to the Future of the Atlantic Basin," *The Future of Energy in the Atlantic Basin* (Washington, D.C., Center for Transatlantic Relations, Johns Hopkins University SAIS, 2015), p.10, http://transatlanticrelations.org/wp-content/uploads/2017/03/Doc-43-text-Future-of-Energy-in-the-Atlantic-Basin-text-final-pdf.pdf (accessed August 25, 2017).

3. "Water, Food and Energy," UN-Water, http://www.unwater.org/water-facts/water-food-and-energy/ (accessed August 25, 2017).

Basin to become largely energy self-sufficient, with trans-Atlantic trade flows and investments increasing the opportunity for greater synergies. In the electric power sector, increasing natural gas supplies offer an opportunity to reduce emissions in the short- to mid-term by replacing higher-emitting coal generation with gas generators that also make possible greater flexibility in managing intermittent renewable resources on the grid, especially when combined with improved storage technologies.

In the words of Daniel Hamilton, Executive Director of the Center for Transatlantic Relations at Johns Hopkins University School of Advanced International Studies (SAIS),

> We are on the cusp of fundamentally changing the way energy is produced, distributed and traded across the entire Atlantic space. Over the next 20 years the Atlantic is likely to become the energy reservoir of the world and a net exporter of many forms of energy to the Indian Ocean and Pacific Ocean basins. The Atlantic is setting the global pace for energy innovation and redrawing global maps for oil, gas, and renewables as new players and technologies emerge, new conventional and unconventional sources come online, energy services boom, and opportunities appear all along the energy supply chain.[4]

Of direct relevance to the future of both energy and transportation in the Atlantic Basin is United Nations Sustainable Development Goal Seven— to ensure access to affordable, reliable, sustainable and modern energy for all by the year 2030.

According to the mid-year 2017 update from the United Nations, there is a significant shortfall in each target area:

> Progress in every area of sustainable energy falls short of what is needed to achieve energy access for all and to meet targets for renewable energy and energy efficiency. Meaningful improvements will require higher levels of financing and bolder policy commitments, together with the willingness of countries to embrace new technologies on a much wider scale.[5]

---

4. Daniel S. Hamilton, Preface to *The Future of Energy in the Atlantic Basin,* op. cit., p. xv.

5. "Progress towards the Sustainable Development Goals: Report of the Secretary-General,"UN Economic and Social Council, May 11, 2017, http://www.un.org/ga/search/view_doc.asp?symbol=E/2017/66&Lang=E (accessed August 25, 2017).

The update further reports the following statistics:

- Globally, 85.3 percent of the population had access to electricity in 2014, an increase of only 0.3 percentage points since 2012. That means that 1.06 billion people, predominantly rural dwellers, still function without electricity. Half of those people live in sub-Saharan Africa.

- Access to clean fuels and technologies for cooking climbed to 57.4 per cent in 2014, up slightly from 56.5 per cent in 2012. More than 3 billion people, the majority of whom are in Asia and sub-Saharan Africa, are cooking without clean fuels and more efficient technologies.

- The share of renewable energy in final energy consumption grew modestly from 2012 to 2014, from 17.9 per cent to 18.3 per cent. Most of the increase was from renewable electricity from water (hydro), solar and wind power. Solar and wind power still make up a relatively minor share of energy consumption, despite their rapid growth in recent years. The challenge is to increase the share of renewable energy in the heat and transport sectors, which together account for 80 per cent of global energy consumption.

- From 2012 to 2014, three quarters of the world's 20 largest energy-consuming countries reduced their energy intensity—the ratio of energy used per unit of GDP. The reduction was driven mainly by greater efficiencies in the industrial and transport sectors. However, that progress is still not sufficient to meet the target of doubling the global rate of improvement in energy efficiency.

The discussion that follows will explore three concepts that, when taken together, characterize a possible future state of energy and transportation in the Atlantic Basin that would accelerate the effort to meet Sustainable Development Goal Seven by 2030:

- *Democratization of Energy*, fueled by a growing desire for local control of the means of energy production and by the availability of new consumer-centric energy options;

- *The Dynamic Electric Grid*, enabled by communications, measurement, monitoring, and sensor and control devices that facilitate the real-time management of electricity demand; and

- *Environmentally Beneficial Electrification,* driven by the shift of primary end-use in the energy and transportation sectors away from carbon-intensive fuels to efficient electrification that promotes environmental gains, efficient use of water resources, and increased agricultural productivity.

When integrated, these three concepts, local control of energy and transportation management through a dynamic electric grid that increasingly enables electricity-driven economies, present a potential path to meeting the challenges being analyzed and addressed in the energy and transportation sectors of the four interdependent continents of the Atlantic Basin.

The Current State of Electrification in the Atlantic Basin: Access and Decarbonization

The figures below depict the latest available global data to highlight some of the differences and similarities across the four Atlantic Basin continents regarding access to electric service. They illuminate some of the unique opportunities and challenges and establish a baseline for contextualizing trends throughout this chapter.

Figure 1 shows the share of populations in the Atlantic Basin with access to electricity. Access to basic electric service is universal or nearly universal across most of the Americas and Europe. Within Latin America and the Caribbean, however, about 5 percent of the overall population has no access to grid electricity, mainly in rural areas of Central America and the mountainous Andean region of Peru and Bolivia. The most significant outlier is Haiti, where more than 60 percent of the population lacks access to electricity. High levels of access are prevalent across North Africa and in South Africa, but access varies widely across sub-Saharan African nations, where up to three quarters of the population are without electricity. Overall, only 35 percent of the African population had access to electricity in 2012, and rapid population growth makes progress even more challenging.[6]

As Figure 2 shows, sub-Saharan Africa is home to the largest share of people without access to electricity. Access rates are higher in urban areas, but electric grids often do not extend to rural areas where 60 percent of the population resides. Despite urbanization rates second only to Asia, most of the population in the region is still rural and is expected to remain so in the coming decades.[7] Rural electrification is a challenge faced previously in the

---

6. "Making Renewable Energy More Accessible in Sub-Saharan Africa," The World Bank, February 13, 2017, http://www.worldbank.org/en/news/feature/2017/02/13/making-renewable-energy-more-accessible-in-sub-saharan-africa (accessed August 25, 2017).

7. Mariama Sow, "Foresight Africa 2016: Urbanization in the African context," Brookings, December, 30, 2015, https://www.brookings.edu/blog/africa-in-focus/2015/12/30/foresight-africa-2016-urbanization-in-the-african-context/ (accessed August 25, 2017).

Figure 1: Share of Population with Access to Electricity (2014)

Source: "SDG 7: Affordable and Clean Energy," *Atlas of Sustainable Development Goals*, The World Bank, 2017, http://datatopics.worldbank.org/sdgatlas/SDG-07-affordable-and-clean-energy.html (accessed August 25, 2017).

other continents of the Atlantic Basin, and the lessons learned there may be able to be applied here.

As shown in Figure 3, even where there is universal or near-universal access to electricity, per capita consumption in developing countries across the Atlantic Basin is significantly lower than in the developed countries of the region. Economic growth and electric usage tend to grow in tandem. This is especially true in rapidly developing countries where growth leads to new demands for electricity from homes and businesses.[8]

---

8. Bosco Astarloa, Julian Critchlow, and Lyubomyr Pelykh, "The Future of Electricity in Fast-Growing Economies," World Economic Forum, January 2016,http://www3.weforum.org/docs/WEF_Future_of_Electricity_2016.pdf (accessed August 25, 2017).

Figure 2: Number of People without Access to Electricity (billions)

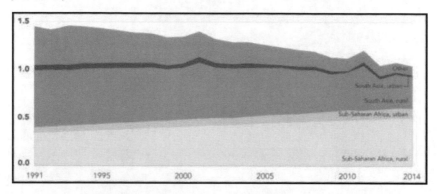

Source: "SDG 7: Affordable and Clean Energy," Atlas of Sustainable Development Goals World Bank, 2017. http://datatopics.worldbank.org/sdgatlas/SDG-07-affordable-and-clean-energy.html.

Figure 3: Electricity Consumption per Capita (2015)

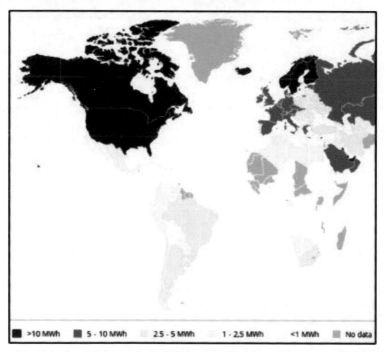

Source: "Electricity: Consumption per Capita (MWh/capita), 2015," Atlas of Energy, International Energy Agency, 2017, http://energyatlas.iea.org/#!/tellmap/-1118783123/1 (accessed September 19, 2017).

Figure 4: Share of Fossil Fuels in Electricity Production (2015)

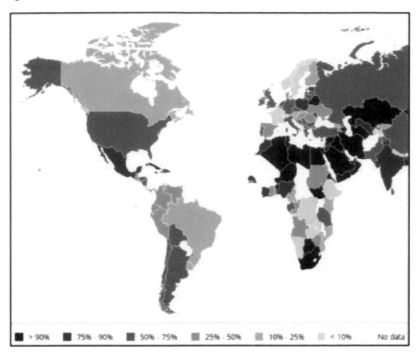

Source: "Share of Fossil Fuels in Electricity Production (%), 2015," Atlas of Energy, International Energy Agency, 2017, http://energyatlas.iea.org/#!/tellmap/-1118783123/2 (accessed September 19, 2017).

As a proxy for the current carbon intensity of electric grids across the Atlantic Basin, Figure 4 shows the share of electric production in each country that comes from fossil fuels. This subtractive look is useful because other sources of electricity are generally non-emitting (hydroelectric, non-hydroelectric renewable, nuclear) or carbon neutral (biomass, waste-to-energy). This map does not distinguish between fossil fuel types, however; and significant shifts from higher emitting coal to lower emitting natural gas have taken place in the United States and, to a lesser extent, in Europe. In the United States, coal has fallen from about half of all electric generation in the late 1990s to 30 percent in 2016 and was surpassed by natural gas generation on an annual basis for the first time in that year. In the EU countries, coal-based generation declined from about 30 percent of all generation to just over 21 percent over the same period, falling behind electricity generated from renewables and nuclear energy.[9]

Taken together, some interesting points can be gleaned from the figures above. First, the developed countries of the Atlantic Basin have made and continue to make significant progress towards decarbonizing their electric grids. Second, many developing countries in Latin America and several in Africa already have low-carbon electric grids. However, as they develop they will need to invest in low-and non-emitting technologies if they are to meet the demands of increasing energy consumption to power their economies without significantly increasing the carbon intensity of their electric sectors.[10] This is especially important as developing economies invest in expanding electric access for homes, businesses, and transportation that will be further discussed in this chapter. Third, similar to the landline-cell tower infrastructure leap, developing countries may decarbonize their grids by leapfrogging over previously sequential waves of adaptation and development.

Democratization of Energy

Throughout the Atlantic Basin there is a deepening interest in local control of energy resources. In fact, the beginnings of an energy cooperative network are being driven by two common interests: local control of energy production and renewable energy availability. European renewable energy cooperatives have emerged in the past ten years, many of which are participating in the European Federation of Renewable Energy Cooperatives (REScoop), a federation with 1,240 members and 650,000 consumers. Among its members are the cooperative association of Germany, DGRV, with 850 co-ops serving

---

9. "Coal power continues market share retreat in U.S. and Europe," *The Economist*, March 7, 2017,http://www.eiu.com/industry/article/455191829/coal-power-continues-market-share-retreat-in-us-and-europe/2017-03-07 (accessed September 5, 2017).

10. There remains the possibility of successfully capturing CO_2 output from coal plants and finding productive uses that could be marketed globally. Electric cooperatives in the United States, partnering with the state of Wyoming and others in the U.S. and Canada, have invested in an Integrated Test Center located at Basin Electric Cooperative's Dry Forks generating station in Wyoming to explore uses and markets for CO_2 output. The X-Prize Foundation has, in turn, offered a U.S.$20 million NRG Cosia Carbon XPRIZE for the successful demonstration of such an outcome. Twenty-three teams from six countries, including Canada, U.S., UK, and Switzerland, represent an incredible diversity of approaches to turn waste (CO_2 emissions) into valuable products such as fish food, fertilizer, carbon nanotubes, and building material. Wyoming Integrated Test Center, http://www.wyomingitc.org/ (accessed September 18, 2017), and NRG Cosia Carbon XPRIZE, https://carbon.xprize.org/teams (accessed September 18, 2017).

150,000 consumers; Enercoop of France, with 10 co-ops serving 23,000 consumers; and Cooperative Energy of Great Britain, serving 250,000 consumers. The Alliance for Rural Electrification, headquartered in Brussels, Belgium, has members across the Atlantic Basin, including electric and energy cooperative representatives.[11]

In the United States 834 electric distribution cooperatives deliver electric service to 19 million meters and 42 million people in 47 states. These cooperatives cover more than half of the nation's landmass.[12] As cooperatives, they are not-for-profit energy service providers, owned and democratically governed by the consumers they serve. Many distribution cooperatives have joined together to form generation and transmission cooperatives (G&Ts) that provide power to distribution co-ops through their own generation facilities or by aggregating wholesale electricity purchases on behalf of their distribution members. The cooperatives, each independently governed and managed, are supported by an extensive, sophisticated cooperative network for capital financing, insurance, research and development, power marketing, information technology, materials supply, and back office support.

In terms of renewable energy development, the most advanced cooperative project globally is located on Kauai, an island of 66,000 people in the state of Hawaii. Like many islands, Kauai historically has been reliant on expensive imported diesel for its electricity. To reduce costs, Kauai Island Utility Cooperative (KIUC) has set a goal of using renewable resources to generate 70 percent of its power by 2030. KIUC has made significant progress towards this goal, with more than 40 percent of its electricity now coming from renewable generation, including solar, hydropower, and biomass. On the sunniest days, solar generation can provide in excess of 90 percent of the island's energy needs. KIUC's newest projects are two large solar arrays with battery storage systems that allow their output to be dispatched more flexibly, even after the sun goes down.[13]

Many electric cooperatives have developed or are in the process of developing electric vehicle recharging policies and, in some cases, have installed charging stations. According to Advanced Energy, a U.S. energy consulting firm, "Electric cooperatives throughout the United States are well underway with implementing strategies to increase electric vehicle (EV) adoption and take advantage of its benefits. Public charging stations are going up, member

---

11. Alliance for Rural Electrification, http://www.ruralelec.org (accessed September 8, 2017).

12. America's Electric Cooperatives, https://www.electric.coop (accessed September 8, 2017).

13. Kaua'I Island Utility Cooperative, http://website.kiuc.coop/ (accessed September 8, 2017).

education events and workshops are being hosted, and incentives are available."[14] As an example, New Hampshire Electric Cooperative in the U.S. offers incentives for the installation of electric vehicle charging stations to its commercial and municipal members. Members can install fast-charging stations and qualify for an incentive of 50 percent of the cost.[15] Much of the longer-distance need for electric vehicle charging in the U.S. will be located in rural areas served by cooperatives.

In addition to electric service, U.S. electric co-ops are deeply involved in their communities, promoting development and revitalization projects, small businesses, job creation, improvement of water and sewer systems, broadband deployment, and assistance in delivery of health care and educational services.

Electric cooperatives throughout Latin American and the Caribbean have renewable energy projects underway. The largest electric cooperative in the world is Cooperativa Rural Electrificación (CRE),[16] headquartered in Santa Cruz, Bolivia. CRE serves 600,000 consumers and is deploying large solar arrays. Costa Rica has four electric cooperatives that rely entirely on electricity generated from hydropower, wind, and solar power. Argentina has more than 500 electric cooperatives, many of which have invested in grid-connected renewable projects. In the Caribbean, Cuba is developing biofuels for use in electricity generation and is pursuing the development of cooperatives as a matter of government policy. In sub-Saharan Africa there are fewer examples of electric cooperative start-ups, but the concept is applicable to the goal of electricity access for all.

Futurist and EU advisor Jeremy Rifkin predicts that an "Energy Commons" will develop as an alternative to the current control of the electricity delivery system by large, investor-owned utilities: "A new Commons model is just beginning to take form, and interestingly enough, it is an outgrowth of an older Commons model for managing electricity that arose in the 1930s to bring electricity to the rural areas of the United States."[17]

---

14. Jonathan Susser, "Electric Vehicle Strategies for Electric Cooperatives," Advanced Energy, February 21, 2017, https://www.advancedenergy.org/2017/02/21/electric-vehicle-strategies-for-electric-cooperatives (accessed September 18, 2017).

15. "Electric Vehicle (EV) Charging Stations are good for business," New Hampshire Electric Cooperative, https://www.nhec.com/ev-commercial-charging/ (accessed September 18, 2017)

16. Cooperativa Rural de Electrificación, http://www.cre.com.bo (accessed August 28, 2018).

17. Jeremy Rifkin, *The Zero Marginal Cost Society* (New York, 2014), p. 206.

Rifkin believes that the cooperative business model is ideally suited for an Internet-based economy:

> The Internet of Things gives the advantage of the lateral power made possible by the new distributed and collaborative communications and energy configuration. The prospect of a new economic infrastructure and paradigm that can reduce marginal costs to near zero makes the private firm, whose very existence depends on sufficient margins to make a profit, less viable. Cooperatives are the only business model that will work in a near zero marginal cost society. Thousands of green energy and electricity cooperatives are springing up in communities around the world, establishing a bottom-up Commons foundation for peer-to-peer sharing of electricity across regional and continental transmission grids. In the European Union, where more people invest in cooperatives than in the stock market—a striking fact—cooperative banks are taking the lead in financing green electricity cooperatives.[18]

Rifkin's observation about European cooperative banking interests and renewable energy is being replicated in the United States. The National Cooperative Bank, in collaboration with the Cooperative Finance Corporation, now offers lending to consumers of electric cooperatives who wish to install rooftop solar systems or to participate in community solar programs that are discussed below.[19] Also, a start-up credit union, Clean Energy Federal Credit Union, has been chartered by the National Credit Union Administration and will offer consumer financing to the 4,300 members of the American Solar Energy Society for the purchase of solar panels and electric or hybrid vehicles and high-efficiency home energy improvements.[20]

Cooperatives operate with a consistent set of principles adopted globally through the International Cooperative Alliance: voluntary and open membership; democratic member control; member economic participation; autonomy and independence; education, training and information; cooperation among cooperatives and concern for community. In addition, cooperatives

---

18. Ibid. pp. 214-215

19. "National Cooperative Bank and CFC Launch Retail Financing Program to Expand Renewable Energy Options for Electric Cooperative Members," National Cooperative Bank, June 12, 2017, https://ncb.coop/media/press-releases/2017/national-cooperative-bank-and-cfc-launch-retail-financing-program-to-expand-renewable-energy-options-for-electric-cooperative-members (accessed September 18, 2017).

20. Clean Energy Credit Union,https://www.cleanenergyfcu.org/ (accessed September 18, 2017).

are based on the values of self-help, self-responsibility, democracy, equality, equity, and solidarity.[21]

The Canadian historian Ian MacPherson saw cooperatives as a critical contributor to the global economy:

> Most co-operatives are effective businesses. That is attested to by the age of many co-operatives around the world and by the rapid growth of new cooperatives. There is some evidence that cooperatives have a better survival rate than capital-driven enterprise. The capacity of the cooperative model to be applied in many different contexts and in pursuit of many kinds of business is remarkable; its ability to strengthen local economies is a much-needed asset in a globalizing world. At the same time, the potential of the international co-operative movement to create an alternative, people-based economic system represents one of its most promising and important opportunities.[22]

A recent report by the International Labor Organization suggests that cooperatives represent a proven model of sustainable development:

> Cooperatives are sustainable enterprises that work for the sustainable development of their local communities through policies approved by their members. Cooperatives and the cooperative movement have been addressing these issues for over 150 years—since the first formal co-operative was established. Similarly, but driven by a global concern of the environmental limits of the planet, the World Commission on Environment and Development (the Brundtland Commission) famously defined the term sustainable development as "meeting the needs of the present generation without compromising the ability of future generations to meet their own needs."

> Despite the fact that sustainable development and the cooperative movement were born out of different motivations, they address—although to different degrees and at different levels—a common ground: to reconcile economic, social and environmental needs, be it the needs of a local community or the needs of the whole world. Accordingly, cooperatives are ideally placed to promote sustainable development

---

21. "What is a Cooperative?" International Co-operative Alliance, https://ica.coop/en/what-co-operative (accessed September 2, 2017).

22. Ian MacPherson, "The Centrality of Values for Co-operative Success in the Market Place," *The Cooperative Business Movement, 1950 to the Present*, (Cambridge, 2012), http://www.academia.edu/4377149/Co_op_values (accessed September 18, 2017).

and foster a Green Economy—which was adopted by Rio+20 as a practical concept and vehicle for achieving sustainability.[23]

A notable example of the impact of local control of energy resources and the power of aggregation is the emergence of community solar programs pioneered by U.S. electric cooperatives. In this approach a large solar array is installed in the cooperative's service area, and individual members are offered the opportunity to purchase or lease one or more solar panels in the array. In return, the individual member receives a rebate on the monthly bill calculated on a rate-of-return basis. The advantage is that consumers receive access to a renewable resource while the cooperative is able to take advantage of its economies of scale to provide that resource at a lower cost. Community solar also makes solar available to all members who want it, including renters or members who cannot (or choose not to) add solar to their rooftops.

There is a great deal of debate across all four Atlantic Basin continents about the best way for consumers to take greater control of their energy services. Some believe that the best way to facilitate this energy future is for utilities to step aside and simply provide a platform for consumers and third-parties to interact with new applications for energy management. One version of this argument is the idea of redefining utilities as distribution system operators (DSOs)[24] that provide only grid management services, allowing the consumer to choose among multiple wholesale power and energy service suppliers. Alternatively, the utility could become a consumer-centric utility,[25] offering or facilitating the same innovative energy services that would otherwise be available through a third-party provider. This model allows the utility to continue to integrate and optimize resources on the system for the benefit of all consumers.

The energy cooperative as a business model functions as both a DSO and an energy management service provider in the form of a consumer-centric

---

23. "Providing clean energy and energy access through cooperatives," International Labour Office Cooperatives Unit, (Geneva, 2013), p. xvii-xviii, http://www.ilo.org/wcmsp5/groups/public/—-ed_emp/—-emp_ent/documents/publication/wcms_233199.pdf (accessed September 18, 2017).

24. For a discussion of DSOs in a European context, see "The Role of Distribution System Operators (DSOs) as Information Hubs," EURELECTRIC, June, 2010,http://www.eurelectric.org (accessed September 5, 2017).

25. Definitions and details of the concept of the "consumer-centric utility" can be found in "The Consumer-Centric Utility Future," National Rural Electric Cooperative Association (NRECA), March 23, 2016,https://www.cooperative.com/public/51st-state/Documents/51st-State-report_FINAL.pdf (accessed September 5, 2017).

utility. The ability to aggregate the benefits and minimize the risks of new products and energy management services is a defining characteristic of the consumer-centric utility. The community solar product mentioned above is an excellent example of a cooperative solution that is both consumer-centric and optimized for the benefit of the entire membership.

Cooperatives can play a central role as consumer-centric utilities that maintain the core infrastructure of the electric system by providing safe and reliable service, system planning and grid operations, long range planning, capital investment, and consumer services. The cooperative business structure can and does also provide an essential safety net for low-income consumers through policies that ensure that all members benefit from an affordable level of service.

The Dynamic Electric Grid

The cooperative model directly addresses the desire of consumers to have a greater say in their energy future through local control and ownership. However, the innovative applications needed to fully achieve this outcome will require advances in how the electric grid is operated with dynamic two-way flows of energy and data. That, in turn, will require advances in communications, measurement, monitoring, and sensor and control technologies.

Related to this evolution is the concept of economic-based grid control. According to *Renewable Energy World*,

> Every day, the number of new power generators from renewable resources joining the world's collective electricity grid goes up. Growing at an equal pace are the people working to keep the balance between supply and demand on that collective grid. More and more, they are turning to an intelligent and interactive networked system based on economics and market mechanisms where transactions are used to manage the grid and ensure reliability and efficiency.[26]

The key point about the evolution of the electric grid is that, beyond the ability to track and analyze energy demand, demand can now be managed

---

26. Jennifer Delony, "A Transactive Energy Future: The Inevitable Rise of Economic-based Grid Control," Renewable Energy World, September 11, 2017, http://www.renewableenergyworld.com/articles/print/volume-20/issue-5/features/solar-wind-storage-finance/a-transactive-energy-future-the-inevitable-rise-of-economic-based-grid-control.html (accessed September 18, 2017).

from the user's side of the system, as for example the ability to remotely adjust a thermostat level using a smart phone. In the future the ability to account for peer-to-peer energy transactions among homeowners and businesses likely will become widespread, representing an interesting application of platform economics.[27]

The evolution of the grid will also enable greater resiliency—i.e. the ability to maintain a reliable operational state or to return to a reliable operation state as quickly as possible during or after a disruptive event, a need that is becoming acutely clear in the face of increasingly severe weather events in the Atlantic Basin.

Cooperatives are innovative developers and implementers of emerging grid technologies. Local control enables the cooperative utility to move nimbly and often without the traditional regulatory oversight required of larger for-profit and crown corporation utilities. Tools and planning models perfected in one geographic area can support accelerated deployment in other geographic areas through networks that fulfill the foundational principle of cooperation among cooperatives.[28]

As an example, tools built by U.S. cooperatives that provide for the integration of utility-operated software systems at the distribution level are now deployed across the Atlantic Basin through MultiSpeak©,[29] an internationally recognized interoperability standard. MultiSpeak©, in turn, is being harmonized with comparable tools developed at the wholesale supply level in Europe through the International Electrotechnical Commission in Brussels.

A second example is in the arena of microgrid development. In the state of North Carolina, North Carolina Electric Membership Cooperative has developed the state's first grid-interconnected microgrid on an island that it serves and has another mainland microgrid in development at an animal confinement facility for waste management and odor control. The island microgrid is an exercise in community resilience, protecting a community that is often in the path of offshore storms and can be used for demand

---

27. Ibid.

28. "Co-op 101: Understanding the Seven Cooperative Principles," NRECA, https://www.electric.coop/seven-cooperative-principles%E2%80%8B/ (accessed September 18, 2017).

29. MultiSpeak© is a utility standard that allows the exchange of data with any system or application commonly used in a distribution utility such as outage detection, accounting, meter reading, or engineering analysis. "What is MultiSpeak?" http://www.multispeak.org/what-is-multispeak/ (accessed September 5, 2017).

response, energy arbitrage, and ancillary services in the regional power market. The resources in the microgrid include a 3-megawatt diesel generator, a Tesla 500-kilowatt / 1 megawatt-hour battery, 15 kilowatts of solar, and 225 internet-connected, consumer-controlled thermostats and water heaters. These resources also can reduce reliance on the main power grid during times of high demand when the island reaches its peak population in the summer, and provide backup power in case mainland power is interrupted.[30] At times of low consumption in the winter, these same resources can be deployed into the regional wholesale market for financial return.

In addition, cooperative organizations are using geographic information system tools for electrification planning in sub-Saharan Africa. These tools require the collection of base data that include transportation infrastructure, electric infrastructure, and demographics, among other items. Such efforts are being integrated with dynamic modeling tools developed by U.S. cooperatives to make cost-effective and reliable grid investments and, in particular, to conduct microgrid analyses that employ more sophisticated modeling and analytic capabilities.

Such analytical tools enable robust grid expansion as well as providing a platform for consumer participation and local control of energy production. They further complement analyses of existing transportation, water, food, and energy systems from a resiliency and sustainability perspective.

Grid modernization and the integration of low-carbon technologies go hand-in-hand. The intensity and approach of such efforts varies substantially between and among the four continents of the Atlantic Basin, and yet there is a common direction driven by two concurrent trends. The first is the rapidly declining cost and increasing efficiency of renewable energy, especially wind and photovoltaic solar. The second is the massive increase in recoverable reserves of natural gas at historically low prices. A third trend, increased research, development, and deployment of energy storage resources, is at an earlier stage but shows potential to contribute to decarbonization, especially when deployed in conjunction with intermittent renewable generation.

Each of these trends — growth of renewables, natural gas supply, and storage technologies will now be expanded upon within the Atlantic Basin con-

---

30. Robert Walton, "How Ocracoke Island's microgrid kept (most of) the lights on during last month's outage," Utility Dive, August 29, 2017, http://www.utilitydive.com/news/how-ocracoke-islands-microgrid-kept-most-of-the-lights-on-during-last-mo/503806/ (accessed September 19, 2017).

text leading to a discussion of the modernization of the electric grid and the evolution of microgrids necessary to optimize the value of each trend to both the energy and transportation sectors.

Growth of Renewables

Deployment of wind and solar power has received significant and ongoing policy support from the U.S. government and the EU governments via incentives and mandates. This has resulted in achieving significant scale and very significant cost reductions, as shown in Figure 5. In the EU, the 2020 Package adopted in 2009 mandates that renewables supply 20 percent of total energy by 2020,[31] and the emissions trading program helps support renewable deployment. In the U.S., federal tax subsidies and state renewable mandates[32] have resulted in significant growth in renewable generation. Between 2005 and 2015, the share of electric generation in the United States from renewable sources shot up dramatically from under 9 percent to over 13 percent, and exceeded 15 percent in 2016.[33] In the EU, renewable generation rose from just under 15 percent in 2005 to nearly 29 percent in 2015.[34] In 2016, wind and solar made up the majority of new capacity additions in both the U.S. and the EU, accounting for about 63 percent[35] and 86 percent,[36] respectively.

Expansion has driven technological improvements, with resulting increased output and cost reductions, in more mature markets like the U.S.

---

31. This target is not just for electric generation.

32. While efforts to pass a national Renewable Portfolio Standard (RPS) have not passed the U.S. Congress, such standards been adopted by 29 states and the District of Columbia (DC), with several others adopting voluntary standards. Recently, some states have extended their standards or increased their goals. In 2016 alone, DC, Oregon, and New York extended and expanded their RPS standards with many other states in ongoing conversations about altering their renewable standards.

33. This is in part due to rapid growth in non-hydro renewables and the end of drought conditions in the western United States that had depressed hydroelectric generation output.

34. "Renewable Energy Statistics," *Eurostat*, June 2017, http://ec.europa.eu/eurostat/statistics-explained/index.php/Renewable_energy_statistics#Electricity (accessed August 25, 2017).

35. "Renewable generation capacity expected to account for most 2016 capacity additions," EIA, January 10, 2017,https://www.eia.gov/todayinenergy/detail.php?id=29492 (accessed August 25, 2017).

36. "Almost 90 percent of new power in Europe from renewable sources in 2016," *The Guardian*, February 9, 2017,https://www.theguardian.com/environment/2017/feb/09/new-energy-europe-renewable-sources-2016 (accessed August 25, 2017).

**Figure 5: U.S. Unsubsidized Levelized Cost of Energy—
Wind/Solar PV (Historical)**

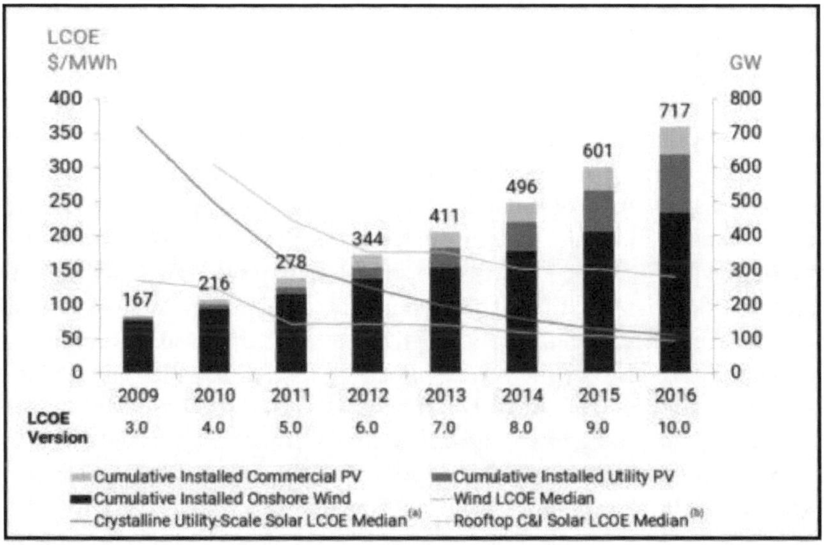

Source: Levelized Cost of Energy Analysis 10.0," Lazard, December, 15 2016, https://www.lazard.com/
perspective/levelized-cost-of-energy-analysis-100/ (accessed August 25, 2017).

and Europe that help to drive down the costs of these resources across the
entire Atlantic Basin.

Hydropower has been the primary source of power generation in Latin
America for several decades and will continue to be developed, although
much of the potential has already been tapped and new projects are in more
difficult to access areas and often face significant popular opposition. Moreover, concerns have increased regarding cyclical droughts.[37]

Non-hydro renewables provide about 2 percent of generation in Latin
America, but these technologies are expected to be the fastest growing
source of electricity over the next five years, as the declining costs and
increasing efficiency of wind and solar generation have made these resources
more economically attractive, compared to fossil generation.[38] In fact, in

---

37. Ramón Espinasa and Carlos G. Sucre, "What Powers Latin America? Patterns and
Challenges," *ReVista: Harvard Review of Latin America*, 2015, https://revista.drclas.harvard.edu/
book/what-powers-latin-america (accessed August 25, 2017).

38. Mae Louise Flato, "Is Latin America the New Global Leader in Renewable Energy?"
Atlantic Council, February 7, 2017,http://www.atlanticcouncil.org/blogs/new-atlanticist/is-
latin-america-the-new-global-leader-in-renewable-energy (accessed August 25, 2017).

2016 the region set records for both wind and solar installations, and Latin America's share of global demand for solar PV is expected to more than double in 2017, reaching 10 percent by 2020.

In Africa, hydropower historically has played a major role in development in the region, especially along the Nile, Niger, and Congo River basins. Excluding South Africa, hydropower accounts for more than half of the installed electric capacity in the sub-Saharan region.[39]

Since 2000 several new hydropower projects totaling more than 3 gigawatts have been added in this region, many involving Chinese financing and construction.[40] There have also been several high profile solar projects. Notably, in Morocco the first phase of the Noor Ouarzazate Power Station came online in 2016. Once the whole facility comes online it will be the world's largest solar facility totaling 580 megawatts. This facility uses concentrated solar thermal panels that are coupled to steam turbines to generate power. Concentrated solar technology is not yet as cost competitive as fossil generation. The Noor Ouarzazate plant includes 80 megawatts of solar PV in combination with 500 megawatts of solar thermal generation. The goal is to add additional solar and wind resources to reduce Morocco's dependence on imported fuel.

Morocco's stable government, extensive electric grid, and robust economy have attracted foreign investment; and the majority of the project funding is from EU development banks, the World Bank, and the African Development Bank, with significant additional contributions from the Moroccan government. Similar but smaller projects also have come online previously in Egypt and South Africa, and there are significant solar PV projects in Ethiopia, Kenya, Uganda, Tanzania, Ghana, and Nigeria.[41]

Wind presents a similar picture, with multiple large projects installed. South Africa leads the continent with more than one gigawatt of installed

39. South Africa accounts for more than half of the installed electric generating capacity in sub-Saharan Africa.Nkiruka Avila, Juan Pablo Carvallo, Brittany Shaw, and Daniel M. Kammen, "The energy challenge in sub-Saharan Africa: A guide for advocates and policy makers (Part 1)," Oxfam, 2017, https://www.oxfamamerica.org/static/media/files/oxfam-RAEL-energySSA-pt1.pdf (accessed August 25, 2017).

40. SzabolcsMagyari, "The up-and-coming African solar: Top 50 announced African solar PV projects," *Solarplaza*, April 11, 2017, https://www.solarplaza.com/channels/top-10s/11689/-and-coming-african-solar-top-50-announced-african-solar-pv-projects/ (accessed September 5, 2017).

41. "Morocco starts construction on 70 MW Noor Ouarzazate IV PV plant," *PV Magazine*, April 3, 2017, https://www.pv-magazine.com/2017/04/03/morocco-starts-construction-on-70-mw-noor-ouarzazate-iv-pv-plant/ (accessed August 25, 2017).

capacity and plans to exceed two gigawatts. Morocco and Egypt each have close to one gigawatt of installed wind. These countries all have fairly advanced electric grids and high access to electricity; but there is also significant wind capacity online in less-developed Ethiopia and planned in Kenya.[42]

In general, sub-Saharan Africa presents a unique challenge, with 650 million people without access to electricity and frequent outages and high prices for those who do have access. Sub-Saharan Africa is the most electricity poor area of the world.

Less capital intensive off-grid solutions using solar PV and batteries offer the most immediate opportunity to provide basic electric service in rural sub-Saharan Africa[43] and underserved portions of Latin America and the Caribbean. In these areas, the falling cost of solar PV and batteries makes this an attractive resource for off-grid electric power. Solar power can charge batteries to power lights at night, charge phones, and power schools in these areas. As electric technologies have become more efficient, more can be done with less. Off-grid solar can provide safer and cleaner lighting and cooking, help students read and study, and save people money since it is cheaper than buying candles and kerosene for illumination or paying for phone charging.[44]

As noted above, the latest update on UN Sustainable Development Goal Seven indicates that progress in affordable and clean energy is far short of what is needed and urges more financing and adoption of successful technologies like off-grid solar on a vastly wider scale. Thus, while other parts of the Atlantic Basin focus on reducing their energy and carbon intensity, for sub-Saharan Africa and other underserved areas of the Atlantic Basin, the focus is on increasing access to basic electricity for productive agriculture, manufacturing, and cleaner cooking and lighting.[45]

---

42. Tony Tiyou, "The five biggest wind energy markets in Africa," *Renewable Energy Focus*, October 19, 2016, http://www.renewableenergyfocus.com/view/44926/the-five-biggest-wind-energy-markets-in-africa/ (accessed August 25, 2017).

43. Alister Doyle, "Vast Moroccan solar power plant is hard act for Africa to follow," *Reuters*, November 5, 2016, http://www.reuters.com/article/us-climatechange-accord-solar-idU.S.KBN1300JI (accessed August 25, 2017).

44. Adam Critchley, "Latin America's Bright Future for Off-Grid Solutions," *Solarplaza*, March 16, 2017, https://latam.unlockingsolarcapital.com/news-english/2017/3/16/latin-americas-bright-future-for-off-grid-solutions (accessed August 25, 2017).

45. Nathalie Risse, "UN Secretary-General Issues Second SDG Progress Report," *SDG Knowledge Hub*, June 8, 2017, http://sdg.iisd.org/news/un-secretary-general-issues-second-sdg-progress-report/ (accessed August 25, 2017).

New Natural Gas Supply

Another factor driving decarbonization of electricity in the Atlantic Basin is the significant expansion of natural gas supply. Natural gas supply is important for energy production as well as for its significant ramping capability essential to integrate increasing amounts of intermittent renewable resources. The trend toward a vastly increased supply and lower and less volatile pricing due to the shale gas revolution in the United States and Canada has captured the most attention, with the potential for increased liquefied natural gas (LNG) export throughout the Atlantic Basin.

Since the early 2000s, with the emergence of hydraulic fracturing, or fracking, the potential recoverable reserves have increased significantly because of the ability of this new technology to drill into areas that were otherwise previously unattainable or not economically feasible.

The U.S. Energy Information Administration (EIA) estimates that at the beginning of 2015, there were 2,355 trillion cubic feet of recoverable dry natural gas reserves in the United States. On the basis of current natural gas consumption levels, this amount of reserves would supply the U.S. for over 80 years with no new unproved reserves found.[46] Natural gas from unconventional sources has already become the largest source of natural gas production in the United States. At current production levels, the EIA forecasts in its 2017 Annual Energy Outlook (AEO) that shale gas and tight oil will account for nearly two-thirds of U.S. natural gas production by 2040, as shown in Figure 6.[47]

Increased supply has led to historically low U.S. spot market prices for natural gas, in the range of U.S.\$2 to U.S.\$5 per MMBTU since 2009. Analysts project that the price of natural gas will stay below U.S.\$4 MMBtu through 2018, a direct result of the increased supply.[48] Over the longer term, prices are projected to stay below U.S.\$5/MMBtu through at least 2030.

Elsewhere in the Atlantic Basin, in addition to increased availability of LNG from North America, there have been significant discoveries of large new offshore natural gas fields in the Eastern Mediterranean, much of whose capacity is expected to be marketed in Europe, assuming pipeline infrastruc-

---

46. "Natural Gas Consumption by End Use," EIA, July 31 2017, https://www.eia.gov/dnav/ng/ng_cons_sum_dcu_nus_a.htm (accessed August 25, 2017).

47. *AEO 2017*, EIA, January 2017, https://www.eia.gov/outlooks/aeo/ (accessed August 25, 2017).

48. "Natural Gas Futures Prices (NYMEX)," EIA, August 23, 2017, https://www.eia.gov/dnav/ng/hist/rngwhhda.htm (accessed August 28, 2017).

Figure 6: U.S. Natural Gas Production, Historic and Projected

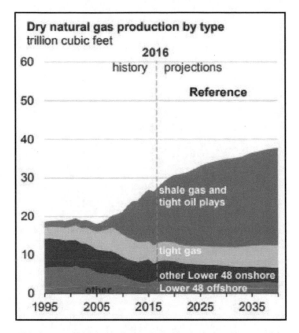

Source: AEO 2017, EIA, January 2017, https://www.eia.gov/outlooks/aeo/ (accessed August 25, 2017).

ture can be built out. European countries are reliant on natural gas imports to meet two-thirds of their demand. At full output, these resources could supply most of the EU's import needs. Accordingly the EU has designated the construction of an Eastern Mediterranean pipeline to allow imports via Greece, a "project of common interest" with the region, streamlining processes and making the project a diplomatic priority, while exploring LNG options. Competition from other sources and challenges to regional cooperation likely will result in failing to reach these levels. Nonetheless, these new sources of gas offer European countries the opportunity to diversify suppliers and lower costs, making natural gas a more competitive source of electricity generation in Europe as well.[49]

---

49. TareqBaconi, "Pipelines and Pipedreams: How the EU can support a regional gas hub in the Eastern Mediterranean," European Council on Foreign Relations, April 21, 2017, http://www.ecfr.eu/publications/summary/pipelines_and_pipedreams_how_the_eu_can_support_a_regional_gas_hub_in_7276 (accessed September 19, 2017).

By offering an economically competitive alternative to coal, natural gas could reduce the emissions impact of the planned retirement of Germany's nuclear plants and help the country meet its energy transition (*Energiewende*) goals. In Germany, natural gas produces more than 12 percent of the country's electricity, just slightly less than the 13 percent produced by those nuclear plants set to retire. Higher-emitting coal, however, produces more than 40 percent of electricity, offering significant opportunities for emissions reduction by switching to lower-emitting natural gas.[50]

Natural gas is already the primary fossil fuel for electric generation in Latin America, supplying about a quarter of the region's generation. The shale gas supply boom most directly affects Mexico, which is the largest export market for the United States, through pipelines rather than LNG. The Latin America and Caribbean region also has significant sources of supply from gas fields in the Andean region of Peru and Bolivia, and from Trinidad and Tobago, a long-time exporter of LNG. The Vaca Muerta shale formation in Argentinian Patagonia, according to Energy Information Agency (EIA) estimates, holds the world's second largest shale gas reserves and the world's fourth largest shale oil reserves.[51]

There are significant opportunities to reduce costs while achieving greater efficiency and emissions reductions by converting existing oil and diesel generation to run on natural gas, especially in the Caribbean. These resources ensure that, along with renewables, natural gas generation will play an important role in meeting increased demand in the region.[52]

While there is great potential for renewables in expanding electric generation in Africa, fossil generation will still be necessary to meet burgeoning demand, expand access, and increase reliability. Increased natural gas supply and lower prices will also offer an opportunity for African countries seeking to expand their generation to do so at lower cost and with lower emissions. Some of the new production in the Eastern Mediterranean will be used to

---

50. Dagmar Dehmer, "Natural gas is key to German Energiewende, says association chief," Euractiv/Der Tagesspiegel, August 24, 2017, https://www.euractiv.com/section/energy/news/natural-gas-is-key-to-german-energiewende-says-association-chief/ (accessed August 25, 2017).

51. Santiago Miret, "Vaca Muerta, Vaca Viva—Argentina's Shale Story," Berkeley Energy & Resources Collaborative, November 19, 2014, http://berc.berkeley.edu/vaca-muerta-vaca-viva-argentinas-shale-story/ (accessed September 18, 2017).

52. Ramón Espinasa and Carlos G. Sucre, "What Powers Latin America? Patterns and Challenges," *ReVista: Harvard Review of Latin America*, 2015, https://revista.drclas.harvard.edu/book/what-powers-latin-america (accessed August 25, 2017).

supply North Africa and Egypt in particular. There are also significant natural gas supplies across Africa and potential for large new discoveries, all of which could help reduce energy costs and boost local investment if they can be developed and delivered.[53]

Storage Technologies

Much of the recent excitement around storage technology has been driven by the increasing production and declining costs of battery technologies. Battery storage has the potential to help increase the flexibility and reliability of intermittent renewable technologies, especially solar PV. While there is not yet wide deployment and experience with combined utility-scale solar PV-battery storage systems, a recent report by the U.S. National Renewable Energy Laboratory (NREL) found that these systems become increasingly financially viable the higher the level of PV penetration. It concluded that while grid-connected solar PV without storage is generally more financially attractive today, by 2020 PV-battery storage systems will be more economic at penetration levels over 15 percent with current solar tax subsidies and at levels of 24 percent or higher even without subsidies. While this study focused on the United States, its conclusions should be broadly applicable in other grid-connected areas in the Atlantic Basin.

Batteries are not the only storage option. There are already dozens of pumped hydro projects deployed around the world. This nearly century-old technology uses inexpensive power overnight, when demand and prices are low, to pump water to an elevated reservoir and then release the energy as needed to spin a turbine and generate during the peak of the day, when demand and prices are high. Less common are compressed air storage systems, which use off-peak power to compress air into a cavern or vessel that is then released to generate electricity. Pumped storage has always had some carbon reduction benefit since it offsets peaking generation from resources such as combustion turbines that tend to have higher emissions. When coupled with renewable generation, such storage systems can act to absorb excess non-emitting energy when it is not needed and shift to it when it is needed. This is especially attractive with wind generation, where output tends to be higher at night when demand is low but can also be used in areas of high solar penetration.

53. Antonio Castellano, Adam Kendall, Mikhail Nikomarov, and TarrynSwemmer, "Powering Africa," McKinsey, February 2015, http://www.mckinsey.com/industries/electric-power-and-natural-gas/our-insights/powering-africa (accessed August 25, 2017).

Advances in grid architecture are also delivering opportunities to aggregate demand side resources to provide storage. "Community Storage" is an emerging term for programs that aggregate distributed energy storage resources that are located throughout a community, such as water heaters, electric vehicles, and interconnected storage batteries to improve the operational efficiency of electric energy services to consumers. The defining characteristic of a community storage program is the coordinated dispatch and optimization of premises-based energy storage resources, often behind a consumer's energy meter, to achieve electric system-wide benefit.[54]

As noted by Keith Dennis of the U.S. National Rural Electric Cooperative Association in *Public Utilities Fortnightly*, electric cooperatives are leaders in community storage:

> As a real-world example of community storage in the U.S., Great River Energy (GRE), a wholesale energy cooperative with 28 distribution co-op members in the state of Minnesota, stores a gigawatt-hour each night, every night, in water heaters in homes across its territory. Some of that energy is sourced from wind generation that would otherwise be curtailed. This storage capacity is valuable, so valuable that Steele-Waseca Electric Cooperative, a distribution cooperative member of GRE, will give any member who signs up to participate in the water heater control program an electric storage water heater at no cost. The member can also purchase the output from solar panels from the community solar project at a discount. This small but exciting project empowers members to contribute to shared environmental goals while saving money by eliminating the cost of purchasing a water heater altogether.[55]

Grid Infrastructure Modernization and Microgrid Development

Renewable energy resources often are not geographically co-located within centers of electricity demand because of the nature of the renewable resource and the fact that scalability requires a large footprint. Significant transmission infrastructure throughout the Atlantic Basin would be necessary to deliver renewable energy from rural or off-shore sources to densely populated centers of electricity demand. Examples throughout the Atlantic Basin include:

---

54. Keith Dennis, "Community Storage—Coming to a Home Near You," Public Utilities Fortnightly, February 2016, https://www.cooperative.com/public/bts/energy-efficiency/Documents/Community-Storage-Public-Utilities-Fortnightly.pdf (accessed August 25, 2017).

55. Ibid.

- The Clean Renewable Energy Zones project to deliver wind power from the Texas panhandle to the state's major cities in the southeast;[56]
- The Madeira transmission line, the world's longest, delivering hydropower from the Amazon Basin to major electricity demand centers near the southeastern coast of Brazil; and
- A proposal for several new transmission lines to deliver off-shore wind power from northern Germany to industrial centers in the south.[57]

Even though solar resources are more widespread and less concentrated, allowing for more flexible siting closer to electricity demand centers, larger solar PV projects face many of the same transmission challenges as wind projects due to their large footprint. Transmission projects, however, often face significant public opposition, making them difficult to site and build on a timely basis.

One way to overcome the transmission challenge is to put greater reliance on distributed energy resources (DERs), including small scale generation, storage, and demand-side management resources that can be positioned closer to the electric demand centers. Historically, electric grids have supported one-way flow of electricity, i.e. from the generator, through the transmission and distribution systems, and finally into productive end-use. Central-station generation[58] was the primary, and in many cases the only, source of electricity. Today, distributed energy resources are becoming more prevalent, necessitating the ability to effectively, and hopefully optimally, handle two-way flows of electricity and two-way flows of data. A longer and more technical version of this point would focus on the grid becoming an agile fractal grid, with the ability to isolate sections of a distribution system for protection purposes and to provide a continuous flow of power from distributed resources when central-station power is unavailable.[59]

---

56. Terrence Henry, "How New Transmission Lines Are Bringing More Wind Power to Texas Cities," National Public Radio, June 26, 2014, https://stateimpact.npr.org/texas/2014/06/26/how-new-transmission-lines-are-bringing-more-wind-power-to-texas-cities/ (accessed August 25, 2017).

57. Benjamin Wehrmann, "The Energiewende's booming flagship braces for stormy times," Clean Energy Wire, June 14, 2017, https://www.cleanenergywire.org/dossiers/onshore-wind-power-germany (accessed August 25, 2017).

58. Large power plants are historically more efficient, and most developed grids have relied on them to provide most generation, which is then delivered by transmission and distribution lines to where it is needed.

59. Craig Miller, Maurice Martin, David Pinney, and George Walker, "Achieving a Resilient and Agile Grid," NRECA, 2014, http://www.electric.coop/wp-content/uploads/2016/07/Achieving_a_Resilient_and_Agile_Grid.pdf (accessed August 25, 2017).

Former U.S. Secretary of Energy Ernest Moniz described the electric grid as "a continent-spanning machine, of immense complexity, which is at its best when it is invisible."[60] This is certainly true throughout the Atlantic Basin, including northern Africa and the more developed areas of sub-Saharan Africa. At the same time, many analysts envision a grid that is made up of smaller, independent or quasi- independent generating entities, or microgrids:

> The "grid of grids" is not necessarily a better model than an integrated grid everywhere and at all times, but there is no doubt that the integration of locally more autonomous generating units needs to be addressed. There are definite advantages to having access to and control of distributed energy resources. Advanced control technology will be very useful to accommodating and then taking advantage of innovative approaches to distributed generation, storage and load control.[61]

As microgrids become more prevalent, the ability to optimize their performance for grid stability and reliability will require the creation of dynamic distribution networks with control and information technologies that operate in real time. This becomes an engineering education challenge, with the likelihood that it can best be achieved through a collaborative trans-Atlantic process. Such developments will evolve differently depending on the context of each national and regional grid. For example, in developed countries like the United States and Germany, which today rely on significant fossil generation, this means upgrading and modernizing a complex and longstanding electric grid to accommodate a changing energy mix. It will be particularly interesting to compare approaches developed in the Americas to those being developed in Germany as critical to the *Energiewende*.

For developing economies across the Atlantic Basin that already have universal or near universal electricity access, the challenge will be to adapt the existing grid to harness additional low- and non-emitting technologies in such a way that development and increased per capita electricity use does not result in runaway growth in greenhouse gas emissions.

For those developing economies in sub-Saharan Africa where access is still limited and electric grids are not fully deployed, especially in rural areas, this might mean developing grids that look very different from those

---

60. Ernest Moniz, "Keynote speech to the Innovative Smart Grid Technologies Conference," IEEE (Washington, February 19, 2014), https://smartgrid.ieee.org/resources/videos/387-ernest-moniz (accessed September 19, 2017).

61. Craig Miller et al, "Achieving a Resilient and Agile Grid."

deployed elsewhere. While wider deployment of grid electricity may represent a longer-term goal, the end result might look very different from the central-station-dominated grids deployed across the Americas and Europe. Just as sub-Saharan Africa has leap-frogged landlines through widespread adoption of mobile phones, there is a possibility that non-grid resources will evolve into microgrids that eventually will be joined together to form a much more decentralized model than seen elsewhere, with a far greater reliance on distributed generation.

Out of necessity, microgrids have been developed in rural areas in the state of Alaska in the U.S.. The Alaska Village Electric Cooperative (AVEC) is the power provider for 33,000 people in 58 small communities in the state's interior, western, and southeastern areas. They are not connected to Alaska's Railbelt electric grid that serves the more densely populated areas between Anchorage and Fairbanks. To serve these communities, AVEC has 50 microgrids (a few communities are close enough to share). Given extreme weather and the lack of road connections, these systems are built with extensive redundancy. The primary fuel is diesel, which is generally expensive and has to be brought in by boat, costing AVEC $26 million last year even at a time of low oil prices. AVEC seeks practical and affordable solutions to reduce fuel costs. The co-op has deployed 34 small wind turbines to help offset fuel costs, saving over $1 million in 2016. At peak output, wind generation exceeds demand, so excess power is diverted to passive loads such as boilers at water treatment plants and other public facilities, reducing their need for diesel. AVEC also makes heat from its diesel engines available for water plants and public buildings.[62]

Ongoing rural electrification in areas of sub-Saharan Africa may provide novel insights into the role of microgrid development for resiliency purposes in mature grids. Local governance models, including cooperatives, for managing transportation, energy, water, and food in emerging economies might also provide learning opportunities for more mature economies.

The dynamic grid, the expansion of renewable generation, and the displacement of fossil generation results in every kilowatt of electricity being consumed more cleanly than the previous vintage of supply. These developments of the grid underlie the value of using more electricity, not only for quality of life and economic prosperity, but also for environmental gain.

62. Derrill Holly, "Are Microgrids the Wave of the Future?" NRECA, June 29, 2017, https://www.electric.coop/microgrids-potential-for-alaska-power/ (accessed August 28, 2017).

Environmentally Beneficial Electrification[63]

Electrification has always been a means to an end, enabling a better quality of life and supporting greater economic prosperity. The availability of high speed communications enabled by electrification as well as the evolving electrification of the transportation sector further enhances positive economic impacts and improves environmental performance and decarbonization efforts.

Modernizing the electric grid, adding real-time control technologies and building out microgrids are the foundations needed for the full development of the concept of environmentally beneficial electrification through the decarbonization of end-uses of electricity and through the electrification of transportation systems. This also has the benefit of creating more resilient energy systems, less likely to suffer from cascading outages experienced in more centralized systems and of being able to be restored individually and then reconnected to the grid.

End-Use Electrification

Historical data from research by the World Bank demonstrates that access to electricity is one of the most powerful economic development multipliers, enabling people around the world to break free from subsistence and economically prosper.[64] Now, more than a century after the advent of electricity, the electric power industry is undergoing a second revolution as the industry dramatically alters not only the fuel mix but also the electric distribution system itself.

Trends in energy generation and end-use technology are changing the environmental value of using electric appliances to produce heat and hot water in buildings. In fact, many experts now believe we are approaching a tipping point: we simply cannot meet the global CO_2 reduction goals if we continue to promote burning fossil fuel on-site in homes and businesses. The strategy of pursuing environmentally beneficial electrification has been

---

63. The concepts and arguments in this section on environmentally beneficial and end-use electrification are taken from Keith Dennis, "Environmentally Beneficial Electrification: Electricity as the End-Use Option," The Electricity Journal, November, 2015, http://www.sciencedirect.com/science/article/pii/S104061901500202X (accessed August 25, 2017).

64. *The Welfare Impact of Rural Electrification: A Reassessment of the Costs and Benefits.*The World Bank Independent Evaluation Group, (Washington, 2008), http://siteresources.worldbank.org/EXTRURELECT/Resources/full_doc.pdf (accessed September 18, 2017).

suggested by the likes of Energy and Environmental Economics (E3)[65] and Lawrence Berkeley National Lab (LBNL)[66] in their assessments of how the state of California will meet its aggressive climate goal and by Jeffrey Sachs in his solutions to address the issue of climate change on a more global scale.[67] Furthermore, this trend is supportive of end-use consumer desires to be more environmentally sustainable in their energy choices, a trend that is at the core of the democratization of energy concept.

Engineering-based analysis demonstrates that electric end-use is the environmentally superior choice over on-site fossil fuel use for space and water heating, cooking, vehicles, agricultural pumping, and other equipment.[68] These trends include a long-term reduction in greenhouse gas intensity of the electric grid, increased efficiency of electric end-use appliances, and the increased need to manage end-use electric demand to help integrate variable renewable resources. As these trends continue to develop, electricity will only increase in environmental performance while on-site fossil fuel use has reached the virtual limits of its efficiency. A 2013 report by Lawrence Berkeley National Lab asserted that "moving away from oil and natural gas and towards electricity is a key decarbonization strategy."[69]

The potential of environmentally beneficial electrification is being recognized in Europe as well. The EU power sector is committed to reducing greenhouse gas emissions by 80 to 95 percent by 2050, and there are calls to promote more efficient electric technologies such as heat pumps to replace

---

65. Amber Mahone, Elaine Hart, Ben Haley, Jim Williams, Sam Borgeson, Nancy Ryan, and Snuller Price, "California PATHWAYS: GHG Scenario Results," E3, April 6, 2017, http://www.ethree.com/wpcontent/uploads/2017/02/E3_PATHWAYS_GHG_Scenarios_Updated_April2015.pdf (accessed September 18, 2017).

66. Max Wei et al., "Scenarios for Meeting California's 2050 Climate Goals: California's Carbon Challenge Phase II: Volume I," LBNL Energy Research and Development Division, September 2013, http://www.energy.ca.gov/2014publications/CEC-500-2014-108/CEC-500-2014-108.pdf (accessed August 28, 2017).

67. Jeffrey Sachs, "Five Questions for Jeffrey Sachs on Decarbonizing the Economy," *Yale Environment360*, July 15, 2014, http://e360.yale.edu/digest/five_questions_for_jeffrey_sachs_on_decarbonizing_the_economy (accessed September 5, 2017).

68. This argument focuses on end-use space and water heating appliances. There are similar opportunities for electrification of vehicles, diesel agricultural pumps, and small internal combustion engines like lawnmowers and commercial blowers.

69. James Nelson et al., "Scenarios for Deep Carbon Emission Reductions from Electricity by 2050 in Western North America Using the Switch Electric Power Sector Planning Model: California's Carbon Challenge Phase II Volume II," LBNL Energy Research and Development Division, February 2013,http://www.energy.ca.gov/2014publications/CEC-500-2014-109/CEC-500-2014-109.pdf (accessed August 28, 2017).

on-site combustion of oil and natural gas for space and water heating.[70] Indeed, the logic of environmentally beneficial electrification is applicable for grid-connected areas throughout the Atlantic Basin.

For less developed areas in the Atlantic Basin, including Haiti and rural sub-Saharan Africa, environmentally beneficial electrification includes cooking using cleaner fuels as part of a transition from the black carbon produced by coal, charcoal, and fuelwood used in traditional cooking, which is simultaneously creating serious health problems, particularly among women and children.[71]

Electrification of Transportation[72]

Ideally, the effort to decarbonize transportation will proceed in tandem with the movement to decarbonize the electric grid. It is interesting to note that some of the earliest applications of environmentally beneficial electrification were focused on seaports and airports, displacing diesel power equipment with electric power equipment (see Chapter Seven). Today, there are a variety of competing technologies seeking to reduce or eliminate direct emissions from transportation.[73] Despite the greatly increased supply of oil and gas in the Atlantic Basin due to fracking and offshore discoveries, there is a growing momentum to displace the internal combustion engine through the introduction of electric vehicles (see Chapters One and Three). In addition, the growing supply of lower-emitting natural gas and biofuels is likely to play a role in this change. This is complemented by the increase in battery production and decline in battery costs that are driving the growth in battery storage in the electric sector.

---

70. Kristian Ruby, "Electrification: A Key Driver for a Decarbonized and Energy Secure Europe," The Energy Collective, April 6, 2016,http://www.theenergycollective.com/aolaru/ 2375457/electrification-a-key-driver-for-a-decarbonized-and-energy-secure-europe(accessed August 25, 2017).

71. For detailed discussions of the environmental and health impacts of black carbon, see Baron, Montgomery and Tuladhar,"An Analysis of Black Carbon Mitigation as a Response to Climate Change," Copenhagen Consensus on Climate, http://www.copenhagen consensus.com/sites/default/files/ap_black_carbon_baron_montgomery_tuladhar_v.4.0.pdf(accessed August 25, 2017) and Janssen, et.al., "Health effects of black carbon," World Health Organization, 2012,http://www.euro.who.int/__data/assets/pdf_file/0004/162535/e96541.pdf (accessed August 25, 2017).

72. The discussion of projections regarding electric vehicle penetration are taken from Brian Sloboda https://www.cooperative.com/public/bts/energy-efficiency/Documents/Member-Advisory-Alleviating-Misconceptions-about-Electric-Vehicles.pdf (accessed August 28, 2017).

73. Direct tailpipe emission from vehicles, rather than life-cycle or source energy.

As this evolution occurs, the same logic underlying end-use environmentally beneficial electrification applies to transportation as well; electricity from a decarbonizing grid will ultimately emit less carbon than direct combustion of fossil fuels. The electrification of the terrestrial transportation sector in the Atlantic Basin will, in many cases, necessitate the development of grid-tied transportation systems. In such a future, decisions will need to be made on the location and ownership of electric vehicle charging stations as well as the role that electric utilities will play.

The year 2017 may be the turning point for the electric vehicle (EV). France and Britain both announced that they would ban sales of petrol and diesel automobiles by 2040.[74] They join Norway, the global leader in electric vehicle adoption, which last year announced a 2025 ban on emitting vehicles. Several other European countries have set goals or targets for EV sales and for the phase out of fossil fueled vehicles.[75] Multiple automobile manufacturers released models that represent true technological innovation. Volvo went so far as to announce that all of its vehicles will either be hybrid or electric by 2019. This announcement was so significant that it took attention away from the much-anticipated assembly line roll-out of the Tesla Model 3.

According to the Center for Automotive Research (CAR), U.S. sales of electrified vehicles in the U.S. were up 16.4 percent in 2017 compared to 2016. The only other vehicle types seeing a sales increase in 2017 were CUV, SUV, and pickup trucks, with increases in the single digits. All other segments experienced negative sales growth. Electrified vehicles (hybrids and electrics) accounted for 3.1 percent of all auto sales, outselling the large car segment and only 2.1 percentage points behind luxury car sales.

Although the EV market is still small, adoption is increasing (see Chapter Three). If current trends continue, significant penetration of electric vehicles is likely over the next 15 years, particularly in suburban areas and bedroom communities for large cities. As shown in Figure 7, electric vehicle sales are projected to surpass internal combustion engine sales by 2038. A Bloomberg New Energy Finance forecast indicates that "adoption of emission-free vehicles will happen more quickly than previously estimated because the cost

---

74. Charlotte Ryan and Jess Shankleman, "U.K. Joins France, Says Goodbye to Fossil-Fuel Cars by 2040," *Bloomberg*, July 25, 2017 https://www.bloomberg.com/news/articles/2017-07-25/u-k-to-ban-diesel-and-petrol-cars-from-2040-daily-telegraph (accessed August 25, 2017).

75. Outside of the Atlantic Basin, China and India (the world's largest and sixth largest automobile markets, respectively) have also announced policies favoring the sale of EVs and curtailment of petrol and diesel vehicles.

Figure 7: Projected Global Market Penetration of Electric Vehicles to 2040

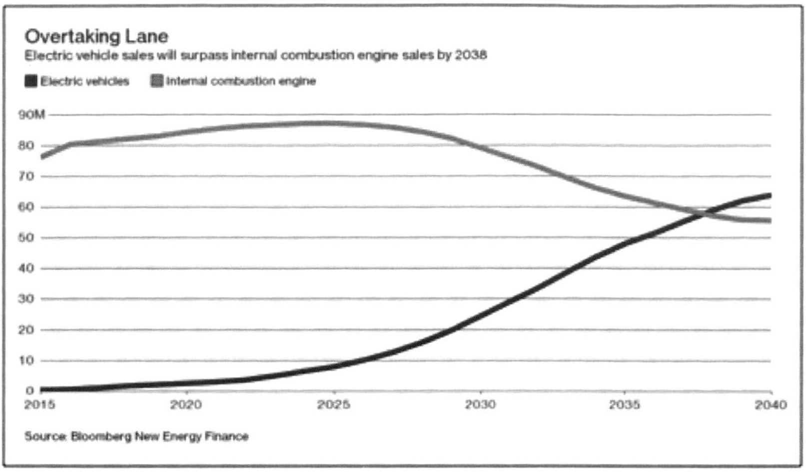

Source: Jess Shankleman, "The Electric Car Revolution Is Accelerating," Bloomberg Businessweek, July 6, 2017, https://www.bloomberg.com/news/articles/2017-07-06/the-electric-car-revolution-is-accelerating (accessed September 18, 2017).

of building cars is falling so fast. The seismic shift will see cars with a plug account for a third of the global auto fleet by 2040 and displace about 8 million barrels a day of oil production—more than the 7 million barrels Saudi Arabia exports today."[76]

Long-term EV market expansion could have a significant impact on electricity markets. A recent report by the Brattle Group[77] suggests that switching to a largely electric fleet by 2050 could increase electricity demand by 56 percent over 2015 electricity sales. This would not only have an impact on utility demand but also on consumers and the environment. The Electric Power Research Institute notes that relative to internal combustion engines,

---

76. Jess Shankleman, "The Electric Car Revolution Is Accelerating," Bloomberg Businessweek, July 6, 2017, https://www.bloomberg.com/news/articles/2017-07-06/the-electric-car-revolution-is-accelerating (accessed September 18, 2017).

77. Peter Maloney, "Brattle: Wider electrification key to averting both climate change and utility death spiral," *Utility Dive*, May 24, 2017, http://www.utilitydive.com/news/brattle-wider-electrification-key-to-averting-both-climate-change-and-util/443369/ (accessed August 25, 2017).

EVs can be more than twice as energy efficient, save 70 percent in fuel costs, and reduce CO_2 emissions by 75 percent.[78]

The speed of adoption of technology advances in decarbonizing electric grids and in electrifying the transportation sector will impact each of the four Atlantic Basin continents differently, but the movement toward environmentally beneficial electrification will inexorably move forward.

Conclusion

There is a long-term value to trans-Atlantic collaboration that tests and accelerates a new energy and transportation future characterized by local control and grid optimization, respectively enabling electrification and being enabled by electrification. Such collaboration would support economic development and prosperity, promote high quality jobs, complement ongoing discussions of resiliency and sustainability of the water-food-energy nexus, and promote community-level investment throughout the Atlantic Basin. The urban/rural rebalancing that could emerge through grid modernization and microgrid development would lead to improved transportation, water, food, and energy security and, hopefully, reduce the level of income disparity.

As has been shown through examples in this article, electric and energy cooperatives are functioning successfully or are under development on all four continents. In addition, economists and futurists point to the cooperative model as fulfilling emerging needs of people for greater control of their energy future. Existing cooperatives can play a catalyzing role in the Atlantic Basin with governments, for-profit corporations, and non-government organizations, innovating around technology development, technology transfer, and human resource development.

Grid modernization holds the key to economic advancement on all four continents. The efficiency of both connected grids and microgrids will be dependent on effectively managing the two-way flow of power and data. A dynamic grid creates for the first time in the history of electrification the opportunity to manage energy demand in real time and to enable a more resilient grid to better manage severe weather-related events. Combined efforts of government, research institutions, and universities are focusing

---

78. Mike Howard, "The City of Tomorrow: Smart, Electric," *EPRI Journal*, July 25, 2017, http://eprijournal.com/the-city-of-tomorrow-smart-electric/ (accessed August 25, 2017).

close attention on the information and control technologies that are in use or under development today. Existing electric utilities and cooperatives have unlimited partnership opportunities in that regard and should proactively engage in demonstration projects with existing research entities. The electrification of transportation systems and the decarbonization of the electric grid through increased penetration of renewable energy resources, each of which are enabled by grid modernization, represent a vision for the future that is environmentally and economically beneficial and, with deliberative actions to encourage local engagement and participation, can be inclusive of all members of society.

Three specific actions would help to accelerate this vision of a trans-Atlantic collaboration:

- Expansion of electricity and energy cooperative development through an intensive education process with government officials, policymakers, economists, and technologists about the cooperative option and the importance of collaboration and cooperation;
- Shared best practices and research and development for grid modernization and end-use energy management through collaborative efforts among government agencies, universities, and research institutions; and
- Public-private partnerships committed to gaining political, financial, technological, and human resource development support for the transition to environmentally beneficial electrification.

Part II

Energy and Land Transportation
in the Atlantic Basin

Chapter Three

Sustainable Mobility in the European Union: Alternative Fuels for Passenger Transport

Eloy Álvarez Pelegry, Jaime Menéndez Sánchez, and Macarena Larrea Basterra[1]

Transportation is responsible of 25 percent of global final energy consumption (2,800 Mtoe in 2016).[2] Some 60 percent of this global transport demand is passenger transportation (or passenger mobility), one of the fastest growing sectors in terms of energy consumption (with an estimated average annual growth rate of 1.5 percent projected to 2040).

Both travel and freight transport are expected to grow faster than any of the other end-uses for refined petroleum over the period to 2040. This is particularly relevant for electricity—which will see its consumption in transport triple over the same period—and for natural gas—the supply of which will increase by nearly 500 percent. This transportation growth will be driven mainly non-OECD countries, especially in freight transport (which is projected to grow by 30 percent between 2015 and 2040, while remaining relatively constant in OECD).[3]

This growth in freight transport will also multiply the possibilities for multimodal transportation, in parallel to increases in industrial production in developing countries, but not in OECD. In fact, more than a half of the increase in the world's freight transportation energy use, together with increasing demand for goods and services, will come from non-OECD countries.

Given the complexity and breadth of the total global transportation sector (which also includes freight and rail, shipping and aviation), this study focuses only on road passenger mobility, the largest segment of the transportation sector.

---

1. The authors would like to thank Manuel Bravo for his suggestions.

2. This figure is estimated based on consumption in 2012 and assuming certain growth of global fuels consumption, and is based on Energy Information Administration, *International Energy Outlook 2016*, https://www.eia.gov/outlooks/archive/ieo16/pdf/0484(2016).pdf.

3. Energy Information Administration, "International Energy Outlook, 2017, https://www.eia.gov/outlooks/ieo/pdf/0484(2017).pdf.

To achieve sustainable mobility efficiency, both demand management and mitigation of environmental impacts must be considered. The automation of transportation, along with information and communication technologies (ICT), could contribute significantly to a sustainable transportation model in the future. Alternative fuels[4] in transportation, such as electricity or natural gas, are also essential for transportation sustainability because of their relatively low emissions.

This chapter begins with a description of the current crossroads of energy and transportation in Europe, and an analysis of this economic and policy intersection over the last decade. Our attention then turns to the electric vehicle and its related issues, focusing the analysis on the leading European countries in electric mobility, and on France (due to its size and continental weight). A similar analysis of gas-fueled vehicles is then undertaken, centering on Italy, the most advanced European country in gas-fueled transportation. Electricity and natural gas are studied and considered as alternative energies for vehicle transportation both at the national level and within the European Union (EU) context. Finally, there is a presentation of the results and main findings of our recent study on passenger mobility in the Basque Country[5] of Spain.[6] The chapter ends with an analysis of the absolute and relative environmental and economic costs and benefits among these alternatives and other fuels available for use in passenger transportation in Europe (BEVs, PHEVs, conventional hybrids, CNG and LPG vehicles).

---

4. By alternative fuel we mean energy sources used to power alternative fuel vehicles, including the following: liquefied petroleum gas (LPG), natural gas (NG), biomethane, hybrid and pure electric energy, hydrogen, E85, biodiesel, biofuel, as stated by the European Commission (see EEA, "New passenger vehicles using alternative fuels," 2017, https://ec.europa.eu/transport/facts-fundings/scoreboard/compare/energy-union-innovation/alternative-fuel_nl).

5. A number of characteristics make the Basque Country an appropriate case to study: its energy, transportation and environmental policies, its entrepreneurial initiatives for the development of electric vehicle penetration and other alternative fuels, as well as its industrial base which is relevant for transportation. Furthermore the size (7,000 km^2) of the Basque Country and its highways and roads infrastructure are of an appropriate size for the practical development and deployment of electric and gas-fueled vehicles. Last but not least, a very detailed database on vehicle displacements between areas and zones within the Basque country allow for useful calculations and analysis.

6. This study considers some of the most relevant countries in terms of penetration and promotion of electric and gas-fueled vehicles in order to extract lessons for achieving a more sustainable passenger transportation sector. Spain is not among these countries; however it is considered when we analyze the impact of the penetration of alternative fuel vehicles in economic and environmental terms.

Figure 1. Evolution of Transportation in the EU-28, 1995–2014

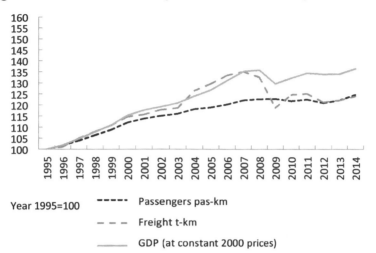

Year 1995=100

----- Passengers pas-km

— — — Freight t-km

———— GDP (at constant 2000 prices)

Notes for Figure 1: 100 = respective levels in 1995. Passengers pas-km means passenger-kilometers (a passenger-kilometer is tabulated when a passenger is carried one kilometer: calculation of pas-km equals the sum of the products obtained by multiplying the number of revenue passengers carried on each passenger travel/transport stage by the stage distance). Freight t-km is a measure of freight carried by a mode of transport, like roads, railways, airways or waterways. It is calculated as T-km equal TLC (total load carried measured in tons) multiplied by TDC (total distance covered measured in kilometers). Source: Álvarez, E. y Menéndez, J., *Energías alternativas para el transporte de pasajeros. El caso de la CAPV: análisis y recomendaciones.* Energy Chair of Orkestra—Basque Institute of Competitiveness, 2017, http://www.orkestra.deusto.es/es/investigacion/publicaciones/cuadernos-orkestra/1150-energias-alternativas-transporte-pasajeros.

Energy and Transportation in Europe[7]

Both as an economic sector and as an infrastructural network ranged across the map, over time European transportation has expanded in parallel with the growth of the European economy (in standard GDP terms). Although freight transport is more sensitive to the evolution and growth of the economy, passenger transportation has also become increasingly tied to economic growth (see Figure 1), and both were pro-cyclical during the last economic crisis.

---

7. For a deeper discussion of EU transportation strategy and policy with respect to infrastructure as well as alternative fuels see the section "EU Transportation Strategy," in Chapter Seven of this volume "The Greening of Maritime Transportation, Energy and Climate Infrastructures in the Atlantic Basin: The Role of Atlantic Port-Citites," by Joao Fonseca Ribeiro.

The most integrated and developed transportation infrastructures are the road and highway networks (even though some European countries, like France, have quality and competitive railways for passenger transportation). As a result, road transport is key within the EU; in terms of passenger-kilometers (pas-km, the standard measure unit employed by the sector), the road segment accounted for 82.5 percent of total EU passenger transport in 2012. As a result, private cars are the key lever within the energy and transport sectors simply because public transportation of passengers (i.e., by bus, train, etc.) is not very significant at the European level.

Transportation accounts for 96 percent of petroleum-derived fuel consumption in the EU. Because of this high level of oil dependency, the economic cost to import most of this crude oil, and the environmental and geopolitical risks associated with it, the EU has established objectives to reduce the weight of petroleum-derived fuels within the transportation energy mix. One way to reduce EU dependency on oil-based transportation fuels would be to reduce the activity of the sector. However, such fossil fuels should be phased out of transportation in a way that does not negatively affect other economic activities.

Indeed, there is a need to move towards sustainable mobility. There is no single definition of sustainable mobility, although many have been proposed. The most widely accepted meaning is that it meets the mobility needs of the present without compromising the ability of future generations to meet their own needs. Other definitions are based on specific conditions such as the satisfaction of demand at affordable prices, facilitated citizen access, or lower energy and material resources consumption.

Since the beginning of the century, but particularly since the COP 21, the EU has committed itself to reducing greenhouse gases (GHG), including CO_2 emissions, and to decreasing oil consumption. The development of new and more efficient vehicles, along with cleaner fuels, has characterized this European aspiration. Among the various technological developments currently restructuring the European vehicle fleet, alternative vehicle fuels should be considered a viable policy option.

The European Commission has developed legislation—some binding and some merely indicative—to address the energy and climate change challenges (including EC directives on air quality [2008], and the promotion of renewables [2009]). The European Commission's *Directive on the Promotion of Clean and Energy Efficient Road Transport Vehicles* must be transposed

Figure 2. Trends in Total Registrations of AFVs, 2000-2015 (Thousand Vehicles)

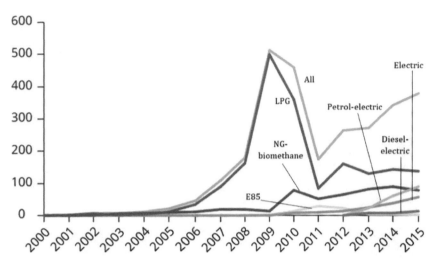

Source: European Environment Agency (EEA), "Monitoring CO2 emissions from new passenger cars and vans in 2015," http://www.eea.europa.eu/publications/monitoring-emissions-cars-and-vans.

to member state legislation. For exampe, in Spain this was done through the Sustainable Economy Act.

But given that the penetration of alternative energy into the transportation sector (see Figure 3) must be increased and intensified, the role of the EU Directive 2014/94/EU (on the *Deployment of Alternative Fuels Infrastructure*, or DAFI) has become the key baseline for the implementation of a National Framework for Action on Alternative Fuel in Transport in each European member state. In this sense all the countries had to prepare a National Framework for Action for the Promotion of Alternative Fuels by the end of 2016.

Despite the development of such rules and others at the European level, the evolution of alternative fuel vehicles has been limited and inconsistent (see Figure 2). In any case, the penetration of alternative fuels must also be supported by the development of new strategic infrastructure, which the EU promotes. Nevertheless, infrastructure costs remain a barrier to development.

Electric vehicles

The penetration of electric vehicles (EV) is not yet significant across the world. However, the global EV fleet surpassed the two-million-unit barrier in 2016, only a year after it had reached the first one million mark in 2015.[8] At the current stage of technological development, high EV price and unmet charging infrastructure requirements remain the main causes behind this still relatively low penetration rate. In addition, the relative differences between electricity and conventional fuel prices must still be seriously considered. However, some European countries are making important efforts to accelerate the rate of EV penetration. Norway and the Netherlands are perhaps the most outstanding countries in this regard. However, for the purposes of this analysis, France is highlighted, due to the relative weight of its economy within Europe and because of some distinctive features of the country and certain challenges it faces in order to increase the penetration rate of EVs. Nevertheless, further references are also made to other relevant European countries such as Germany and Sweden, as well as to the Netherlands and Norway.

France

Some distinctive features distinguish France from most of its European partners: (1) the size of its economy and population; (2) the notably low CO_2 emissions generated by its electricity sector (100 g/kWh) mainly due to the penetration of nuclear (76.5 percent) and renewables (17.4 percent) in the electricity generation mix;[9] (3) the strong French automotive industry; and (4) clear French policies supporting EV deployment.

Since 2009–2010 France has implemented significant regulations for promoting alternative fuels in transportation. Electric mobility has been given a noticeable boost by the National Action Framework and the Energy Transition Law. Furthermore, the various pieces of legislation that since 2009 have pursued cleaner air and lower GHG emissions are also important, as they have supported the development of electric vehicles and recharging infrastructure.

---

8. International Energy Agency (IEA), *Global EV Outlook 2017. Two million and counting*, International Energy Agency, 2017 https://www.iea.org/publications/freepublications/publication/GlobalEVOutlook2017.pdf.

9. Réseau de transport d´électricité, Power Generation by Energy Source, 2016. http://www.rte-france.com/en/eco2mix/eco2mix-mix-energetique-en. Only Norway and Sweden have electricity mixes with lower percentages of CO_2 emissions.

In October 2016 Ségolène Royal, the Minister for Ecology, Sustainable Development and Energy, announced that the EV car stock in France has surpassed 100,000 units. By June 2017, France represented one third of the EU's pure or battery electric (BEV) vehicle stock, while Germany accounted for one sixth. Indeed, in terms of pure electric (or BEV) vehicles, France leads the European Union.[10] However, if one were to compare national levels of pure electric *plus* plug-in hybrid electric vehicles (i.e., BEV+PHEV[11]), France would still account for one fifth of all the EVs in the EU (although, in this case, France would trail the Netherlands, and Germany would be right behind it.)[12] Although such levels of EV penetration might seem significant, it should be noted that registered EVs account for only 1.1 percent of the total French vehicle fleet in the Paris region.

However, the development of EV charging infrastructure in France has been unequalled in Europe and highly concentrated in some areas. As with all EU countries, there are clear differences between regions within France. While most analyses of EVs are country-focused, a regional philosophy should be considered, as there can be important differences inside a country.

Since 2014, the number of charging points has increased significantly— four-fold between 2014 and 2015 (compared to a three-fold increase in Norway and a doubling in Germany and Sweden). This same growth is paralleled in the EU as a whole: the greatest increase of charging points in Europe occurred during the 2014–2016 period. In 2016, there were more than 14,360 charging points in Europe (up from 1,800 in 2012), of which more than 468 were fast charging points.

The EU-financed Corri-Door project has facilitated the installation of 180 fast charging points (with 80 km between each charging point). The French Energy Transition Law for Green Development established the objective of one million charging points by 2030. In fact, France has since raised the target to seven million charging points by 2030.

This rapid rollout of EV infrastructure is at least partly due to the fact that France has a strong incentive system that provides up to 10,000 euros (€) for the purchase of an electric vehicle, among other benefits. Furthermore, the vehicle manufacturing industry wields significant influence over the promotion and rollout of electric vehicles. The leading model in France

---

10. At the broader European level, Norway would stand out with the greatest stock of EV.

11. PHEV means plug-in hybrid electric vehicle.

12. EAFO, *European Alternative Fuels Observatory*, 2017, http://www.eafo.eu/.

in terms of sales—the Renault ZOE—is also the leader across the continent, including in the EU, EFTA and Turkey.[13]

Norway

Despite the EV numbers of France, no EU country matches the electric vehicle stock of Norway. If we consider the EU and Norway together, Norway would make up 20 percent of all electric vehicles in this broader Europe while France would represent 15 percent. The main difference between Norway and France is that the former accounts for only 1 percent of the total population and 1 percent of the total passenger car fleet of Norway+EU, and France 14 percent and 13 percent, respectively.

Norway is therefore the leading European country in terms of the penetration share and size of its EV fleet (with 133,260 electric vehicles in 2016). This significant EV deployment is the result of a long trajectory that began in the 1990s and has continued to enjoy a consensus of political support among national parties since then. This trend is set to continue, given that from 2025 all new vehicles in Norway (such as private cars, city buses and light vans) must be zero-emission vehicles, while GHG emissions from transportation must be cut by 50 percent by 2030, according to Norwegian national legislation.

Norway is not, however, a member state of the EU. As a consequence, Norway does not have a National Framework for Action on Alternative Fuels in Transport. However, it does belong to the European Economic Area (EEA) through which Norway can participate in the EU market. The creation of this broader market space, together with the articulation of several EU northern policies, has forged a close link between EU and Norwegian policies. In Norway, therefore, the relevant equivalent to the member states' National Framework for Action on Alternative Fuel in Transport is the National Transport Plan (NTP), which has been organized in two distinct phases: the NTP 2014–2023 and the NTP 2018–2029.

The NTP adopts the concept of the zero-emission vehicle. As a result, the NTP does not support any particular concrete technology (such as electric vehicles), but rather aims to cut transportation emissions by allowing different kinds of vehicles to be developed. This is similar to the philosophy underpinning European policy, as expressed in the 2014/94/EU Directive (which allows for different kinds of alternative fuels, including liquified

---

13. EAFO, op. cit., 2017.

petroleum gases, or LPG), although the Norwegian objectives are more rigorously in line with the objective of a low carbon economy.

Among the main incentives for the implementation of the NTP, the Norwegian Government has exempted BEVs (including fuel cell vehicles, or FCVs) from the vehicle registration tax. There is also a reduced property tax for BEVs and FCVs, along with an exemption from the value-added (VAT). Direct exemptions amounted to nearly 40 percent in 2015, when EVs accounted for some 23 percent of total vehicle sales.

By 2030, a 30 percent sales rate for EVs is expected to be in effect in Norway, and a 250,000-strong EV fleet is projected for 2020.[14] In anticipation, the Government has launched a public funding plan to set up two multiple-mode charging points every 50 kilometers on major highways.

Germany

Because of its automotive industry, Germany is especially relevant to any discussion of European mobility. Nevertheless, the country's penetration rate has not been high enough to place Germany's EV fleet among the leaders in Europe. In 2016, the country had a stock of only 72,730 EVs. The EV market share in 2017 was only 1.26 percent, and is not expected to exceed double digits by 2020, unlike France and the Netherlands.[15]

However, Germany needs to develop an EV market in order to retain its position as a leading automotive supplier (see Chapter One). The Alliance of German Car Manufacturers (BMW, Daimler AG, Volkswagen and Ford) has set targets for what would be Europe's largest network of Combined Charging System (CCS) fast charging points. By the end of 2017, 400 charging points are to be put in place across Europe (and several thousand by 2020).[16]

With a time horizon to 2020, Germany has instituted a program of support for electric vehicle development, with a total budget of € 1.2 billion (of which the Federal Government contributes half).[17] The Federal Government

---

14. Ibid.

15. IEA, *Global EV Outlook 2016: Beyond one million electric cars*, International Energy Agency, 2016 https://www.iea.org/publications/freepublications/publication/Global_EV_Outlook_2016.pdf.

16. IRENA, *Electric vehicles: Technology Brief*, International Renewable Energy Agency, 2017 http://www.irena.org/DocumentDownloads/Publications/IRENA_Electric_Vehicles_2017.pdf.

17. BMWi, *Fifth "Energy Transition" Monitoring Report: The Energy of the Future, 2015 Reporting Year*, German Federal Ministry for Economic Affairs and Energy, 2016 https://www.bmwi.de/Redaktion/EN/Publikationen/monitoring-report-2016.html.

has dedicated €300 million of this budget to improving the charging infrastructure. This program also includes direct incentives of €4,000 for the purchase of BEVs and €3,000 for PHEVs. In addition, for those vehicles registered before December 31, 2015, there is a property tax exemption for ten years, and for five years for those registered between that date and December 31, 2020.[18] Such taxes vary with engine power and CO_2 emissions.[19]

Other incentives for BEVs include free car parks (or reserved parking spaces) and legal access to bus lanes,[20] although some of these are applied differently, depending on the Länder (or regional government).[21] Another priority objective of the German Government is to reduce administrative obstacles to the installation of private charging points.

The Netherlands

In the Netherlands, there were 112,010 EVs registered in the transportation fleet in 2016, along with 26,700 charging points (mainly standard ones, as opposed to fast charging outlets). These relatively high numbers are partly due to an important political pact in the Netherlands: the National Energy Agreement for Sustainable Growth, organized with the participation of 40 organizations, including public institutions and private market agents, with the aim of reducing CO_2 emissions in transport by 17 percent in 2030 and 60 percent in 2050. The agreement includes a specific chapter for mobility complemented by the Sustainable Fuels Vision, which states that by the year 2035 all new vehicles sold in the country must be emissions-free.[22]

Vehicles with zero emissions are exempt from registration tax. There is a progressive tax system that varies with the CO_2 emissions of the vehicle. There is no aid for the purchase or installation of infrastructure at national level but there is in certain regions.

Tax incentives have been the main driver for electromobility in the Netherlands since 2015. Between 2017 and 2020 further major changes in the

---

18. EAFO, 2017.

19. Tietge, U., Mock, P., Lutsey, N. and Campestrini, A., *Comparison of leading electric vehicle policy and deployment in Europe*, White Paper, The International Council on Clean Transportation (ICCT), 2016 http://www.theicct.org/sites/default/files/publications/ICCT_EVpolicies-Europe-201605.pdf.

20. EAFO, op. cit., 2017.

21. IEA, op. cit., 2016.

22. EAFO, op. cit., 2017.

Dutch tax system are expected; such changes would mainly affect PHEVs, the tax benefits of which would be progressively reduced towards the level of conventional vehicles.

Sweden

With 29,330 EVs and 2,738 charging points (nearly half of them fast), Sweden is aiming for a 70 percent reduction of CO_2 emissions in the transport sector by 2030.[23] To this end, in 2015, SEK 1.925 billion (aproximately €202 million) was earmarked for local climate change investments between 2015 and 2018. These policies will be strengthened by the end of 2017 with the *Klimatklivet* program, which in total will contribute SEK 1.6 billion by 2020. The government also supports the installation of 40 percent of the charging points, with investment in 3,849 points to date.[24]

Sweden provides a premium aid (*Supermiljöbilspremie*) of SEK 20,000 (aproximately €2,100) for PHEV purchases, provided CO_2 emissions do not exceed 50 g/km and SEK 40,000 (approximately €4,200) for the BEV.[25] The government expects to revise this program in 2018. However, some uncertainty hangs over this program, given that there have occurred some interruptions of the incentives which have had a considerable impact on the penetration ratio of Swedish EVs. Nevertheless, this incentives policy has driven Sweden into one of the best EV positions among European countries: in 2016 Sweden accounted for 3.41 percent of EV registrations, just behind Norway and the Netherlands.

There is also an exemption to the payment of the annual circulation tax for five years.[26] Since 2011, it has also been possible for municipalities or the Transport Administration to create parking spaces dedicated exclusively to electric vehicles.[27]

The current situation in these five emblematic European countries is summarized in Table 1.

23. Tietge, op. cit., 2017.

24. Government of Sweden, *Sveriges handlingsprogram för infrastrukturen för alternative drivmedel i enlighet med direktiv 2014/94/EU, 2016* http://www.regeringen.se/informationsmaterial/2016/11/sveriges-handlingsprogram-for-infrastrukturen-for-alternativa-drivmedel-i-enlighet-med-direktiv-201494eu/.

25. EAFO, op. cit., 2017.

26. Ibid.

27. Government of Sweden, op. cit.

Table 1. Energy and Transportation in Europe, Selected Data from Selected Countries

	France	Germany	Netherlands	Norway	Sweden
Share of EV registrations over total registrations (%)	1.46	0.73	6.39	28.76	3.41
EVs stock	84,000	72,730	112,010	133,260	29,330
Total public available charging points	15,843	17,953	26,700	8,157	2,738
Targets for share of EV registrations over total registrations (%)	20	6	10	30*	--
EVs stock per charging points	5.3	4	4.2	16.7	11.1

Source: Álvarez et al., 2017, based on EAFO, 2017; Tietge et al., 2016; IEA, 2017 and 2016. Note: registration targets represent an average for the period 2016-2020. (-) data not available. (*) objective for 2030.

Penetration and Other Relevant Ratios

The wide variety of policies and results in each country reveals great differences, but no clearly obvious relationship among the various factors that can lead (or not) to higher EV penetration. To identify the circumstances that most stimulate the development of electric mobility, the economic, social, environmental and technical characteristics of each country should be analyzed and compared.

One leading economic driver is the provision of incentives. Given their relevance for the development of electric vehicles, Table 2 presents the level of incentives provided as a percentage of the vehicle final price, along with the country's relative position in terms of incentives and EV penetration. The position of Norway stands out, as the relative incentives of the other countries have not achieved an apparently proportional level of penetration.

The level of GDP per capita (adjusted for purchase power parity) is another determinant of growth in EV registrations. Yet other factors to consider are vehicle price (which varies between countries) and the price differential between conventional fuels and electricity. Finally, the dominant type of local dwellings is also important: people living in detached or semi-detached housing are likely to be more inclined to buy an EV because it is easier for them to have their own charging point at home. We have also ana-

Table 2. Estimated Effect of Direct Incentives in 2016

		France	Germany	Netherlands	Norway	Sweden
Share of EV registrations over total registrations	%	1.46	0.73	6.39	28.76	3.41
	Position	4	5	2	1	3
Percentage of the direct incentive on the final price of vehicle	%	25.6	10	16.8	39.5	10.6
	Position	2	5	3	1	4

Source: Álvarez et al., 2017, based on EAFO, 2017; Tietge et al., 2016; IEA, 2017 and 2016.

lyzed other factors affecting the penetration rate of EVs (e.g., the relationship between area and population density with the density of charging infrastructure); however, they do not show clear results.[28]

One relationship that does stand out is that between EV registrations and the level of electricity-generated CO_2 emissions in each country. Often, countries with higher emissions present lower EV registrations. However, this does not appear to be a clear causal relationship. Consider that from the consumer point of view—which has a tendency to take into account only the tank to wheels (TTW) chain of emissions—an EV emits zero emissions; but for technicians and governments, the policy point of view should incorporate the system to wheels (STW) chain of emissions (at least for GHGs)— a more inclusive accounting cycle of emissions that also captures the carbon footprint of the power sector that supplies electricity to EVs.[29] This means that consumers generally do not consider the nature of the electricity mix in their decisions. But although the generation mix is not a determining driver of EV penetration, it does directly affect the level of emissions reduction at each level of EV penetration. Decarbonization of the power mix remains the central fulcrum which allows EV penetration to further reduce emissions.

---

28. For more, see Álvarez et al., 2017.
29. For more, see section on environmental aspects later in this chapter.

Figure 3. Consumption of Natural Gas in Transportation in Selected EU countries, 2005–2014

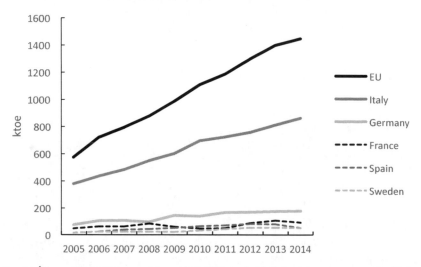

Source: Álvarez et al., 2017, based on Eurostat, 2017. Note: the Netherlands is not represented in this figure. Although it is considered an important case for natural gas vehicles, the Dutch consumption volume is too negligible, compared with the others shown here, to be to captured by the graph.

Gas-Fueled Vehicles

Natural gas is another alternative transportation fuel that could contribute to a reduction of the transport sector's GHG emissions. In this chapter, we refer mainly to the use of compressed natural gas (CNG) by private cars engaged in passenger transportation. Heavy transport vehicles should also be mentioned, given that in case of road or maritime freight transport, there is a trend toward the use of liquefied natural gas (LNG), although freight transport is not dealt with directly in this analysis.[30]

The number of vehicles worldwide running on natural gas has grown at an average annual rate of 20 percent over the last 10 years. Despite this global growth, EU sales have registered a slowdown in recent years: in 2016 sales of gas-fueled passenger cars were only 40 percent of their 2008 levels.[31]

---

30. For a discussion of LNG as a fuel for road freight and maritime cargo, see Chapter Seven of this volume "The Greening of Maritime Transportation, Energy and Climate Infrastructures in the Atlantic Basin: The Role of Atlantic Port-Cities," by Joao Fonseca Ribeiro.

31. (EAFO, 2017).

Table 3. CNG Refueling Infrastructure, Leading EU Countries, 2016

Country	Public CNG Refueling Stations	Passengers Vehicles per CNG Refueling Station
Italy	1,104	808
Germany	883	104
Sweden	169	307
Netherlands	162	61
France	43	178
Spain	45	42

Source: EAFO, 2017 and NGVA 2017.[32]

Today Italy stands out as the largest European consumer of natural gas used in transport. Gas is also used as a transportation fuel in the Netherlands, Germany and Sweden.

With respect to gas vehicle infrastructure, 70 percent of the gas refueling stations in the EU are found in just two countries: Italy and Germany (see Table 3). The number of vehicles per refueling station varies from 808 to 79 vehicles/station in Italy and the Netherlands, respectively.

An important factor affecting the use of such vehicles is the price of natural gas, which remains volatile, given that it is still relatively tightly linked to oil prices (themselves volatile). Still, the final price of natural gas—the sum of the international price plus the supply and distribution costs, and taxes—has fallen. Not only did the natural gas price differential widen with respect to diesel across Europe during 2016; gas prices are also currently below those for low-sulfur fuel oil.

Italy

Italy has developed the use of natural gas in transportation more than any other country in the EU (see Figure 4), and now has the most natural gas vehicles (967,090 in June 2017) and refueling stations (1,104 in 2016). The use of gas for transport began more than 30 years ago, and has sustained a

---

32. NGVA, Statistical Report 2017. https://www.ngva.eu/downloads/NGVA_Europe_Statistical_Report-2017.pdf.

Figure 4. Evolution of natural gas consumption and gas-fueled vehicles in Italy

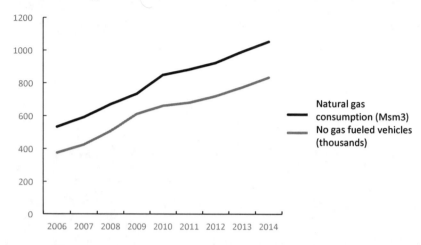

Source: Álvarez et al., 2017 based on Eurostat, 2017[33] and ANFIA, 2015.[34]

growth rate of 9 percent per year. This increased demand has stimulated the development not just of an industry for the conversion of vehicles and the production of related equipment, but also of new standards and legislation. Nevertheless, natural gas still accounts only for 3 percent of total energy consumption in Italian road transport.

The natural gas used in transport is consumed mainly in the form of compressed natural gas (CNG) in low-consumption vehicles: small and medium-sized low-capacity vehicles with high levels of utilization (more than 20,000km/year). As a result, their acquisition—without incentives or subsidies—would be amortized over five to seven years (which is the average fleet renewal period).

The market was initially developed through: (1) a strategy to promote the consumption of own energy sources; and (2) the promotion of the vehicle conversion industry. Vehicle conversions were encouraged through a subsidy of € 600 € to € 2,400 per vehicle. A significant number of stakeholders, however, also have an interest in this market (R&D centers, international

33. Eurostat, 2017.
34. ANFIA, Associazione Nazionale Filiera Industria Automobilistica, 2015. www.anfia.it.

Figure 5. Gasoline, Diesel and Natural Gas Prices, Italy, November 2016

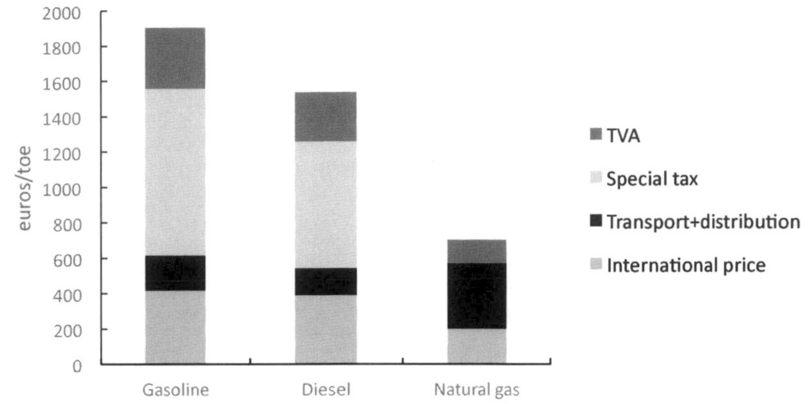

Source: Álvarez et al., 2017.

organizations such as UNECE [United Nations Economic Commission for Europe], etc.).

Italy is also the European leader in the development of regulation for gas-fueled vehicles. In Italy, natural gas enjoys an exemption/reduction of the minimum excise duty of 2.6 €/GJ (set by Directive 2003/96/EC). The Blue Corridors project,[35] with its build-up of LNG and CNG refueling stations, will also facilitate the development of the gas infrastructures in Europe, and not only for freight transport.[36]

---

35. European Commission, Good Practice Examples Appendix D - LNG Blue Corridors Project Fact Sheet, 2016. https://ec.europa.eu/transport/sites/transport/files/themes/urban/studies/doc/2016-01-alternative-fuels-implementation-good-practices-appendix-d.pdf

36. LNG Blue Corridors is a European project financed by the Seventh Framework Programme (FP7). The project is co-funded by the European Commission to the amount of €7.96 million (of €14.33 million in total investments), involving 27 partners from 11 countries, all members of Natural Gas Vehicle Association (NGVA) Europe. The aim is to establish LNG as a real alternative for medium- and long-distance transport—first as a complementary fuel and later as an adequate substitute for diesel. The project has defined a roadmap of LNG refuelling points along four corridors covering: (1) the Atlantic area; (2) the Mediterranean region and (3) connecting Europe's South with the North and its (4) West and East. To help catalzye a sustainable transport network for Europe, the project's goal is: (a) to construct approximately 14 new LNG or L-CNG refueling stations (both permanent and mobile) at critical locations along the Blue Corridors; and (b) to rollout a fleet of some 100 heavy duty vehicles (HDV) powered by LNG.

Somewhat in contrast to the case of EVs, the price of natural gas is key to the penetration of gas-fueled vehicles. This gas price driver is further reinforced by the relatively small difference between the price of conventional vehicles (running on gasoline and diesel) and that of gas-fueled vehicles. In this respect, the prices of gas for transport have an advantage over conventional fuels (gasoline and diesel), given that they are exempted from taxes (see Figure 5).

The Netherlands

The Netherlands is the largest natural gas *producer* in the EU. However the use of natural gas as a transportation fuel in the country is a relatively recent development and began only in 2005 with the construction of the first CNG refueling facilities.

The country sees the use of natural gas as fuel in light vehicles as a transitional solution to promote the use of biogas. Therefore, there is no forecasted expansion of the natural gas distribution network and the current network of 145 supply stations (in 2016) seems to be sufficient given current Dutch plans.

Following a government stimulus program for natural gas-fueled company cars in 2011, natural gas consumption in transportation grew at an average annual rate of 30 percent while the number of gas-powered vehicles increased from 4,000 to 11,000. However, this amount of gas-powered vehicles represents only 0.15 percent of the total fleet, and the total consumption of natural gas in transport does not yet exceed 0.2 percent of total energy consumption.

Natural gas vehicles in the Netherlands enjoy the benefit of reduced taxes, but such benefits are limited. The natural gas energy tax, although considerably lower than that for conventional fuels, remains above the minimum stipulated by the EU. Furthermore, the Netherlands does not take advantage of the kind of tax reductions or exemptions that natural gas fuels enjoy in other countries such as Italy or Spain. In the Netherlands, taxation on vehicle ownership (registration, circulation, and income from the private use of company vehicles) is based on the vehicle's CO_2 emissions per kilometer.

Germany

Germany has 100,000 gas-fueled vehicles and 913 refueling stations. As a part of the national strategy to reduce dependence on oil in the transport

Figure 6. Gas Consumption in Transportation and Gas-fueled Vehicles, the Netherlands, 2006–2016

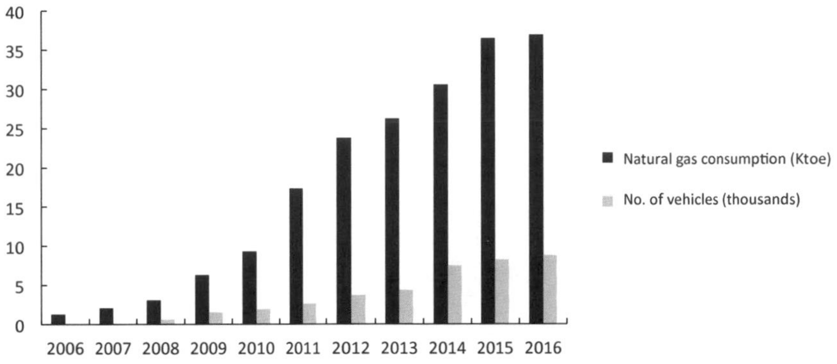

Source: Álvarez et. al. 2017. Note: Ktoe = thousand tons of oil equivalent.

sector, in 2010 Germany launched the *Initiativ Erdgasmobilität* (Initiative for Mobility Based on Natural Gas).

The German government *does not* envisage providing any incentives for the purchase of gas vehicles at present. However, under the Action Program for Climate Protection 2020 (*Aktionsprogramms Klimaschutz 2020*) of 2014, the government took additional measures aimed at expanding the use of LNG as a transportation fuel for both maritime (and inland) shipping and for heavy road transport. The program also proposes a reduction of the energy tax on natural gas as of 2018.

The German government is working with the LNG Platform in road transport, with the collaboration of the automotive industry and other stakeholders, to develop measures to achieve the established target of a 4 percent contribution from natural gas to the energy mix of road transport in 2020. The specific measures under consideration include: a) promoting the installation of LNG service and refueling stations based on the production of biogas and synthetic natural gas; b) encouraging the conversion of CNG service and refueling stations for use by local passenger and commercial vehicles; c) establishing prices for tolls in the natural gas network; d) improving semi-public service and refueling stations for fleet operators; and e) special rights for commercial vehicles operating with CNG/LNG. Biomethane is also important in the Germany strategy to boost natural gas in transport.

Figure 7. Gas Consumption in Transportation and Gas-fueled Vehicles, Germany, 2006–2015

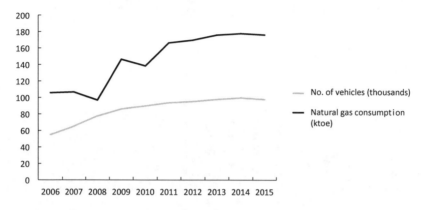

Source: Álvarez et. al. 2017. Note: ktoe = thousand tons of oil equivalent.

Sweden

Gas represents 1.8 percent of total energy consumed in road transportation in Sweden, where there are currently some 52,000 gas-powered vehicles, 2,300 buses (15 percent of the entire fleet and 40 percent of total gas consumption in transport) and 205 public service and refueling stations.[37]

The Swedish parliament has accepted the government's ambitious goal to achieve a vehicle fleet that does not depend on fossil fuels by 2030.[38] This objective is a first step towards the broader objective of achieving zero net CO_2 emissions by 2050. To generate even less CO_2 emissions from gas-fueled vehicles, Sweden is also promoting the use of biogas mixed with natural gas.

In March 2017, the government proposed a new climate action framework, and a new law was expected to be approved in June. The new targets establish zero net GHG emissions in 2045 and a 70 percent reduction in emissions in 2030 (compared with 2010). Therefore, the government must develop political measures to achieve these objectives. Among these measures, the most important are taxes on energy and CO_2, and a VAT of 25 percent added to each conventional fuel, such that taxes will represent a greater weight in the final price.

---

37. NGVA Europe, 2016. https://www.ngva.eu/.

38. Government of Sweden, *Proposition 2008/09.162*, 2009.

Figure 8. Gas Consumption in Transportation and Gas-fueled Vehicles, Sweden, 2006–2015

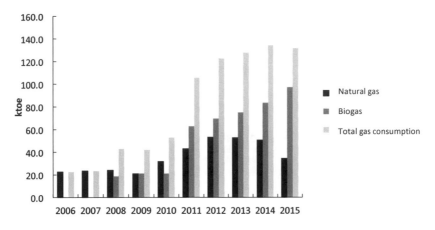

Source: Álvarez et. al. 2017. Note: ktoe = thousand tons of oil equivalent.

Further relevant data from the European countries examined above are summarized in Table 4.

Table 4. Natural Gas Use in Transportation in Europe, Summary Data from Selected European Countries

Netherlands	Germany	Sweden
Focus on a long-term goal for electricity rather than on natural gas in light duty transport.	Germany is the second leading country in the EU in natural gas refueling infrastructures	Clear goals for transport emissions reduction.
Clear orientation to biogas.	Number of vehicles per refueling station is below other European countries with less infrastructure.	Encourages the use of biogas, which has significantly increased its weight (75%) within the fuels of natural gas vehicles (NGVs).
11,000 CNG vehicles	100,000 CNG vehicles	52,000 CNG vehicles
35,000 toe natural gas consumed in transport	180,000 toe natural gas (of which 36,000 toe is biogas)	30,000 toe natural gas (of which 90,000 toe is biogas

Source: own elaboration. Note: toe = tons of oil equivalent.

Alternative Fuels for Passenger Transportation: Environmental Benefits and Costs

To assess the costs and benefits of deeper penetration of alternative fuels in European transportation, our recent study, *Energías alternativas para el transporte de pasajeros. El caso de la CAPV: análisis y recomendaciones* (Alternative Energies for Passenger Transportation), analyzed a range of available alternative vehicle and energy/fuel types, incorporating assumptions and data on the technologies and fuels currently used in the vehicle fleet, vehicle and energy prices, and necessary supply infrastructures and investment.[39] The sections that follow present and analyse the main economic and environmental characteristics of each type of alternative fuel vehicles (AFVs), along with the main findings of the study.

Economic Aspects

One important issue for the penetration of alternative transportation fuels is the cost of electric vehicle (EV) charging infrastructures and compressed natural gas (CNG) refueling points. For biofuels, because there is already a supply infrastructure in place, there is no need for additional investment in infrastructures. In the case of liquefied petroleum gases (LPG), some new infrastructure investments would need to be considered.

For conventional vehicles, current prices are around € 14,000–16,000 per vehicle. EVs are priced at € 34,000 in our study and CNG vehicles at € 25,000.[40] These figures are based on current market prices. A price of € 26,000 has been assumed for conventional hybrids.

The cost of electrical charging points on public roads has been assumed to be in the range of € 7,500 to € 10,000 for conventional charging and € 35,000 to € 50,000 for fast charging. For home charging points, with power levels of 3.7–22 kW, a cost of between € 2,200 and € 2,400 per point is considered. In the case of CNG refueling stations, costs vary depending on the

---

39. Eloy Álvarez y Jaime Menéndez, *Energías alternativas para el transporte de pasajeros. El caso de la CAPV: análisis y recomendaciones*. Energy Chair of Orkestra—Basque Institute of Competitiveness, 2017, http://www.orkestra.deusto.es/es/investigacion/publicaciones/cuadernos-orkestra/1150-energias-alternativas-transporte-pasajeros.

40. According to industry sources, a vehicle with a maximum authorized weight (MAW) of 3,500 kg, might have a purchase cost of € 28,000 + VAT, whereas under a 5-year renting arrangement, the cost would be € 1,254.87, not including VAT. For a vehicle with an MAW of 5,000 kg, the price would be around € 29,000 plus VAT.

Figure 9. Comparative Evolution of Estimated TCO (€/km), Conventional and Alternative Fuel Vehicles

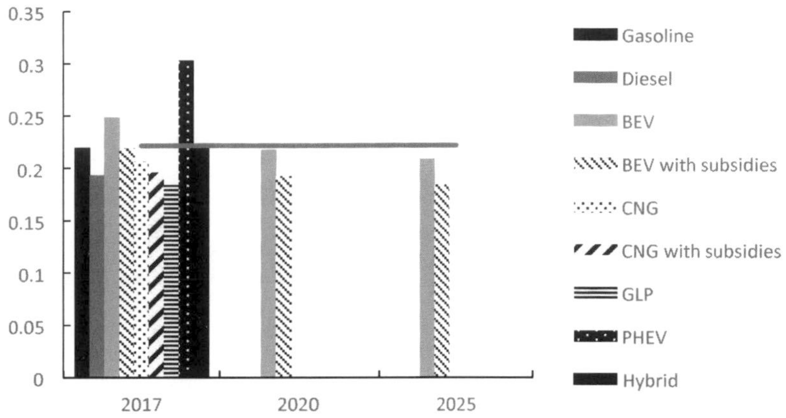

Source: Álvarez and Menéndez, 2017.

capacity and filling type (slow or fast): from a minimum of US$5,000 to a maximum of US$700,000.

From an economic point of view, it is also important to consider vehicle and fuel prices. The price of the vehicle and the cost of the fuel over its lifetime, together with other costs of use (maintenance and others) make up the total cost of ownership for the owner (TCO). Based on the assumptions we have made, our estimates suggest that TCO of AFVs will equalize with that of conventional vehicles by 2025 (see Figure 9).

The TCO may have an impact on the preferences of citizens for one or another technology. It should be kept in mind that, in the end, the decision of which type of car to buy will be taken by the consumer. Along with conventional vehicles, both natural gas or LPG vehicles are sufficiently proven technologies with high production volumes. However, EV technology (and batteries in particular) remain on the learning curve. Therefore, future reductions in their price may affect the TCO.

According to forecasts in 2014 by McKinsey & Company, the price of batteries is projected to fall from 383 US$/kWh in 2015 to US$197/kWh in 2020 and US$163/kWh in 2025—a cost reduction of more than 50 percent over the coming decade.[41] Because battery costs currently represent around

41. McKinsey & Company, *Evolution. Electric vehicles in Europe: gearing up for a new phase?* 2014. http://www.mckinsey.com/~/media/McKinsey%20Offices/Netherlands/Latest%20thinking/PDFs/Electric-Vehicle-Report-EN_AS%20FINAL.ashx.

Table 5. Future Batteries Prices, Forecasts from Various Sources (US$/kWh unless indicated)

Source	2020	2022	2025	2030
Nykvist and Nilson	200-450	-	150-250	150-250
Lux Research			175	
Stockholm Environment Institute			150	
DOE	125	-	-	-
OEM	-	100	-	-
McKinsey	200	-	163	-
Element Energy	-	-	-	215
Fraunhofer (€/kWh)	100-300	-	-	-
General Motors	-	100	-	-
SET-Plan (€/kWh)	200			
Highest and lowest	High: 100 Low: 450	High: 100 Low: 200	High: 150 Low: 250	High: 150 Low: 250

Source: Álvarez and Menéndez, 2017. Note 1: Figures of this table are represented in the currency in which study was conducted. Most of them in US$, unless the Fraunhofer study and the SET-Plan, where the currency employed is €. Note 2: Where more than one type of battery prices were offered, the lithium-ion battery was chosen.

35 percent of the price of EVs, these and other cost reductions could easily bring the TCO of EVs to approximately that of gasoline and natural gas vehicles (as seen in Figure 9).

In line with this cost reduction trend, the European Commission, through the European Strategic Energy Technology Plan (SET-Plan) has set the target for the costs of lithium-ion batteries of € 200/kWh between 2020 and 2030.[42] Some uncertainty remains around the future price of batteries given that projections vary widely among the various institutions producing them. A comparison of several battery cost projections is presented in Table 5.

---

42. European Commission, *Materials Roadmap Enabling Low Carbon Energy Technologies*. Commission staff working paper, SEC(2011) 1609 final, 2011. https://setis.ec.europa.eu/activities/materials-roadmap/Materials_Roadmap_EN.pdf/view.

Environmental Aspects

In a comparative environmental analysis of alternative fuels and vehicle technologies, the first distinction that must be made is between air pollutants and greenhouse gas emissions (GHGs). This is because each distinct yet related set of emissions operates on a different scale of impact and potential damage. Air pollutant emissions have a greater direct impact when people are exposed to them at the local level, and their main risk is related to health when they are inhaled. On the other hand, the GHG emissions present the global risk of climate change. But although GHGs do not represent a direct or immediate problem for citizens, at the global scale, however, their generalized effects build up in the pipeline and eventually have concrete, if indirect, impacts everywhere.

Following from this, the place where air pollutant emissions take place does matter. This happens where vehicles are driven, which generally means greater and more direct exposure to air pollutants among urban populations. On the other hand, the place where GHG emissions take place does not specifically matter: their direct destination is the general atmosphere (and the oceans) that all of us share.

This is why each category of transportation emissions (air pollutants and GHGs) should be analyzed within the frame of different scales (or emissions cycles), depending on their origin and the geographical reach of their potential damage. A smaller scale (or shorter cycle)—used in the case of air pollutants—is known as *from tank to wheels* (TTW) and represents only those emissions that are generated on vehicle roads.[43] A more global scale—used in the case of GHGs—covers the entire chain of emissions. Known as *from well to wheels* (WTW), this scale includes not only the emissions directly from the vehicle, but also from the production, treatment and transportation of the fuel before it reaches the vehicle.

The analysis in this chapter (and based upon our previous study) therefore considers both TTW and WTW emissions scales, because both are critical to an understanding of the broader environmental implications of each fuel. Furthermore, the emissions that each country produces within its own national energy system are typically generated in a cycle somewhere between the WTW and TTW scales. This is especially relevant for the analysis of the electric vehicle, given that its environmental impact (i.e., emissions reductions)

---

43. Not only the emissions produced from the combustion of fuel inside the engine should be considered, but also those produced by the erosion of the wheels and the road when the vehicle is moving (which throws particulate pollution into the atmosphere).

Figure 10. Comparison of TTW, STW and WTW

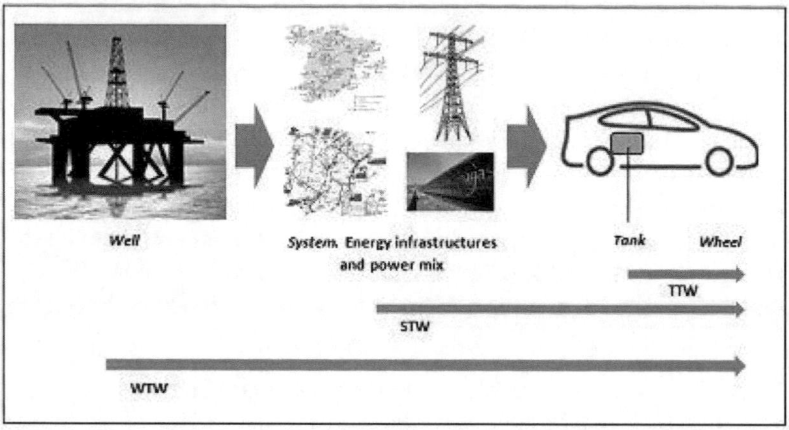

Source: Álvarez and Menéndez, 2017.

is directly related to the structure of the national power mix and the level of emissions resulting from electricity generation. Therefore, this scale—called from *system to wheels* (STW)—has been also calculated and estimated. An illustration of these three different scales appears in Figure 10.

Both CO_2 and air pollutant emissions in the TTW, STW and WTW calculations vary by type of energy, and it is important to remain aware of the differences between them (as illustrated in Figure 11). Both the STW and WTW measures for BEV (and also partly for PHEV, when it is charged) depend on the emissions of the particular national electricity generation mix. Such estimates of emissions levels, then, are more than likely to change in the coming years, given the overall trend toward decarbonization of the power sector. Therefore, to make a homogenous comparison between technologies with 2020+[44] projection values and BEVs, we have estimated and projected lower GHG emissions in future, primarily given the expected increasing penetration of renewable energies (RE). This future RE penetration trend will partly affect the scale of emissions projections for PHEV (in periods of charging), but the main difference is a marked positive effect on the emissions projections for BEV.

Figure 12 presents TTW and STW emissions estimates for air pollutants (NOx and PM). The WTW scale of the emissions chain is not shown because

---

44. 2020+ refers to any vehicle model that is produced from that year.

Figure 11. CO$_2$e Emissions (TTW, STW and WTW) for Each Vehicle Type

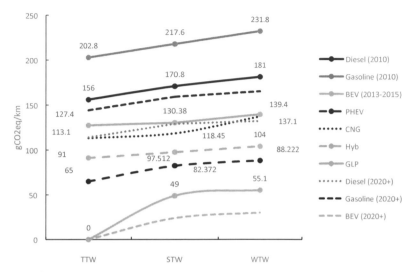

Source: Álvarez and Menéndez, 2017. Note: For the sake of clarity, diesel, gasoline and AFV 2020+ emissions are stated again here: Diesel (gCO$_2$e/km): TTW 114, STW 129, WTW 132. Gasoline (gCO$_2$e/km): TTW 144, STW 159, WTW 165. BEV (gCO$_2$e/km): STW 24, WTW 30.

it is much less relevant for local emissions. Our 2020+ projections for air pollutant emissions foresee reductions for BEV, but PHEV would also generate net pollutant emissions reductions (to the extent that they rely on charging).

Incorporating the above data, Table 6 presents the main assumptions underlying the different emissions estimates (GHG, NOx and particulate matter) for TTW, STW and WTW and for each vehicle type. This lays the foundation for an analysis of possible future scenarios for alternative fuels penetration into the passenger transportation sector.

Scenarios for Alternative Energies in European Transportation: Approaches and Main Findings

Because of their relatively low emissions, alternative fuels,[45] such as electricity or natural gas, are critical for future transportation sustainability.

---

45. In this section, four alternative technologies are analyzed: BEVs, PHEVs, CNG and LPG. Additionally, conventional hybrid cars are included (Hyb), as well as conventional cars (CONV).

Figure 12. Pollutant Emissions, TTW and STW, by Vehicle Type

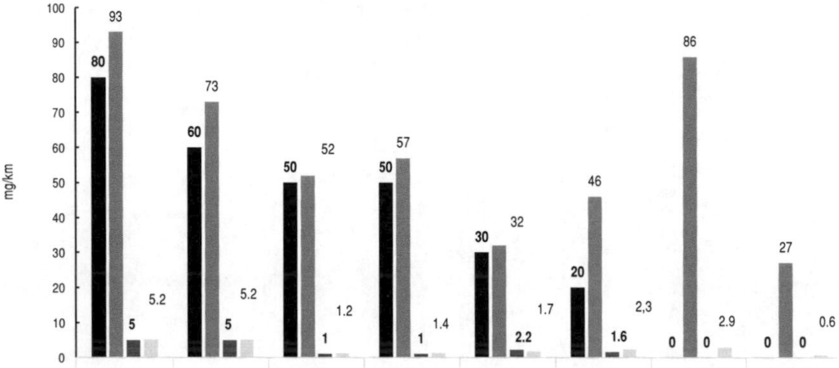

	Diesel	Gasoline	LPG	CNG	Hyb	PHEV	BEV (2013-2015)	BEV (2020+)
■ NOx TTW	80	60	50	50	30	20	0	0
■ NOx STW	93	73	52	57	32	46	86	27
■ PM TTW	5	5	1	1	2.2	1.6	0	0
▫ PM STW	5.2	5.2	1.2	1.4	1.7	2.4	2.9	0.6

■ NOx TTW ■ NOx STW ■ PM TTW ▫ PM STW

Source: Álvarez and Menéndez, 2017. Note 1: The particulate emissions which derive from electricity con-sumption are known as PM10. Note 2: Substantial reductions of NO_x are foreseen in the electric system for the years to come.

The penetration of these energies into the transportation fuel mix will have both environmental and economic implications. To analyze and compare these impacts, we have framed our estimates and projections around two different approaches for the penetration pace of alternative energy fuels in the mix and alternative energy vehicles in the fleet: (1) the immediate, overnight replacement of the existing conventional car fleet by one other single type of fuel/technology; and (2) a gradual, progressive replacement of the current fleet (conventional) with a combination of alternative energy vehicles (see Figure 13).

The first approach assumes complete (100 percent) replacement (overnight) of the current conventional car fleet by one single type/technol-ogy of alternative fuels/vehicles, while the second approach assumes ultimate incorporation of different combinations of technologies in the mix. The sec-ond approach assumes progressive penetrations with different rates of replacement of conventional vehicles by alternative electric vehicles.

Because of the availability close at hand of a high-quality and relatively complete data set on passenger mobility, we have conducted this exercise

Table 6. Summary of the Main Assumptions of the Study's Emissions Estimates and Projections

Type of vehicle	TTW emissions GHG (gCO$_2$e/km)	TTW emissions NOx (mg/km)	TTW emissions PM (mg/km)	STW emissions GHG (gCO$_2$e/km)	STW emissions NOx (mg/km)	STW emissions PM (mg/km)	WTW emissions GHG (gCO$_2$e/km)
Petrol (2010)	203	60	5	218	73	5.2	232
Diesel (2010)	156	80	5	171	93	5.2	181
BEV (battery electric vehicle) (2013–2015)	0	0	0	48.5	86	2.9	55
PHEV (plug-in hybrid) (2020+)	65	20	1.6	86	46	2.4	88
CNG (compressed natural gas) (2020+)	113	50	1	118	57	1.4	137
LPG (liquefied petroleum gas) (2020+)	127	50	1	130	52	1.2	139
Hyb (hybrid) (2020+)	91	30	2.2	98	32	2.3	104

Relevant at local/zone scale: TTW emissions (NO$_x$, PM). Relevant at the scale of the mainland energy system: STW emissions (NO$_x$, PM)

Source: Álvarez and Menéndez, 2017. Note: Substantial reductions of NO$_x$ are foreseen in the electric system for the years to come.

for the Basque Country, a European region (both industrial and rural) located in the north of Spain, and bordering on Pyrenees and France. This region has developed a transportation survey which tabulates the daily number of trips made by passenger cars among and between different areas and zones.[46] Based on such survey data, Álvarez and Menéndez (2017) generated a range of simulated projections for the Basque Country, with a study set covering 72 percent of the total automobile journeys in the region.

---

46. Government of Basque Country, *Estudio de la Movilidad de la Comunidad Autónoma Vasca 2011*, 2012. http://www.CAPV.eus/contenidos/documentacion/em2011/ es_def/adjuntos/Movilidad%20Encuesta%202011.pdf

Figure 13. Approaches and Scenarios

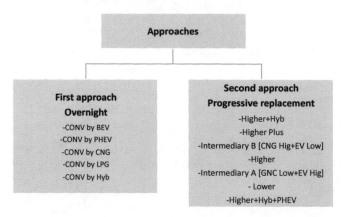

Source: own elaboration.

In the first approach, called Overnight[47]—the assumed immediate and complete replacement of the existing conventional car fleet by a single alternative vehicle type—the compete substitution of the current fleet, for instance, with electric vehicles—results in an extra accumulated net cost of around €4.8 billion (over and above the those for the existing conventional fleet). CO_2 emissions would decline by between 1.5 and 1.8 $MtCO_2e$/year (WTW and TTW, respectively) in perpetuity. NOx and particulates fall by 741 tons/year and 76 tons/year (TTW), respectively.

Given the diverging economic and environmental impacts of such a fleet replacement (i.e., higher economic costs and lower emissions), no single fuel/technology can claim the best results according to all of the criteria. Only by focusing on a single impact does one or another alternative fuel/technology emerge as clearly the most suitable. Table 7 lays out the different criteria for assessment: (1) fuel savings; (2) CO_2 specific cost (the ratio of the cost of vehicle and infrastructure to the amount of CO_2 reductions); (3) reduction of environmental cost (in which a price for NO_x and PM are considered); and (4) specific contribution to the CO_2 reduction targets of the Basque Country. Broadly speaking, electric and hybrid vehicles present good relative positions/results for most of the criteria.

---

47. This substitution exercise, however, is a hypothetical, not a real, analysis, It provides ordered figures for comparing the results of the alternatives. It also forms a basis for the progressive replacements analysed later.

Table 7. Order of Alternatives, Overnight replacement approach results against different criteria

	Fuel saving	Specific cost CO_2	Reduction in environmental costs	Contribution to meeting GHG reduction targets
CONV by BEV	1	4	3	1
CONV by PHEV	3	5	1	2
CONV by CNG	2	3	4	4
CONV by LPG	4	1	5	5
CONV by Hyb	5	2	1	3

Source: Álvarez and Menéndez, 2017. Note: Basic sensitivity analyses carried out demonstrates no significant changes with the reference scenarios, therefore results can be judged as robust.

In the second approach, the progressive replacement of the conventional fleet with alternative energies/technologies, different ultimate shares of each energy/technology (BEV, PHEV, CNG, LPG and Hyb) are projected for the future.

Based on different rates of penetration, several basic cases or assumptions are established, assuming higher or lower EV penetration (EV Superior and EV Inferior). The same is assumed and projected for gas (CNG Superior or CNG Inferior). Furthermore, basic hypothesis about the penetration of conventional Hybrids and LPG are considered. The combination of these hypotheses results in different rates of penetration leading to different potential scenarios, as can be observed in Figure 14. It can be observed that alternative fuels vehicles (AFV) penetration corresponds with a decline of the conventional vehicle penetration rates.

Therefore, conventional vehicles will gradually be replaced by alternative energies. As a result, alternative fuel vehicles will coexist with conventional vehicles for some time. By 2030, however, alternative fuel vehicles (including conventional hybrids) could represent more than a half of the total passenger vehicle fleet in the territory. Table 8 presents the range of the simulated projections.

An example of the economic and environmental impact of the scenarios in terms of: (1) greater cost of vehicles; (2) investment in new infrastructure; and (3) the reduction of GHG and air pollutant emissions can be found in Annex 1.

Figure 14. Progressive Introduction of AFVs to 2035 in the Basque Country, No. of Vehicles

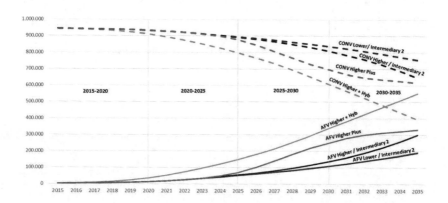

Source: Álvarez and Menéndez, 2017.

Table 8. Cumulative Impacts of AFV Penetration by 2035 under Progressive Replacement

Criterion	Minimum	Maximum
Extra net cost in vehicles	€500 mn	€2,300 mn
Infrastructure investment requirements	€80 mn	€180 mn
Fuel savings	€770 mn	€1,900 mn
CO2 emissions reductions	2 MtCO$_2$e	5 MtCO$_2$e
NOx emissions reductions	860 tons	2,300 tons
Particulate emissions reductions	100 tons	200 tons

Source: own elaboration.

As with the Overnight fleet replacement scenarios in Table 7, the analysis of the progressive replacement scenarios according to the same criteria is presented in Table 9.

There is *no single best option in terms of both economic and environmental impacts*. Each alternative stands out with respect to one or more scenarios and criteria. In any case, *a higher penetration of battery electric cars and hybrids provides the best overall results*.[48]

---

48. For scenarios information and results, see Annex 1.

Table 9. Order of Alternatives, Progressive Replacement by AFV

	Fuel saving	Specific cost of CO_2	Savings in environmental costs	Climate contribution
Higher + Hyb	1	4	1	1
Higher Plus	3	3	3	3
Intermediary B	6	5	6	6
Higher	4	7	4	4
Intermediary A	5	2	5	5
Lower	7	1	7	7
Higher + Hyb + PHEV	2	6	1	2

Source: Álvarez and Menéndez, 2017.

Conclusions and Recommendations

For at least two decades, the EU has been highly concerned with the issue of transportation, both in terms of mobility and trade infrastructure (i.e., TEN-T) and with respect to alternative fuels and emissions. Given the still positive relationship between GDP and both passenger and freight mobility, the transportation sector is expected to continue to grow, contributing still more emissions to those also released by the power, building and land sectors.

As a result, the EU and its member states have developed and passed a range of legislation to reduce greenhouse gas and air pollutant emissions (NOx and particles) across most emitting sectors, including transportation.

Although GHGs are principally an issue at the global scale, air pollutant emissions have more local and regional implications. However, both groups of emissions, and the nature and effects of policies to reduce them, are relevant for the transportation sector—GHGs from the top-down and air pollutants from the bottom up.

But European transportation has no future without a sustainability framework. Sustainable mobility rests on three foundational pillars of social, economic and environmental sustainability. Policy to develop and deploy different alternative transportation fuels, vehicles and infrastructures can also contribute to sustainable mobility in all these ways, although with different relative economic and environmental impacts.

The current European leaders in the promotion of alternative fuels and vehicles are: (1) France (EU) and (2) Norway (non-EU) in electric vehicles, and (3) Italy in natural gas vehicles.

An analysis of these (and a range of other relevant EU) countries reveals that two factors stand out as important for the pace of EV roll-out and penetration: (1) facilitative policies and (2) appropriate incentives. A number of other economic and market parameters are also highly relevant: (3) GDP per capita, (4) vehicle prices, the (5) relative price of fuel, along with (6) the dominant type of housing, are among the most important, although none is dominant in their influence. On the other hand, the energy mix *does not appear* to be a noticeable factor affecting the rate of penetration of EVs or the pace of EV infrastructure roll-out.

Italy is the most important EU country in terms of compressed natural gas vehicles. This is largely the result of a long-running continuity in Italian gas policies. Germany and Sweden—also European leaders in gas fuels—are both actively developing a biogas policy to help supply gas-fueled vehicles.

In one of our study's progressive replacement scenarios for the relatively small but emblematic Spanish-European region of the Basque Country, alternative fuel vehicles (mainly BEV but also conventional hybrids-AFV Superior+Hyb) are seen to gradually displace conventional vehicles from the fleet and would constitute more than half of passenger light-vehicles by 2035. Although the initial policy effort and economic investment implied would not be irrelevant, both would dwindle over time.

In our multicriteria evaluation, no single best solution emerges from among the range of alternative fuel vehicle options widely available in Europe (BEVs, PHEVs, CNG, LPGs and also conventional hybrids). However, the best policy option would promote a combination of alternative fuel vehicles—mainly EVs but also conventional hybrids (and in some parts of Europe, CNG vehicles)—to progressively displace conventional fossil-fuel vehicles from the vehicle fleet.

Thus, the EU and its member states are attempting to promote and develop sustainable mobility across Europe to help achieve its energy efficiency, renewable fuels and emissions reduction commitments.

Many stakeholders must be considered, including consumers, operators, OEMs, component manufacturers, and others, but vehicle owners and purchasers are the key, indispensable agents. New regulation and other local measures aimed at vehicle owners (such as free parking places for alternative fuel vehicles) can therefore provide powerful levers to support the penetration of alternative fuel vehicles.

But to meet the challenge of facilitating alternative fuels and vehicles as an emissions reduction strategy, requires genuine commitment from governments in the form of incentives for the purchase of alternative fuel vehicles and the deployment of charging and refueling infrastructures.

Therefore, it would be wise to allocate sufficient public budget lines to provide for infrastructures and incentives to offset at least some of the extra costs of alternative fuel vehicles in order to achieve the significant environmental benefits of GHG and air pollutant emissions reductions.

Annex 1: Alternative Fuel Vehicles Penetration Scenarios

The study develops several scenarios, each assuming different penetration rates for each AFV. Here, only one of them, progressive replacement with only BEVs, is described as a representative example. In this case, the main assumption is that EV sales are strictly BEV (based on the probability that this technology could become the main segment of EU market). This assumed immediate market displacement of PHEV and conventional hybrids by pure battery EVs gives rise to rapid BEV deployment and an acceleration of battery development within the automotive and fuels industries that produces a faster drop in battery prices over time, and that facilitates the achievement of the objectives of OEMs.

For CNG vehicles this scenario assumes optimistic growth. For LPGs the assumptions are the same in all the scenarios as it is the most developed alternative fuel. Conventional hybrid vehicles would be displaced by the growing BEV market.

The results show an increase in extra infrastructure investment. This may be due, to a certain extent, to the way penetration is achieved. Unlike other cases considered, BEV penetration implies higher costs in the first stages, but a subsequent stabilization of replacement costs in later stages.

Figure 15. Progressive Replacement, only BEVs, Investment Costs, Number of Vehicles, Emissions Reduction and Fuel Savings

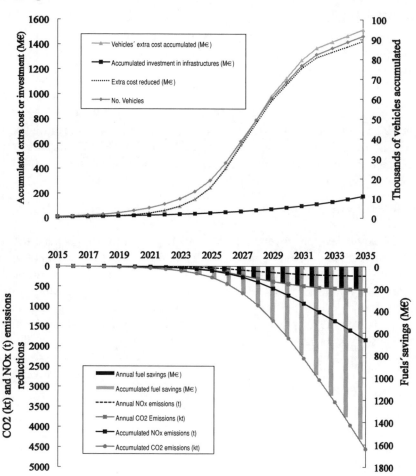

Source: Álvarez and Menéndez, 2017.

Chapter Four

The Energy of Transportation: A Focus on Latin American Urban Transportation

Lisa Viscidi and Rebecca O'Connor

Latin America faces unique transportation challenges. As a developing region, Latin America's growth in oil demand and greenhouse gas (GHG) emissions is closely linked to economic growth. Latin America is largely a region of middle income countries, with sizeable and fast-growing middle classes that enjoy improving purchasing power. As a result, demand for private light-duty vehicles is mushrooming. Demand for heavy-duty vehicles used mainly to transport commercial goods is also growing as economies expand.

This contrasts sharply with developed countries like the United States and Europe where oil demand and emissions have peaked as populations are scarcely growing, most adults already own cars, and improved energy efficiency has led to declines in energy and emissions intensity. Latin America also contrasts with lower income regions, such as Africa, where much smaller portions of the population can afford private vehicles and car ownership is growing at a slower clip (see Chapter Five).

Latin America is also unique in its high rate of urbanization—some 80 percent of inhabitants live in cities. This reality exacerbates problems of congestion and air pollution, but it also creates opportunities to meet much of the population's need with public mass transit. Finally, Latin America also suffers from extremely weak fuel efficiency, vehicle emissions, and fuel quality standards and enforcement. As a result, each kilometer driven consumes more fuel and emits more pollutants than in countries with stronger regulation.

Addressing the transportation challenge requires an integrated approach. Firstly, Latin American countries need to stem the growth in demand for private cars by improving public transportation systems and non-motorized transportation options, such as cycling and walking. These solutions would also reduce the growing problem of traffic congestion. Many Latin American cities have seen great success in public transportation systems. The region pioneered the bus rapid transit (BRT) system and boasts the largest number of BRT systems in the world. However, public transportation systems in Latin America are no longer adequate to meet the demands of passengers, and most cities have not done enough to promote alternative forms of transportation.

Secondly, Latin American countries urgently need to improve fuel efficiency and fuel quality. Experience from other countries, such as the United States, demonstrates that developing and implementing more stringent fuel economy standards can have the largest impact on reducing oil demand of any policy measure. In addition, Latin America is far behind the developed world in imposing fuel quality standards, which not only contributes to GHG emissions but also increases local air pollution, with detrimental effects on human health.

Thirdly, Latin American countries need to do more to diversify fuel sources for transportation. In the long term, it is most important to transition to electric vehicles (EVs), which provide the most viable pathway to zero emissions transportation. While some countries in the region have instituted policies and incentives to promote electric mobility, Latin America has a long way to go toward large-scale use of EVs, and EV markets are tiny compared to many in Europe, Asia, and the United States. Other lower carbon fuel sources, such as natural gas and biofuels, have helped to reduce emissions from the transportation sector in some Latin American countries, and there is potential to expand these markets.

This chapter analyzes the transportation challenge in Latin America and provides critical policy solutions. The chapter focuses on passenger road transportation because although freight transport is responsible for about half of Latin American road carbon emissions, there is more potential to reduce emissions from passenger transport. This is in part because Latin America's high urbanization rate, which is projected to reach almost 90 percent of the population in 2050,[1] makes it feasible for mass public and non-motorized transportation to cover a large portion of the population's mobility needs. Indeed, urban population density is inversely correlated with GHG emissions from land transport.[2] In addition, there is great potential to expand

---

1. Comisión Económica para América Latina y el Caribe, "Estimaciones y proyecciones de población total, urbana y rural, y económicamente activa" (Revisión 2017) https://www.cepal.org/es/temas/proyecciones-demograficas/estimaciones-proyecciones-poblacion-total-urbana-rural-economicamente-activa (accessed September 29, 2017)

2. Ralph Sims, Roberto Schaeffer, Felix Creutzig, Xochitl Cruz-Núñez, Marcio D'Agosto, Delia Dimitriu, Maria Josefina Figueroa Meza, Lew Fulton, Shigeki Kobayash, Oliver Lah, Alan McKinnon, Peter Newman, Minggao Ouyang (China), James Jay Schauer (USA), Daniel Sperling, Geetam Tiwari, "Transport" in *Climate Change 2014: Mitigation of Climate*

electrification for passenger vehicles but current battery technology does not allow heavy-duty vehicles to travel the long distances needed for freight transport. Meanwhile, non-road transport—including marine, aviation, and rail—remains very limited making up only one quarter of the region's carbon emissions from transportation.

The Transportation Challenge in Latin America

A Rapidly Growing Vehicle Fleet

Latin America's vehicle fleet is growing rapidly—it is projected to triple in the next 25 years and grow to more than 200 million vehicles by 2050 (see Table 1).[3] The region also has the fastest growing motorization rate in the world—approximately 4.5 percent per year.[4] Since 2000, the motorization rate has almost doubled from 100 vehicles per 1000 inhabitants to 170 per 1000 inhabitants.[5]

Vehicle fleet growth in Latin America is more closely correlated with purchasing power and growing numbers of people entering the middle class than with population growth.[6] Between 2006 and 2016 the region's middle class almost doubled, from 99 million to 186 million people.[7] Historically, the vast majority of Latin Americans have relied on public transportation. Of the region's 570 million inhabitants, 200 million use public transportation on a

Change. Contribution of Working Group III to the Fifth Assessment Report of the Intergovernmental Panel on Climate Change ed. Elizabeth Deakin and Suzana Kahn Ribeiro (Cambridge, United Kingdom and New York, NY, USA 2014), p. 619 https://www.ipcc.ch/pdf/assessment-report/ar5/wg3/ ipcc_wg3_ar5_chapter8.pdf (accessed September 28, 2017).

3. United Nations Environment Program, "Movilidad Eléctrica: Oportunidades para Latinoamérica" (October 10, 2016), p. 3 http://www.pnuma.org/cambio_climatico/publicaciones/ informe_movilidad_electrica.pdf (accessed July 5, 2017).

4. "Regional Experiences to Keep Latin America Green and Growing," The World Bank Group, (June 26, 2013) http://www.worldbank.org/en/news/feature/2013/06/26/latin-america-green-growth (accessed July 5, 2017).

5. Walter Vergara, Jørgen Villy Fenhann, and Marco Christian Schletz, "Zero Carbon Latin America - A Pathway for Net Decarbonisation of the Regional Economy by Mid-Century," UNEP DTU Partnership (2015), p. 29 http://orbit.dtu.dk/files/123115955/Zero_Carbon_Latin_America_rev.pdf (accessed July 5, 2017).

6. Walter Vergara, Jørgen Villy Fenhann, and Marco Christian Schletz, "Zero Carbon Latin America - A Pathway for Net Decarbonisation of the Regional Economy by Mid-Century," UNEP DTU Partnership (2015), p. 70 http://orbit.dtu.dk/files/123115955/Zero_Carbon_Latin_America_rev.pdf (accessed July 5, 2017).

7. Suzanne Duryea and Marcos Robles, "Social Pulse in Latin America and the Caribbean 2016: Realities & Perspectives" Inter-American Development Bank (October 5, 2016), p. 15 (accessed July 10, 2017).

Table 1: Latin America's Vehicle Fleet

Country	Light-Duty Vehicle Fleet, 2015	Annual Rate of Light Vehicle Fleet Growth (%), 2010-2020	Heavy-Duty Vehicle Fleet, 2012	Total vehicles/1000 inhabitants, 2012
Brazil	30,708,965	4.2	7,619,436	383.8
Mexico	14,310,339	3.0	380,342	281.5
Argentina	10,387,029	3.4	593,476	279.1
Chile	2,907,383	5.2	201,531	226.0
Colombia	2,149,446	7.9	306,012	196.5
Venezuela	2,016,744	3.3	914,985	N/A
Peru	1,346,450	9.5	106,151	70.2
Dominican Republic	638,258	4.4	363,439	285.0
Costa Rica	518,407	5.3	195,784	237.2
Uruguay	498,828	4.5	53,762	502.9
Ecuador	413,303	3.8	128,874**	112.0
Panama	330,367	7.6	21,912	127.0
Bolivia	299,084	5.5	98,688	108.0
Paraguay	222,174	5.3	242,257**	166.1
El Salvador	212,753	4.4	61,046	94.0
Honduras	143,905	4.7	59,151*	134.2
Nicaragua	71,261	4.5	42,721	85.5

Source: United Nations Environment Program, 2016 Inter-American Development Bank "Freight Transport and Logistics" 2015. Note: Guatemala not included *Data corresponds to 2010 ** Data based on extrapolation from 2008-2011

daily basis.[8] The region also has the highest per capita bus use in the world.[9] Many cities in the region—like Bogotá, Medellín, Lima, and Quito—rely on public transportation for more than half of passenger trips in a typical workday and others—like Mexico City and Panama City—rely on public transportation for more than 70 percent of passenger trips in a typical workday.[10] By com-

8. Union Internationale des Transports Publics, "Metro Latin America—Prospects and Trends," (October 2016), p. 2 http://www.latinamerica.uitp.org/sites/default/files/Relat%C3%B3rio%20Metr%C3%B4s_UITP%20Am%C3%A9rica%20Latina_ENG.pdf (accessed July 18, 2017).

9. UNEP, "Movilidad Eléctrica," p. 10.

10. "Compare Systems Indicators," *Global BRT Data*, *BRTData.org* (2017) http://brtdata.org/panorama/systems (accessed July 15, 2017).

parison, private transportation makes up between 78 and 94 percent of passengers trips in a typical workday in Los Angeles and Miami, respectively, and public transport represents just 5 and 3 percent respectively.[11]

However, as the middle class continues to grow and larger numbers of people enjoy more purchasing power, motorization rates and the number of automobiles in circulation are climbing in cities across the region that are already facing serious urban congestion, emissions, and air quality problems. In Mexico City, the motorization rate grew from 308 vehicles to 593 vehicles per 1000 inhabitants between 2005 and 2015.[12] Over the same period, the number of registered vehicles in circulation nearly doubled to 4.9 million.[13] In 2030, Mexico and Brazil—the two largest automobile markets in the region— are projected to represent 5 percent of global light-duty vehicle sales.[14]

Freight transportation is another growing source of vehicles on the road. In Latin America, freight is dominated by diesel-fueled road transport due to insufficient infrastructure to move most goods by rail, air, and marine transport. The number of light, medium, and heavy-duty freight trucks in the region has grown rapidly over the past 15 years along with GDP. In addition to its growing stock of vehicles, Latin America's road freight fleet is also traveling more total kilometers every year as demand for freight transport increases. The region's total vehicle-kilometers—a unit measuring total annual distance covered by a given fleet—for road freight transport nearly doubled between 2000 and 2015.[15] The share of freight transport by rail in Latin America is very small but growing. Brazil, Mexico, and Colombia represent 90 percent of freight by rail in the region, and 62 percent of freight rail transport is dedicated to mining projects.[16] Freight transport by rail is

---

11. Vergara et al., "Zero Carbon Latin America," p. 28.

12. Instituto Nacional de Estadística y Geografía, "Transporte—Índice de Motorización por entidad federativa, 2000 a 2015," Dirección de Estadísticas del Medio Ambiente con base en: Dirección de Estadísticas (July 5, 2017) http://www3.inegi.org.mx/sistemas/sisept/default.aspx?t=mamb137&s=est&c=21690 (accessed July 12, 2017).

13. Instituto Nacional de Estadística y Geografía, "Transporte—Automóviles registrados en circulación por entidad federativa, 2005 a 2015," Estadísticas económicas: Estadística de vehículos de motor registrados en circulación (July 5, 2017) http://www3.inegi.org.mx/sistemas/sisept/default.aspx?t=mamb373&s=est&c=35939 (accessed July 12, 2017).

14. Global Fuel Economy Initiative, "Fuel Economy State of the World 2016—Time for global action" (2016), p. 34 https://www.globalfueleconomy.org/media/203446/gfei-state-of-the-world-report-2016.pdf (accessed July 10, 2017).

15. International Energy Agency, "The Future of Trucks—Implications for Energy and the Environment" (2017), p. 26https://www.iea.org/publications/freepublications/publication/TheFutureofTrucksImplicationsforEnergyandtheTheFutureof.pdf (accessed July 12, 2017).

16. Vergara et al., "Zero Carbon Latin America," p. 33.

Figure 1: Oil Demand by Subsector in Latin America and the Caribbean, 2015 & 2040

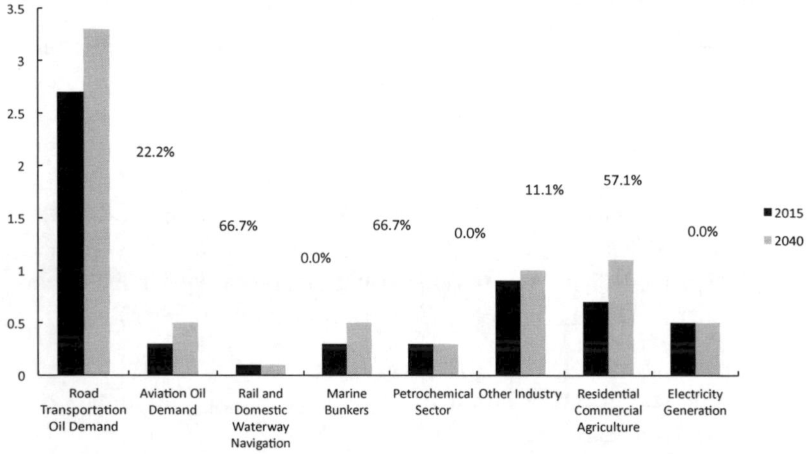

Source: Organization of Petroleum Exporting Countries.

much more carbon efficient than road-based freight transportation. Air transport is also used for small amounts of domestic freight transport, and the region's international freight transfers also include small percentages of air and marine transport.

Energy Demand for Transportation

As the number of vehicles on the road grows, the demand for fuel grows as well. Globally, the transport sector is responsible for more than half of all oil demand and is growing more quickly than all other energy demand sectors, at about 2 percent per year.[17]

Latin America is the third fastest-growing region for oil demand after Asia and the Middle East, currently representing about 9.2 percent of the world total, or 9.2 million b/d.[18] Road transportation fuels, particularly gasoline and diesel, make up the lion's share of Latin American oil demand, with the Organization of Petroleum Exporting Countries (OPEC) projecting a 22 percent increase in Latin America between 2015 and 2040, compared to a

---

17. IEA, "The Future of Trucks" p. 11.

18. Barragan, Ricardo, "Latin America: Petroleum Product Demand Forecast" (September 13, 2017) https://stratasadvisors.com/Insights/091317-GRP-Petroleum-Demand-Latin-America (accessed September 29, 2017).

Figure 2: Breakdown of Fuels Used in the Transport Sector in Latin America and the Caribbean

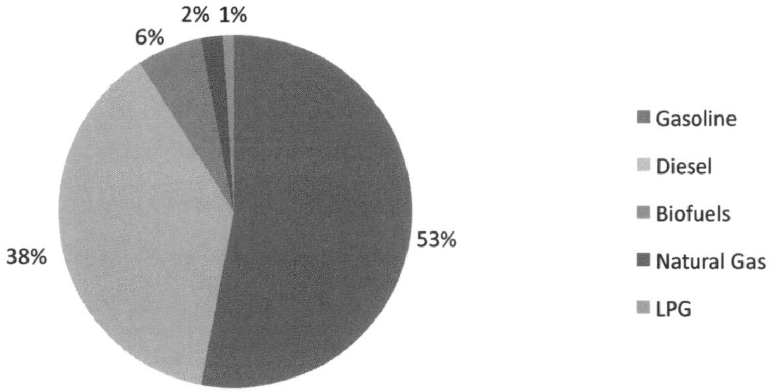

Source: Vergara et al., "Zero Carbon Latin America," p. 34.

15 percent global average increase for this subsector. The aviation and marine bunker subsectors in Latin America will see even larger growth rates over the period but are starting from a very low base and will remain a relatively small source of oil demand (See Figure 1).[19]

Gasoline, the primary fuel used for passenger cars in Latin America, makes up the largest share of the region's transport sector fuels with 53 percent, followed by diesel, commonly used for freight trucks, with 38 percent, and smaller amounts of biofuels, natural gas, and liquid petroleum gas (see Figure 2).[20] Biofuels use is most ubiquitous in Brazil where it represents 17 percent of energy demand for transportation. [21] Gasoline demand in Brazil and Mexico alone represents almost 2 million b/d, or about 30 percent of regional refined product demand.[22] In countries like Colombia and Argentina,

19. Organization of the Petroleum Exporting Countries (OPEC), "2016 World Oil Outlook: Oil supply and demand Outlook to 2040" (2016) https://woo.opec.org/index.php/oil-supply-and-demand-outlook-2040/data-download (accessed September 28, 2017).

20. Enerdata (2015), cited in Vergara et al., "Zero Carbon Latin America," p. 34.

21. Olivia Brajterman, "Introdução de veículos elétricos e impactos sobre o setor energético brasileiro" (March 2016) http://www.ppe.ufrj.br/ppe/production/tesis/brajterman.pdf (accessed September 27, 2017).

22. Barragan, Ricardo, "Latin America: Petroleum Product Demand Forecast" (September 13, 2017) https://stratasadvisors.com/Insights/091317-GRP-Petroleum-Demand-Latin-America (accessed September 29, 2017).

liquid petroleum gas and compressed natural gas also supply an important part of transportation fuels.

Latin America imports a large share of its oil products due to inadequate refining capacity. In 2016, the region imported 730,000 b/d of middle distillate and 830,000 b/d of motor gasoline, half of which went to just three countries: Mexico, Colombia and Brazil.[23]

Impact on GHG Emissions, Pollution and Congestion

Booming oil demand is leading to higher emissions. Latin America overall still has low per capita emissions from the transport sector compared to developed countries due mainly to lower per capita car ownership, as most of the region's inhabitants continue to use public transportation. While Latin America has an average of almost 200 cars per 1,000 inhabitants, Europe and North America have 600 and 800 cars per 1,000 inhabitants, respectively.[24] But as private transportation use increases, so do emissions. The transport sector made up 15 percent of Latin America and the Caribbean's 2013 GHG emissions with 586.56 $MtCO_2e$—a 60 percent increase from a decade earlier.[25] As the largest countries in the region Brazil and Mexico have the highest transport-related emissions. However, Venezuela and Argentina, which each have smaller populations than Colombia, have higher emissions due to higher rates of car ownership and, particularly in the case of Venezuela, the use of less fuel-efficient cars (see Figure 3).

Transport sector carbon dioxide (CO_2) emissions are heavily concentrated in road transport (73 percent) with smaller amounts from international and domestic marine, and air transport, and just 1 percent from rail (see Figure 4).[26] Within road transport, freight and passenger transport are each responsible for about half of emissions. Heavy-duty trucks are particularly carbon intensive, contributing 28 percent of road emissions with only 2.5 million vehicles (see Table 2). In the passenger segment, private automobiles are

---

23. Barragan, Ricardo, "Latin America: Petroleum Product Demand Forecast" (September 13, 2017) https://stratasadvisors.com/Insights/091317-GRP-Petroleum-Demand-Latin-America (accessed September 29, 2017).

24. Vergara et al., "Zero Carbon Latin America," p. 29.

25. "CAIT Climate Data Explorer—Historical Emissions," *World Resources Institute* (2017) http://cait.wri.org/historical (accessed July 13, 2017). Note: Includes emissions from land use change. GHG emissions include carbon dioxide (CO_2), methane (CH4), nitrous oxide (N_2O), hydrofluorocarbons (HFCs), perfluorocarbons (PFCs), and sulfur hexafluoride (SF6).

26. Vergara et al., "Zero Carbon Latin America," pp. 26–27.

Figure 3: Transportation Sector CO$_2$ Emissions from Fuel Combustion by Country, 2014 (mn tons)

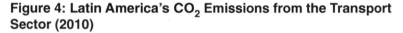

Source: OECD/International Energy Agency, "World CO$_2$ Emissions from Fuel Combustion Database Documentation" (2016). Note: "Other " includes: Dominican Republic, Costa Rica, Paraguay, Panama, Uruguay, Honduras, Trinidad and Tobago, El Salvador, Nicaragua, Jamaica, Cuba, Haiti, Curaçao, Suriname and "other non-OECD Americas"

Figure 4: Latin America's CO$_2$ Emissions from the Transport Sector (2010)

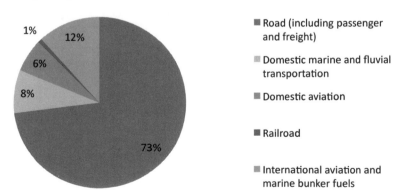

Source: ANTF (2011), CAIT (2015), EPA (2015) and IEA (2015), cited in Vergara et al., "Zero Carbon Latin America," p. 27.

Table 2: Estimated size and emissions from the domestic road fleet in Latin America

Mode	Number of vehicles (millions)	Kilometers per year (thousands)	Fuel efficiency (kilometers per liter)	Metric tons of CO_2 equivalent (MtCO$_2$e)
Private autos	59.4	12	11	150
Taxis	2.2	60	11	27
Motorcycles	10.7	12		5
Standard buses	0.6	40	3.8	12
Articulated buses	0.02	60	3.8	1
Minibuses	1.0	40	2.8	33
Light trucks	5	13	3.2	47
Medium duty trucks	5.4	22	2.7	77
Heavy duty trucks	2.5	50	2.5	134
Total	86.8			486

Source: CAF (2010), CEPROEC (2015), Barbero (2014) and EPA (2015), cited in Vergara et al., "Zero Carbon Latin America," p. 27.

by far the largest source of emissions, while the region's bus fleet accounts for less than 10 percent of road transport emissions.

Left unchecked, emissions from the transport sector will increase dramatically. Globally, the transport sector is the fastest growing source of emissions, with a projected 70 percent increase by 2050.[27] In Latin America, emissions from the transport sector are projected to grow by 114 percent in a business-as-usual scenario by 2050, with total regional emissions reaching nearly 7 gigatons of CO_2 equivalent (GtCO$_2$e) by 2050 (see Table 3).[28] Although the region's transport sector emissions are growing from a smaller base, they are projected to grow more than 1.5 times as fast as global transport sector emissions.

---

27. UNEP, "Movilidad Eléctrica," p. 4.

28. Walter Vergara, Ana R. Rios, Galindo Paliza, Luis Miguel, Pablo Gutman, Paul Isbell, Paul Hugo Suding, and Jose Luis Samaniego, "El desafío climático y de desarrollo en América Latina y el Caribe: Opciones para un desarrollo resiliente al clima y bajo en carbono," Inter-American Development Bank (2013) pp. 14–15 https://publications.iadb.org/bitstream/handle/11319/456/Libro%20Final%20Dic%209%202014.pdf?sequence=4&isAllowed=y (accessed July 6, 2017).

Table 3: Projected business-as-usual emissions by sector,* Latin America and the Caribbean (Gt, %)

Sector	2010	2050	Percent change	Main cause(s)
Business as usual emissions trajectory	4.73	6.73	+42	
Electricity	0.24	0.54	+125	Carbonization
Industry	0.33	0.66	+100	Economic growth
Industrial Products	0.11	0.23	+109	Economic growth
Residential/Commercial	0.18	0.21	+17	Economic growth
Transport	0.56	1.2	+114	Motorization, urbanization
Land Use	1.6	0.67	-58	Decrease in deforestation
Total CO2 emissions	3.3	4.56	+38	Energy demand
CH4	1	1.5	+50	Livestock, agriculture
N2O	0.34	0.63	+85	Fertilizer use

*Vergara et al.'s business as usual scenario is based on the Latin America and the Caribbean regional projections in the International Institute for Applied Systems Analysis' (IIASA) Global Energy Assessment (GEA) Database. The BAU scenario is based on the GEA's MESSAGE (Model for Energy Supply Strategy Alternatives and their General Environmental Impact), which is a "hypothetical no-policy baseline describing the evolution of the energy system in the absence of any transformational policies for the demand- or supply-side of the energy system." Gt = gigaton.

Source: CAF (2010), CEPROEC (2015), Barbero (2014) and EPA (2015), cited in Vergara et al., "Zero Carbon Latin America," p. 47–49.

In addition to the global impacts of Latin America's transport emissions on climate change, pollution from vehicles also causes severe health problems for local populations, particularly in urban areas. Many Latin American cities regularly declare emergency levels of pollution. Smog—visible air pollution created when emissions combine with atmospheric conditions like sunlight and heat—is prevalent in cities across the region like Mexico City, where 90 percent of the city's smog comes from the transportation sector.[29] Mexico's *Hoy no circula* program limits the days and hours vehicles in Mexico City and the neighboring State of Mexico can be on the road based

---

29. Institute for Transportation and Development Policy, "Sustainable Transport—Santiago, Chile, Putting Pedestrians First," (Winter 2017) N. 28, p. 4 https://3gozaa3xxbpb499ejp30lxc8-wpengine.netdna-ssl.com/wp-content/uploads/2017/01/ST28.12.28.pdf (accessed July 14, 2017).

on each vehicle's emissions level. In April 2016, smog in the city reached its highest levels in decades, requiring emergency measures to further restrict vehicles. Santiago has a similar program, which restricts vehicles on a rotating basis based on the last digit of their license plates. Santiago also has a serious air quality problem and frequently issues advisories at the "alert," "pre-emergency," and "emergency" levels. The transport sector contributes more than a third of Santiago's GHG emissions and 40 percent of its pollution.[30] On an annual basis, according to Plume Labs' index, Santiago has an average of 119 days with moderate pollution, 135 with high pollution, 88 with very high pollution, 6 with excessive pollution, and just 16 with fresh air.[31] Certain vehicles in each city—like electric and hybrid vehicles—are exempt from such restrictions. São Paulo, Bogotá, and Quito also have similar programs.

The amount and type of pollution each vehicle emits depends on both its vehicle emissions standard and the fuel it uses. Compared to gasoline, diesel provides better fuel economy and lower overall GHG emissions.[32] But diesel emits more nitrogen oxides (NO_x) and particulate matter, two important contributors to smog formation. Diesel-powered vehicles also emit more black carbon than gasoline vehicles, though both are a significant source of the pollutant.

Air pollution—largely from the transport sector—has important and costly impacts on human health, such as increased risk of stroke, heart disease, chronic and acute respiratory diseases like asthma, and lung cancer. Emissions from the transport sector include both long-lived climate pollutants like CO_2 and short-lived climate pollutants like black carbon and ozone. While long-lived climate pollutants are more often the target of national emissions reductions goals and policies because of their role in longer-term climate change, short-lived climate pollutants have more immediate impacts on human health.

---

30. Camila Albertini, "Amplían Etiquetado de Eficiencia Energética a Vehículos Comerciales, Eléctricos e Híbridos," *Publimetro Chile* (June 28, 2017) https://www.publimetro.cl/cl/noticias/2017/06/28/autos-mas-eficientes-segun-etiquetado.html (accessed July 18, 2017).

31. "Live Pollution and Air Quality Forecasts," *Santiago Air Report, Plume Labs* (2017) https://air.plumelabs.com/en/year/santiago (accessed July 18, 2017).

32. Thomas Klier and Joshua Linn, "Comparing US and EU Approaches to Regulating Automotive Emissions and Fuel Economy," Policy Brief No. 16-03, Resources for the Future (April 2016), p. 2 http://www.rff.org/files/document/file/RFF-PB-16-03.pdf (accessed July 14, 2017).

Figure 5: Ambient Air Quality Levels & Guidelines

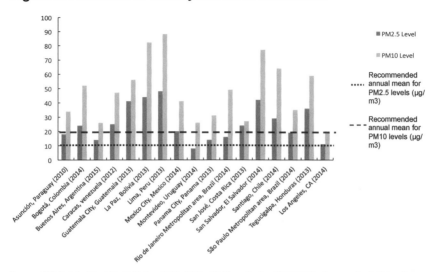

Source: "Global Ambient Air Pollution," *World Health Organization* (2017) http://maps.who.int/airpollution/ (accessed July 19, 2017).

A recent United Nations Environment Program (UNEP) report estimates that air pollution causes at least 50,000 premature deaths per year in Latin America.[33] Almost every capital city in Latin America exceeds the recommended annual limits for $PM_{2.5}$ and PM_{10} emissions (see Figure 5). Air pollution also imposes enormous monetary costs on Latin American economies; UNEP estimates that Mexico alone spends US$40 billion in pollution-related health costs, half of which can be directly attributed to the transport sector.[34]

Reducing short-lived climate pollutants from the transport sector can be a particularly attractive public policy option, as it can improve local health outcomes with direct benefits for communities while contributing to achieving national climate commitments. Stricter fuel efficiency and vehicle emissions standards, for example, reduce short-lived climate pollutants, improving air quality with associated health benefits while lowering CO_2 levels. Mexico's 2013 fuel economy standards are expected to yield more

33. UNEP, "Movilidad Eléctrica," p. 3; World Health Organization, "Reducing Global Health Risks through Mitigation of Short-Lived Climate Pollutants—Scoping Report for Policymakers" (2015), p. 1 http://www.who.int/phe/publications/climate-reducing-health-risks/en/ (accessed July 11, 2017)

34. UNEP, "Movilidad Eléctrica," p. 3.

Figure 6: Extra Hours per Year Spent in Traffic (based on 230 days of commuting)

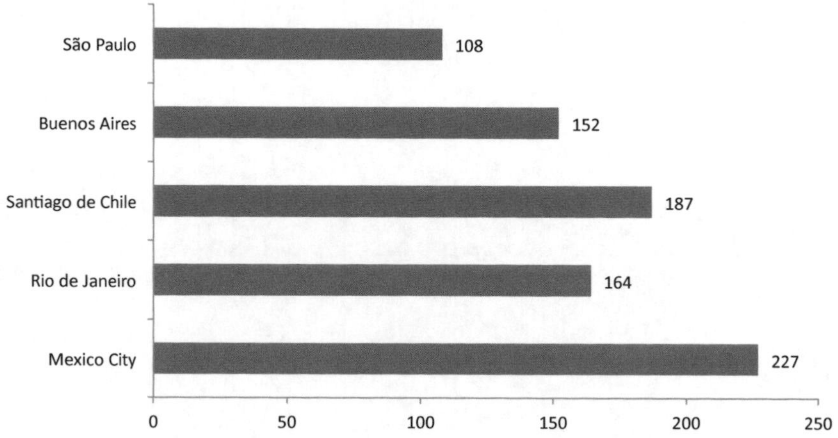

Source: "TomTom Traffic Index," *TomTom International BV* (2017) https://www.tomtom.com/en_gb/trafficindex/ (accessed July 15, 2017).

than US$2 billion in cost savings from health benefits by 2032.[35] Increased use of mass transportation also has similar co-benefits. Fuel quality improvements—like ultra-low-sulfur diesel use with diesel particle filters—have an important impact on short-lived climate pollutants and improve air quality, but do not have the associated CO_2 reduction benefit.

Latin America's transportation challenge is in many ways exacerbated by high levels of urbanization. In some countries—like Brazil, Venezuela, Chile, and Argentina—the percentage of the population living in cities is even higher than the regional average of 80 percent. 67 cities in the region are home to more than one million inhabitants, with many more expected to surpass this threshold in the next decade.[36] As a result of this population density and insufficient infrastructure to support it, many of the region's cities are extremely congested, with commuters spending hours sitting in traffic every day (See Figure 6). Mexico City and Bogotá often rank among the most congested cities in the world.

35. International Council on Clean Transportation, "Policy Update: Mexico's LDV CO_2 and Fuel Economy Standards," (July 2013), p. 3 http://www.theicct.org/sites/default/files/publications/ICCTupdate_Mexico_LDVstandards_july2013.pdf (accessed July 18, 2017).

36. United Nations, "The World's Cities in 2016: Data Booklet," (2016), p. 5 http://www.un.org/en/development/desa/population/publications/pdf/urbanization/the_worlds_cities_in_2016_data_booklet.pdf (accessed July 18, 2017).

Weak Standards and Enforcement

Latin America has very weak standards for vehicle emissions, fuel quality, and fuel economy, meaning that each vehicle has higher levels of emissions than the average vehicle in developed countries, which generally have stricter standards. Mexico is currently the only country in Latin America with mandatory fuel economy regulations in place. Approximately 83 percent of the global car market had fuel economy regulations in place as of 2016, but the remaining 17 percent of the market is largely in Latin America and Southeast Asia, regions expected to see some of the most rapid growth in car ownership in the coming years.[37]

Fuel economy regulations create standards for manufacturers on how efficiently vehicle fleets must use fuel. Countries can apply standards per vehicle or per manufacturer (or both), though manufacturer level standards are most common worldwide. For example, the newest Corporate Average Fuel Economy (CAFE) Standards in the United States—released in November 2016—established a minimum fleet-wide average fuel economy of 36 miles per gallon for all cars and light trucks by 2025.[38] Mexico's standards, first published in 2013 for vehicle model years 2014-2016, are based on the United States' CAFE standards but are slightly less stringent—requiring 1 percent less efficiency for cars and 2 percent less for light trucks—with an average fuel economy of 14.6 kilometers/liter.[39] Though the establishment of these standards is an important step, weak enforcement mechanisms that rely on self-reporting from manufacturers limit their impact.

Though no other country in the region has mandatory fuel economy standards in place, Brazil and Chile have economic incentives to encourage consumers to purchase more efficient vehicles. In 2013, Chile instituted a mandatory labeling system—the first of its kind in the region—to provide consumers with more information about city and highway vehicle mileage as well as CO_2 emissions. In 2014, Chile instituted an even stronger incentive: a progressive tax on new vehicle purchases calculated in relation to fuel efficiency and NO_x emissions. Brazil's INOVAR AUTO program, approved in 2012, incentivizes the production of more fuel-efficient vehicles by providing a 30 percent reduction on Brazil's IPI tax on industrialized products.

---

37. GFEI, "Fuel Economy State of the World 2016," p. 31.

38. Ben Wolfgang, "EPA Locks in Fuel Economy Standards through 2025, Calls for 36 Miles per Gallon," *The Washington Times,* January 13, 2017 http://www.washingtontimes.com/news/2017/jan/13/epa-locks-fuel-economy-standards-through-2025/ (accessed July 11, 2017).

39. ICCT, "Policy Update," p. 1.

Table 4: Emissions Standards in Latin America

Country	Light-duty vehicles	Heavy-duty vehicles
Chile	Euro 5	Euro V
Argentina	Euro 5	Euro V
Mexico	Euro 4	Euro IV
Colombia	Euro 4	Euro IV
Peru	Euro 3	Euro III
Uruguay	Euro 3	Euro III
Ecuador	Euro 1	Euro II
Costa Rica	Euro 1	Euro I

Source: Natural Resource Defense Council, 2014 United Nations Environment Program, "Status of Fuel Quality and Vehicle Emission Standards—Latin America and the Caribbean," (November 2016), http://staging.unep.org/transport/New/PCFV/pdf/Maps_Matrices/LAC/matrix/LAC_FuelsVeh_November2016.pdf (accessed July 18, 2017) "Propuesta para actualización de normas de emisión para vehículos pesados en la región latinoamericana," Centro Mario Molina Chile (April 27, 2017) http://portal.mma.gob.cl/wp-content/uploads/2016/11/Gianni-Lopez-Recomendaciones-para-avanzar-con-la-normativa-de-vehiculos-pesados-en-la-region-latinoamericana.pdf (accessed July 18, 2017) Natural Resource Defense Council, "Dumping Dirty Diesels in Latin America: Reducing Black Carbon and Air Pollution from Diesel Engines in Latin American Countries," (November 2014), p. 9 https://www.nrdc.org/sites/default/files/latin-america-diesel-pollution-report.pdf (accessed July 18, 2017).

Many countries in the region have standards regulating vehicle emissions of local air pollutants, but these are also lagging. Instead of regulating how efficiently cars must run, vehicle emissions standards regulate maximum amounts of pollutants—like CO_2, particulate matter, and NO_x—that are permitted in tailpipe emissions from diesel and gasoline vehicles. Chile and Argentina have the most ambitious emissions standards in place, but none of the countries in the region have implemented Euro 6/VI standards[40]— the most recent of the European Union emissions standards, which are used to measure vehicle emissions in many parts of the world (See Table 4). Successive Euro emissions standards permit lower amounts of CO_2, NO_x, and particulate matter. Many countries in the region are considering stricter standards, and some already have stricter sub-national regulations to combat air

---

40. Light-duty vehicle emissions standards are generally referred to with Arabic numerals, while heavy-duty vehicle emissions standards are generally referred to with Roman numerals.

pollution. For example, Santiago mandates Euro VI standards for heavy-duty vehicles.

Fuel quality standards are closely linked to vehicle emissions standards. At both a global and regional level, fuel quality regulations for diesel and gasoline focus on lowering sulfur content, which generally requires refinery upgrades. To a lesser extent, other gasoline regulations focus on octane, benzene, aromatics and olefins and other diesel regulations focus on cetane, density, lubricity, polyaromatics and cold flow. In Latin America, existing and planned sulfur content regulations vary widely for both gasoline and diesel. Chile and Ecuador are currently the most ambitious, with restrictions allowing only 0-10 parts per million (ppm) of sulfur in gasoline and 10-15ppm of sulfur in diesel. Venezuela and Peru are among the least stringent, allowing 501-2500ppm in gasoline and >2000ppm in diesel.[41]

Used car imports are still prevalent throughout the region, exacerbating the problem of low fuel economy and vehicle emissions standards. A growing number of countries—Argentina (with some exceptions), Brazil, Chile, Colombia, Ecuador, Uruguay, and Venezuela—have banned the practice, but others have much less stringent restrictions on used car imports, or none at all.

Latin America's truck fleet is also very old and, as a result, has low fuel efficiency and fuel economy standards and high levels of emissions. Chile has the youngest truck fleet in the region, with an average age of 10 years, while Nicaragua has the oldest, with an average age of 23 years.[42] Because of limited access to finance, developing countries typically have lower levels of truck scrappage, or removal of the oldest vehicles from the fleet, though rapid increases in sales in recent years have driven down the average fleet age.

Clean Transport Pathways in Latin America

Climate Commitments for the Transport Sector

The Paris Agreement, adopted in December 2015 at the 21st United Nations Framework Convention on Climate Change (UNFCCC) conference of the parties (COP21), is the most ambitious global pact to limit GHG emis-

41. Stratas Advisors, "Global Fuel Quality Developments," (June 6–7, 2016), pp. 11 and 15 http://staging.unep.org/Transport/new/PCFV/pdf/11gpm/11gpm_PCFV_HuimingLi.pdf (accessed July 18, 2017).

42. "Freight Transport and Logistics Statistics Yearbook," *Inter-American Development Bank* (April, 2015) https://publications.iadb.org/handle/11319/6885 (accessed July 18, 2017).

sions to date. The agreement, which had been signed by 195 countries and ratified by 166 as of September 2017, establishes the goal of limiting the increase in global average temperature to "well below 2 degrees Celsius (2°C) above pre-industrial levels and [pursuing] efforts to limit the temperature increase to 1.5 °C above pre-industrial levels, recognizing that this would significantly reduce the risks and impacts of climate change."[43] Though the agreement itself notes that even if every country fulfilled its non-binding nationally determined contribution (NDC) warming would still exceed 2°C, the NDCs are meant to be evaluated and intensified every five years. Notably, the agreement also established a minimum US$100 billion/year goal in climate finance for developing countries.

As a region, Latin America is extremely supportive of efforts to combat climate change. Three quarters of Latin American citizens—more than in most parts of the world—consider climate change to be a very serious problem that is now harming people.[44] Of the Latin American countries that signed the accord, 15 of 18 have already ratified it. The region's NDCs are relatively ambitious, pledging to reduce emissions across all sectors through a wide array of measures, including increasing renewable energy generation, expanding energy efficiency, reducing deforestation, and introducing cleaner forms of transportation. However, only Costa Rica's NDC ranks as "2°C compatible", according to the Climate Action Tracker.[45] Brazil, Mexico and Peru's NDCs are considered "insufficient," or inconsistent with limiting global warming below 2°C as they would require comparably greater reductions on the part of other countries, while Argentina's NDC is ranked as "highly insufficient" and Chile's is "critically insufficient."[46]

The transport sector receives specific mention in almost every one of Latin America's NDCs—proposed measures include the establishment of

---

43. United Nations Framework Convention on Climate Change, "Adoption of the Paris Agreement," (November–December 2015), p. 21 https://unfccc.int/resource/docs/2015/cop21/eng/l09.pdf (accessed September 27, 2017).

44. Bruce Stokes, Richard Wike and Jill Carle, "Global Concern about Climate Change, Broad Support for Limiting Emissions—U.S., China Less Worried; Partisan Divides in Key Countries," *Pew Research Center—Global Attitudes and Trends* (November 5, 2015) http://www.pewglobal.org/2015/11/05/global-concern-about-climate-change-broad-support-for-limiting-emissions/# (accessed July 15, 2017).

45. "Climate Action Tracker," *Climate Action Tracker Partners* (2017) http://climateactiontracker.org/countries.html (accessed September 28, 2017).

46. Ibid. Note: The Climate Action Tracker rates (I)NDCs, long-term targets and current policies against whether they are consistent with a country's fair share effort to achieve the Paris Agreement 1.5°C temperature goal. For more detail on methodology, see: http://climateactiontracker.org/methodology.html.

taxes on vehicle imports, incentives for purchasing electric and hybrid vehicles and using cleaner fuels, and transportation network planning. For example, Chile highlights the contribution of diesel-fueled transport to black carbon and $PM_{2.5}$ emissions in Chilean cities as a priority for mitigation in its NDC. Guatemala includes creating fiscal incentives and subsidies focused on clean energy use in public and private transport as one of its intended mitigation actions.

The transport sector is also the focus of many nationally appropriate mitigation actions (NAMAs). Also part of the UNFCCC framework, NAMAs are policy instruments or implementation tools that translate goals into country-specific action plans. In Brazil, the city of Belo Horizonte has a Comprehensive Mobility Plan NAMA –*planmobBH*– which focuses on creating a more sustainable urban transportation system. The NAMA includes plans to improve public transportation, fare integration, and infrastructure for the promotion of non-motorized transportation across the metro area. This would lead to a cumulative estimated GHG emissions savings of 9 $MtCO_2e$ between 2008 and 2030, a 39 percent reduction in particulate matter by 2030, and a 50 percent reduction in travel time by 2030.[47] In Peru's TRANSPerú Sustainable Urban Transport NAMA—which is expected to reduce GHG emissions by 5.6 to 9.9 $MtCO_2e$ between 2016 and 2025—focuses on developing better fuel economy standards and fuel efficiency standards for light vehicles, developing integrated public mass transport systems, modernizing the public transport fleet, improving urban transport management, and improving non-motorized transportation in Lima and Callao.[48] One of Mexico's NAMAs focuses on the renewal of its car fleet, with the goal of reducing the average age of the country's fleet from 14.8 years to 11.2 years by substituting 500,000 vehicles aged 15 years or older.[49] The NAMA is expected to reduce GHG emissions by 2.63 $MtCO_2e$ per year.[50]

---

47. Transport NAMA Database, "Comprehensive mobility plan for Belo Horizonte (Brazil)," *GIZ* (2010) http://www.transport-namadatabase.org/comprehensive-mobility-plan-for-belo-horizonte-brasil/ (accessed July 18, 2017).

48. Deutsche Gesellschaft für Internationale Zusammenarbeit, "TRANSPerú—Sustainable Urban Transport NAMA Peru," (2015), p. 48 http://transferproject.org/wp-content/uploads/2015/12/GIZ-TRANSfer_Full-NAMA-Concept-Doc-TRANSPeru-EN-online.pdf (accessed July 18, 2017).

49. Transport NAMA Database, "Car fleet renewal in Mexico," *GIZ* (2014) http://www.transport-namadatabase.org/car-fleet-renewal-in-mexico-2/ (accessed July 18, 2017).

50. United Nations Framework Convention on Climate Change, "NS-162 - Car Fleet Renewal in Mexico," Public NAMA (2014) http://www4.unfccc.int/sites/nama/_layouts/un/fccc/nama/NamaSeekingSupportForPreparation.aspx?ID=95&viewOnly=1 (accessed July 27, 2017).

Globally, the transport sector receives specific mention in three quarters of NDCs.[51] In order to limit warming to 2°C by 2025, projections from the International Energy Agency (IEA) indicate 23 percent of reductions must come from the transport sector.[52] At a global level, the costs of meeting additional demand under a 2 degree Celsius scenario can actually be lower than under a 6 degree Celsius business-as-usual scenario, according to the IEA.[53] Urban areas are the focus of most emissions reductions measures, as they can deliver 40 percent of emissions reductions from the transport sector under the 2 degree Celsius scenario.[54]

Reducing emissions from the transport sector requires an integrated approach that combines increasing the use of mass public transportation and non-motorized transportation, improving energy efficiency and vehicle technology, and using cleaner or zero-carbon fuels. These same three approaches should be applied to Latin America to reduce GHG emissions. Many of these measures will also generate improvements in air pollution, human health, and urban congestion.

Increasing the Use of Mass Public Transportation and Non-Motorized Transportation

As Latin America looks to meet increasing demand for transportation while reducing emissions, expanding mass public transportation and non-motorized transportation is crucial. The region's public transportation systems already move large numbers of people every day, but additional investment to expand and improve existing infrastructure is necessary to meet growing demand, provide a practical and convenient alternative to private transportation, and reduce emissions. Latin America's population is

51. Ernesto Monter, "Supporting Decarbonization Efforts in the Transport Sector in Latin America and the Caribbean," presented at *Energy and Transportation in the Atlantic Basin, Jean Monnet Network on Atlantic Studies* (July 20, 2017) http://jeanmonnetnetwork.com.br/wp-content/uploads/2017/08/Ernesto-Monter-Supporting-Decarbonization-Efforts-in-LAC-Transportation-Sectors.pdf.

52. International Energy Agency, "Energy Technology Perspectives 2015—Mobilising Innovation to Accelerate Climate Action," (2015), p. 73 http://www.iea.org/publications/freepublications/publication/ETP2015.pdf (accessed July 21, 2017).

53. International Energy Agency, "Energy Technology Perspectives 2016—Towards Sustainable Urban Energy Systems, Executive Summary" (2016), p. 3 https://www.iea.org/publications/freepublications/publication/EnergyTechnologyPerspectives2016_ExecutiveSummary_EnglishVersion.pdf (accessed July 27, 2017).

54. Ibid., pp. 7–8.

Table 5: Bus Rapid Transit Statistics by Region

Regions	Passengers per Day	Number of Cities
Africa	468,178 (1.46%)	4 (2.43%)
Asia	9,293,372 (29%)	42 (25.6%)
Europe	1,566,580 (4.88%)	44 (26.82%)
Latin America	19,470,072 (60.75%)	54 (32.92%)
Northern America	810,513 (2.52%)	16 (9.75%)
Oceania	436,200 (1.36%)	4 (2.43%)
Total	32,044,915	164

Source: "Compare Systems Indicators," Global BRT Data, BRTData.org (2017)
http://brtdata.org/panorama/systems (accessed September 27, 2017).

projected to grow by 23.6 percent between 2015 and 2050[55], adding to demand for both public and private transportation.

Bus Rapid Transit (BRT)

BRT systems are one of the most important forms of public transportation in the region. These systems combine dedicated lanes for bus transportation with off-board fare collection to provide quick and effective mass transportation, but require a much smaller infrastructure investment than metro or urban rail systems. BRTs in Latin America move almost 20 million passengers per day across 54 cities—60.75 percent of the daily worldwide BRT passenger total (see Table 5).[56]

Many of Latin America's BRT systems are among the most advanced in the world. Belo Horizonte's MOVE and Bogotá's TransMilenio, for example, are reference points for international best practices in the Institute for Transportation and Development Policy's BRT Standard, which evaluates systems based on criteria like frequency of service, corridor location, and integration with other forms of public transportation.[57] Belo Horizonte's MOVE BRT—which received the highest "gold" classification—provides high capacity service along high demand corridors and makes good use of scarce space

55. The World Bank, "Population Dashboard" in *Health, Nutrition and Population* (2015) http://datatopics.worldbank.org/health/population (accessed September 27, 2017).

56. "Compare Systems Indicators," Global BRT Data, BRTData.org (2017) http://brtdata.org/panorama/systems (accessed September 27, 2017).

57. "About the BRT Standard," *Institute for Transportation and Development Policy* (2016) https://www.itdp.org/library/standards-and-guides/the-bus-rapid-transit-standard/about-the-brt-standard/ (accessed July 14, 2017).

in the city center. Bogotá's TransMilenio—also classified as "gold"—has been among the most successful BRT systems, moving passengers equal to or better than many metro systems. BRT corridors in Curitiba, Rio de Janeiro, Medellín, Guadalajara, and Lima also received the premier "gold" score. However, many of these systems suffer from overcrowding and need to increase the network and service frequency and introduce off-board fare collection and express service.

In addition to these improvements to existing BRTs, there is appetite for new BRT corridors in the region. Though the rate of urbanization in Latin American cities has slowed, urban populations are still growing every year, putting additional stress on already heavily strained urban transportation systems. The region's Rapid Transit to Resident Ratios (RTR)—an Institute for Transportation and Development Policy metric which compares the length of rapid transit lines (metro, rail, and BRT) with a country's urban population (a higher RTR indicates more kilometers of transit per urban resident)—are still relatively low. Chile and Ecuador have the highest RTRs in the region (between 20 and 30).[58] Between 2004 and 2014, Brazil's RTR increased from 8.3 to 10.7, as rapid transit growth outpaced urban population growth and Colombia's RTR grew from 0 to 10.1 between 1994 and 2014. Mexico also saw important RTR growth from about 5.5 to 8.4 over the same period.[59] The rest of the region has an RTR of less than 10. By comparison, the United States' RTR is 14.3 and Germany's is 81.6.

In addition to reducing GHG emissions from the transport sector, the introduction of BRT systems has also been shown to improve road safety and air quality. In TransMilenio's first two years of operation, traffic collisions, pedestrian accidents, and related deaths along Bogotá's main BRT corridor fell by 94 percent.[60] In the year after TransMilenio was rolled out, Bogotá also saw a 44 percent reduction in sulfur dioxide, a 24 percent reduction in PM_{10}, and a 7 percent reduction in NO_2.[61]

---

58. "Infographic: Rapid Transit to Resident Ratio (RTR)," *Institute for Transportation and Development Policy* (January 29, 2016) https://www.itdp.org/wp-content/uploads/2016/01/2015-itdp-infographic-spread-1206.pdf (accessed July 19, 2017).

59. Walter Hook, Colin Hughes and Jacob Mason, "Best Practice in National Support for Urban Transportation," *Institute for Transportation and Development Policy* (February 2015), p. 5-6 https://3gozaa3xxbpb499ejp30lxc8-wpengine.netdna-ssl.com/wp-content/uploads/2014/05/Best-Practices-in-National-Support-for-Urban-Transport_ITDP.pdf (accessed September 29, 2017).

60. "C40 Cities in Action: How Bike-Share and BRT Are Accelerating across the World," Sustainability Management Capstone, Earth Institute, Columbia University (2013), p. 10 http://sustainability.ei.columbia.edu/files/2014/01/C40-CITIES-IN-ACTION_Fall-2013-.pdf (accessed July 19, 2017).

61. Ibid., p. 39

Latin American countries are working on developing and rolling out a number of new BRT systems in the coming years. BRT Transbrasil will be Rio de Janeiro's fourth BRT, adding 28 stations, 4 terminals and 15 pedestrian walkways spanning 32 kilometers at a cost of US$416 million.[62] The Transbrasil corridor will be integrated into the city's Transcarioca bus system and will serve about 900,000 passengers per day. Asunción, Paraguay is developing an 18.4 kilometer BRT system, which will connect the capital with the cities of Fernando de la Mora and San Lorenzo. The system—financed with a loan from the Inter-American Development Bank—includes 26 stations and electric-powered buses with an estimated cost of US$167 million and will have a capacity of 300,000 passengers per day.[63]

Metro and Light Rail Systems

A number of cities in the region also rely heavily on metro systems, which carry 20 million people per day in 22 cities across ten countries.[64] Mexico City's metro system ranks among the ten largest in the world and serves approximately 6 million passengers per day—almost one third of the city's metro area population.[65] São Paulo's metro system, the second largest, moves more than 4.5 million passengers per day.[66] Santiago and Caracas also see both high volumes and high rates of metro use. By 2021, the region's metro ridership is expected to grow by almost 5 million passengers per day.[67]

Latin American countries are working to build new metro systems and expand existing metro and light rail systems. Quito is in the process of building its first metro line, which will cover 23 kilometers and include 15 stations, 6 of which will be connected to the existing bus network. The project—which will have a 369,000 passenger per day capacity—will cost an estimated US$1.7 billion and will save US$14 million per year in fuel costs.[68] Lima's Metro Line 2, an ongoing project with an estimated cost of US$5.8 billion, will include 35 kilometers of new urban rail and will integrate with the city's

---

62. "BRT Transbrasil," *Business News Americas*, 2017 https://www.bnamericas.com/project-profile/en/btr-transbrasil-btr-transbrasil (accessed July 21, 2017).

63. "Bus rapid transit (BRT) Metrobus Asunción stretches No. 2 and No. 3," *Business News Americas*, 2017 https://www.bnamericas.com/project-profile/en/btr-transbrasil-btr-transbrasil (accessed July 21, 2017).

64. UITP, "Metro Latin America," p. 2.

65. "Subways," *Metropolitan Transportation Authority* (2017) http://web.mta.info/nyct/facts/ ffsubway.htm (accessed July 11, 2017); UITP, "Metro Latin America," pp. 1–2.

66. UITP, "Metro Latin America," pp. 1–2.

67. Ibid., p. 5.

68. "Quito Metro Line 1," *The World Bank Group* (2017) http://projects.worldbank.org/P144489/ecuador-quito-metro-line-one?lang=en&tab=overview (accessed July 21, 2017).

existing Line 1 and BRT system, reducing public transport travel times for passengers by up to 75 minutes.[69] São Paulo, Santiago, and Panama City are also in the process of adding lines to their existing metro systems.

When building new mass transit systems, cities have many factors to consider. BRT systems are much less costly to build than metro and light rail systems and take less time to implement; they can generally be deployed in five years or less, while metro systems can take decades. But metro and light rail systems can carry more passengers—typically 35,000 per hour per direction compared to 2,000-10,000 on BRT—and have a lower per-passenger operation and maintenance cost.[70] Rail systems are also generally entirely electric, which provides an advantage in terms of emissions reductions, especially in Latin America where electricity is largely generated from hydropower.

Non-Motorized Transport

In addition, increasing access to and convenience of non-motorized transport is an important part of sustainable urban mobility plans. Many cities in the region have made important investments in this space in recent years. When compared to other forms of transportation, cycling infrastructure and bicycle-sharing programs are much less costly, require less space, have no emissions, and can be deployed in a matter of months. Bicycle-sharing programs range in cost from less than US$5 million in cities like in Toronto, Portland and Istanbul to US$40 million in New York City and US$140 million in Paris.[71]

More than 12 cities in Latin America have adopted bicycle-sharing programs in recent years, including Mexico City, Rio de Janeiro, São Paulo, and Buenos Aires.[72] Mexico's ECOBICI program is very popular and demand is growing quickly. The program began operation in February 2010 with 84 stations and 1,200 bicycles and by 2016 had grown to 452 stations and more than 6,000 bicycles.[73] The program regularly sees more than

69. "Peru Lima Metro Line 2 Project," *The World Bank Group* (2017) http://projects.worldbank.org/P145610?lang=en (accessed July 21, 2017).

70. Jacques Drouin, "Why Latin America's Urban Transport Is on Track," *World Economic Forum* (May 6, 2015) https://www.weforum.org/agenda/2015/05/why-latin-americas-urban-transport-is-on-track/ (accessed July 21, 2017).

71. "C40 Cities in Action," Columbia University, p. 9.

72. "Cycling Gains Ground on Latin American Streets," *The World Bank Group* (June 24, 2015) http://www.worldbank.org/en/news/feature/2015/06/24/el-pedaleo-gana-espacio-en-las-calles-latinoamericanas (accessed July 21, 2017).

73. "¿Qué es ECOBICI?" *CMS CDMX, Oficialía Mayor de la Ciudad de México* (2016) https://www.ecobici.cdmx.gob.mx/es/informacion-del-servicio/que-es-ecobici (accessed July 21, 2017).

Figure 7: Daily Bicycle Use in Latin America, 2015

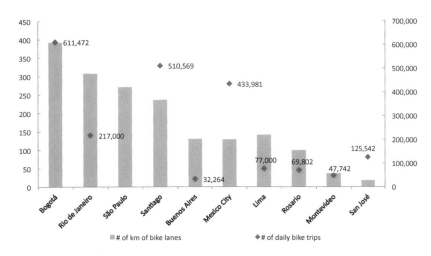

Source: Inter-American Development Bank, "Ciclo-inclusión en América Latina y el Caribe: Guía para impulsar el uso de la bicicleta" (February 2015), p. 3 https://publications.iadb.org/handle/11319/6808 (accessed July 19, 2017).

30,000 rides per weekday, sometimes reaching almost 40,000, and users span 43 *colonias* (neighborhoods) and 3 *delegaciones* (boroughs) covering 35km[2].[74] Rio de Janeiro's bicycle-sharing system—Bike Rio—began operating in 2011 with 60 stations and expanded to 260 stations with 2,600 bicycles covering more of the city in 2014.[75] The city has 450 kilometers of cycling lanes—the second largest in Latin America (after Bogotá) (see Figure 7).[76] Rio recently announced it will modernize its entire bicycle fleet and all 260 stations with more modern technology, including a new payment interface that will accept the *Bilhete Único Carioca*, the city's bus and metro payment system. Investments in cycling infrastructure to create more space for cyclists have also paid off in Santiago, where the number of cyclists on

---

74. "¿Qué es ECOBICI?" *Oficialía Mayor de la Ciudad de México*; "Estadísticas de ECOBICI" *CMS CDMX, Oficialía Mayor de la Ciudad de México* (2017) https://www.ecobici.cdmx.gob.mx/es/informacion-del-servicio/que-es-ecobici (accessed July 21, 2017).

75. Gustavo Ribeiro, "Bike Rio passará por recauchutagem," *O Dia*, June 18, 2017 http://odia.ig.com.br/rio-de-janeiro/observatorio/2017-06-18/bike-rio-passara-por-recauchutagem.html (accessed July 26, 2017).

76. "Biking in Rio," *Rio.com LLC* (2017) http://www.rio.com/practical-rio/biking-rio (accessed July 27, 2017).

the road has grown by up to 25 percent a year in the past decade and now accounts for 6 percent of all journeys.[77]

Investments in pedestrian-friendly infrastructure like sidewalks and lighting also encourage non-motorized transport. Over the past 12 years, Mexico City's government has converted five kilometers—approximately 30 streets—into pedestrian-only or pedestrian-priority streets. These investments will continue in 2017 with updates to make three major roadways more pedestrian and bicycle friendly with an investment of more than US$2 million.

Improving Energy Efficiency and Vehicle Technology

Improving fuel economy, vehicle emissions, and fuel quality standards is also crucial for Latin America, both to reduce GHG emissions and to improve air quality in cities.

Between 2014 and 2015, non-OECD countries have seen faster fuel economy improvements than OECD countries, as improvement trends slowed in the United States (from 2.3 percent to 0.5 percent) and reversed in Japan (worsened by 4.5 percent) while large non-OECD markets like Brazil, China and Malaysia saw improvements.[78] Mandatory fuel economy standards can yield enormous results. Mexico's environment ministry estimates that its standards, implemented in 2013, will save 710 million barrels of fuel and avoid 265 million tons of CO_2 emissions by 2032.[79] Fuel economy standards for heavy-duty vehicles lag particularly far behind, both in Latin America and globally. Only four countries in the world—Canada, China, Japan, and the United States—have fuel economy regulations for heavy-duty vehicles.[80] Mexico is considering implementing heavy-duty fuel economy regulations. More stringent fuel economy standards can raise vehicle prices, but they also generate cost savings for owners as a result of having to use less fuel. Analyses of proposed regulations typically include information about this "payback period"—how long it takes for savings in fuel costs to compensate

77. Gideon Long, "'Get yourself a bike, perico!': how cycling is challenging Santiago's social barriers," *The Guardian*, July 21, 2016 https://www.theguardian.com/cities/2016/jul/21/cycling-challenging-santiago-chile-social-barriers (accessed July 15, 2017).

78. Global Fuel Economy Initiative, "International Comparison of Light-Duty Vehicle Fuel Economy 2005-2015: Ten Years of Fuel Economy Benchmarking" (2017), p.19 https://www.globalfueleconomy.org/media/418761/wp15-ldv-comparison.pdf (accessed September 27, 2017).

79. ICCT, "Policy Update," p. 3.

80. International Energy Agency, "Global EV Outlook 2017," (2017), p. 12.

for the higher upfront cost.[81] Fuel economy standards can sometimes inadvertently encourage consumers to choose private transportation over public transportation because of the low cost of fuel. To avoid this, fuel economy standards can be accompanied by stronger fuel taxes.

Beyond establishing fuel economy regulations, enforcement and verification mechanisms must also be considered. At a global level, some countries have independent certification and inspection systems, some are reliant on manufacturers to self-police, some rely on import statistics, and others have no inspection criteria at all. Vehicle certification processes in Latin America lag far behind, with the notable exception of Chile, according to UNEP.[82] Many countries depend on information from tests developed by vehicle manufacturers themselves, and in some countries, only a sworn declaration by an importer's legal representative is required with no further inspection. Though Mexico's fuel economy standards are the most stringent in the region, they lack incentives for enforcement and, like the United States CAFE standards, rely heavily on self-reporting.

There are also a host of economic incentives for vehicle efficiency that countries can implement. A feebate—like Chile's progressive tax based on fuel efficiency and NO_x emissions—defines a 'pivot point' in emissions levels and taxes vehicles above the pivot point while providing monetary incentives to those below the pivot point.[83] Feebates have the advantage of being fiscally neutral, as payments to low-carbon vehicle owners are financed with taxes on high-carbon vehicle owners. France has applied this policy since 2008 with success.

Countries may also choose to implement a labeling system with different levels depending on efficiency and emissions standards with clear benefits for each level. Labeling systems simplify the application of a feebate and can also be used to exempt vehicles from circulation restrictions. For example, vehicles with Chile's *sello verde*, or green seal, are exempt from Santiago's vehicle restriction program and vehicles in Mexico with a zero or double zero label as well as EVs are exempt from the *Hoy no circula* program.

A vehicle registration tax that corresponds to vehicle emissions levels can also incentivize consumers to purchase more efficient vehicles. Offering incentives for taxi owners to buy newer models with a rebate dependent on

---

81. GFEI, "Fuel Economy State of the World 2016," p. 34.
82. UNEP, "Movilidad Eléctrica," p 31.
83. Ibid., p. 59.

the vehicle's fuel efficiency can also pay dividends in converting this high-use vehicle fleet. Some countries—like Chile and Mexico—employ a combination of these options.

Secondhand car imports will continue to be problematic for reducing emissions from the transport sector and for improving air quality, especially in countries with developing economies. Globally, an estimated 25-35 million light-duty vehicles move internationally as secondhand vehicles every year.[84] By 2030, the volume of secondhand vehicle trade will equal new car sales in the European Union and China combined.[85] Though many Latin American countries have banned used car imports, many others still allow it. Costa Rica, for example, has made several attempts to ban used car imports but the measures have not passed Congress. As a result, 80 percent of the fleet is more than ten years old.[86]

Countries in the region should also consider implementing stricter emissions requirements for new vehicles, though in countries that continue to import used cars, these emissions restrictions will not have as significant an impact. Vehicle emissions regulations should be developed considering the significant difference between laboratory and real-world conditions. The International Council on Clean Transportation estimates that in 2014, CO_2 emissions from vehicles were on average 40 percent higher than testing condition estimates.[87] In recent years, portable emissions monitoring systems (PEMS), which allow real-time measurement of hydrocarbon, CO, CO_2, NO_x, and particulate matter emissions, have gained traction for producing more accurate results. In fact, Euro VI standards require PEMS for heavy-duty vehicles.

Fuel quality standards are also making strides in the region. Though some countries plan to progressively lower sulfur content or leave regulations untouched, a few have chosen to "leapfrog" to a much more rigorous standard. For example, by 2020 Peru will tighten its gasoline sulfur content

84. Roger Gorham, "Prospects for 'Decarbonization' of African Transport," presented at *Energy and Transportation in the Atlantic Basin, Jean Monnet Network on Atlantic Studies* (July 20, 2017) http://jeanmonnetnetwork.com.br/wp-content/uploads/2017/08/Gorham-Prospects-for-Decarbonization-of-African-Transportation.pdf.

85. Roger Gorham, "Prospects for 'Decarbonization' of African Transport," presented at Energy and Transportation in the Atlantic Basin, Jean Monnet Network on Atlantic Studies (July 20, 2017) http://jeanmonnetnetwork.com.br/wp-content/uploads/2017/08/Gorham-Prospects-for-Decarbonization-of-African-Transportation.pdf.

86. UNEP, "Status of Fuel Quality."

87. ICCT, "From laboratory to road: A 2015 update," (2015) cited in UNEP, "Movilidad Eléctrica," p. 58.

restrictions from 501-2500ppm to 31-50ppm and its diesel sulfur content restrictions from >2000ppm to 10-15ppm. Mexico will also significantly restrict sulfur limits in diesel, moving from 351-500ppm to 10-15ppm by 2020. Several countries around the world, including Brazil, also have stricter sub-national regulations.

Using Cleaner or Zero-Carbon Fuels

Electric Vehicles

In the longer term, however, to decarbonize the transport sector Latin America will need to vastly expand alternative vehicles markets, particularly EVs. As Latin America's vehicle fleet continues to grow rapidly—with the IEA projecting the fleet will triple by 2050[88]—EV expansion is vital to avoid huge increases in demand for fossil fuels and emissions from the transport sector. UNEP estimates that an accelerated rollout of electric mobility in the region would result in emissions reductions of 1.4 Gt of CO_2 and fuel cost savings of US$85 billion between 2016 and 2050.[89] With about half of its electricity coming from renewable sources, Latin America is particularly well positioned to gain from widespread EV adoption. Even in countries where fossil fuels still make up a large source of electricity generation, EVs can offer huge benefits in terms of urban air quality. As electricity generation from intermittent renewable energy sources like wind and solar grows, EVs can also offer an important form of energy storage as vehicle-to-grid technology—when electricity is stored in EV batteries and later fed back to the grid—is further developed.

EV markets are still in a very early stage, and strong policy incentives are needed to promote widespread adoption. The global stock of electric cars surpassed 2 million vehicles in 2016, growing from 1.26 million in 2015 and just 180,000 in 2012.[90] Ten countries make up 95 percent of electric car sales; China and the United States are the two largest markets, followed by Norway, the United Kingdom, France, Germany, the Netherlands, and Sweden (see Chapter Three). Electric cars represent more than 1 percent of market share in just six countries—Norway (29 percent), the

---

88. UNEP, "Movilidad Eléctrica," p. 3.

89. Ibid., p. 3.

90. International Energy Agency, "Global EV Outlook 2017," (2017), p. 5 https://www.iea.org/publications/freepublications/publication/GlobalEVOutlook2017.pdf (accessed July 24, 2017).

Netherlands (6.4 percent), Sweden (3.4 percent), France (~1.5 percent), the United Kingdom (~1.5 percent) and China (~1.5 percent).[91]

Latin America faces many barriers to increasing EV uptake with few of the incentives that have spurred sales in other regions (see Table 6). High upfront costs and a lack of public charging infrastructure are the foremost obstacles, although the price difference between electric and conventional vehicles is expected to decrease dramatically in the coming years as lithium-ion battery costs fall and the price of conventional vehicles rises with increasingly strict fuel economy demands. Lithium-ion battery costs have dropped drastically in recent years—from US$1,000 per kilowatt hour (kWh) in 2010 to US$273/kWh in 2016—and are projected to continue falling.[92] Estimates suggest prices will fall to just US$73/kWh by 2030.[93] Stricter fuel economy and vehicle emissions standards are also necessary for EVs to compete successfully with conventional vehicles as they incentivize manufacturers to invest in EV technologies. Concerns about grid reliability, competition from other industries, and fuel subsidies also continue to pose significant challenges for EV uptake in the region.

Fuel subsidies have been particularly problematic in Venezuela, Mexico, Ecuador, Argentina, and Colombia (in 2017 Mexico changed its fuel pricing policies to align domestic fuel prices with international oil prices). These five countries spent US$29 billion on gasoline and diesel subsidies in 2013—26 percent of global fuel subsidy spending.[94] When fuel subsidies are in place, the cost per kilometer driven falls, encouraging consumers to choose private transportation over public transportation and preventing the development of alternative vehicles markets. In countries with large fuel subsidies like Mexico, cost per kilometer for conventional vehicles is about US$0.05, while countries like Uruguay which tax fossil fuels have a cost of more than US$0.11 per kilometer, according to UNEP.[95] EV costs per kilometer can be as low as US$0.008, depending on the cost of electricity. In countries like Mexico and Argentina with generous electricity subsidies, EV cost per

91. Ibid., p. 12.

92. "The Long-Term Outlook for Electric Vehicle Adoption," *Bloomberg Finance*, August 2, 2017 https://bloomberg.cwebcast.com/ses/yHxPvxgMWCQhQn-GScF7pA~~?ek=26664507-22b1-402c-8798-d8ad89681bad (accessed July 27, 2017).

93. Ibid.

94. CEPAL (2014) cited in UNEP, "Movilidad Eléctrica," p. 60. ICCT, "From laboratory to road: A 2015 update," cited in UNEP, "Movilidad Eléctrica," p. 58.

95. Centro de Estudio de la Regulación Económica de los Servicios Públicos Universidad de Belgrano (2016), cited in UNEP, "Movilidad Eléctrica," p. 61.

kilometer is less than US$0.01. In countries with high electricity costs like Uruguay, the cost is around US$0.03 per kilometer.

Many countries in the region have fiscal and non-fiscal incentives in place to encourage the purchase of EVs, though they have not yet been sufficient to meaningfully expand the market. These include a range of measures like tax exemptions or reductions, exemptions from vehicle circulation restrictions, separate electricity metering and lower tariffs for residential vehicle recharging, and access to preferential parking and driving lanes.

Brazil is the region's most important market with almost 4,800 EVs and hybrid EVs (just 300 are 100 percent electric),[96] though expansion has been slow and faces many obstacles. The industry faces strong opposition from Brazil's powerful ethanol lobby and a limited charging network that has expanded slowly due to regulations that prevent power sales by third parties. In Rio de Janeiro, the country's second largest city, there are less than five public EV charging stations. A bill in Brazil's lower house of Congress aims to expand this network by requiring electric utilities to install EV charging stations on public roads as well as in residential and commercial areas. But despite its large size and some promising developments in recent years, like expanded electric bus fleets and more EV brands available for retail purchase, projections for the next ten years show timid growth. Furthermore, unlike in Europe, where battery electric vehicles (BEVs) offer the greatest prospects for emissions reductions (see Chapter 3), analysis suggests that in Brazil conventional hybrid vehicles would do more to lower emissions than all-electric vehicles. A recent study found that although large-scale BEV penetration (82 percent of sales in 2050) would reduce total primary energy demand, it would increase GHG emissions because the use of ethanol would decline considerably and Brazil would have to increase coal-fired power generation to meet additional electricity demand for cars.[97]

Latin America's second largest country, Mexico, is also a large potential market for EVs with the domestic car market projected to reach seventy million vehicles by 2030.[98] Most of the major EV brands, such as Tesla, Nissan

96. "Carro elétrico: o futuro já está entre nós," *Associação Brasileira do Veículo Elétrico* (July 14, 2017) http://www.abve.org.br/noticias/carro-eletrico-o-futuro-ja-esta-entre-nos (accessed July 19, 2017).

97. Olivia Brajterman, "Introdução de veículos elétricos e impactos sobre o setor energético brasileiro" (March 2016) http://www.ppe.ufrj.br/ppe/production/tesis/brajterman.pdf (accessed September 27, 2017).

98. Estefanía Marchán and Lisa Viscidi, "Green Transportation—The Outlook for Electric Vehicles in Latin America," *The Inter-American Dialogue* (October, 2015), p. 7

LEAF, and the BMW i3 and i8, are available for purchase there, though the current fleet remains small with about five hundred EVs.[99] Mexico offers some incentives to purchase EVs, such as exemption from a new vehicle tax, differentiated electricity tariffs for home charging, and exemption from traffic restrictions. However, for the most part, these incentives are not enough to compensate for the high upfront cost of EVs, limited network of public charging infrastructure, and high and unpredictable cost of electricity.

Costa Rica, the most ambitious Latin American country in terms of GHG emissions reduction goals, is an emerging leader in Latin America in electric mobility. Aiming to reach zero net emissions by 2085, Costa Rica is increasingly focusing on cutting emissions from the transportation sector given that about 80 percent of installed capacity already comes from renewable energy. Its NDC specifically mentions plans to increase electric transportation. A new law that has been proposed for debate in congress would lower the cost of EVs up to 44 percent by reducing the sales tax, consumption tax, and import tax on a sliding scale depending on the price of the vehicle for a period of five years.[100] Costa Rica's electric utility, the Costa Rican Electricity Institute (ICE) recently announced it would purchase a fleet of one hundred EVs and one hundred charging stations to incentivize EV use in the public sector.[101]

There is also potential for electric motorcycle, bicycle, and bus growth in the region. Latin America currently has a fleet of 16 million conventional motorcycles, 5 percent of the global market.[102] Electrifying the region's bus fleet is an opportunity to reduce both GHG emissions and short-lived climate pollutants from high-use vehicles. The global stock of electric buses is just 345,000, the vast majority of which are found in China.[103] However, many

---

http://www.thedialogue.org/wp-content/uploads/2015/10/Green-Transportation-The-Outlook-for-Electric-Vehicles-in-Latin-America.pdf (accessed July 24, 2017).

99. "Alto costo y falta de incentivos limitan compra de autos eléctricos," *El Informador, Unión Editorialista*, September 10, 2016 http://www.informador.com.mx/tecnologia/2016/681425/6/alto-costo-y-falta-de-incentivos-limitan-compra-de-autos-electricos.htm (accessed July 27, 2017).

100. "Costa Rica: costo de vehículos eléctricos podría bajar casi a la mitad," *Estrategia y Negocios* (magazine), *OPSA Honduras*, May 22, 2017 http://www.estrategiaynegocios.net/lasclavesdeldia/1073216-330/costa-rica-costo-de-veh%C3%ADculos-el%C3%A9ctricos-podr%C3%ADa-bajar-casi-a-la-mitad (accessed July 27, 2017).

101. "Empresa estatal de Costa Rica usará 100 autos eléctricos para fomentar su uso," *Elpais.Cr*, May 5, 2017 http://www.elpais.cr/2017/05/05/empresa-estatal-de-costa-rica-usara-100-autos-electricos-para-fomentar-su-uso/ (accessed July 24, 2017).

102. UNEP, "Movilidad Eléctrica," p. 15.

103. International Energy Agency, "Global EV Outlook 2017," (2017), p. 28.

Table 6: Benchmarking Electric Vehicle Conditions in Latin America

Country	Low-Carbon Power Generation	Emissions Reduction Targets	Road Access Incentives	Financial Incentives	Extensive Public Charging Infrastructure	Electricity Incentives	Fuel Economy Economic Incentives
Colombia	Yes	Yes	Yes	Yes			
Mexico		Yes	Yes	Yes		Yes	Yes
Brazil	Yes	Yes	Yes	Yes			Yes
Chile		Yes	Yes	Yes			Yes
Costa Rica	Yes	Yes	Yes				

Source: Estefanía Marchán and Lisa Viscidi, "Green Transportation—The Outlook for Electric Vehicles in Latin America," The Inter-American Dialogue (October, 2015), p. 11 http://www.thedialogue.org/wp-content/uploads/2015/10/Green-Transportation-The-Outlook-for-Electric-Vehicles-in-Latin-America.pdf (accessed July 24, 2017) and own elaboration.

Latin American cities—like Bogotá, Medellín, and Mexico City—have begun electric bus pilot projects, and studies based on Quito and Santiago show that electric buses are less costly over their life cycle than hybrid or conventional diesel buses.[104]

Biofuels

Biofuels can also be cost-competitive alternative fuel options for long-distance transport, though they still represent an extremely small share of transport sector fuels in the region. In Latin America and the Caribbean, biofuels make up just 6 percent of transport sector fuels,[105] though they are widely used in Brazil. As a result of the country's Pro-Álcool Program, developed in 1975 to reduce dependence on oil imports, more than 70 percent of Brazil's light vehicle fleet is made up of hydrous ethanol and flex-fuel vehicles.[106] Even Brazil's gasoline has a high level of ethanol; the current requirement is a 27 percent ethanol blend.[107] Brazil also mandates biodiesel blending, though on a smaller scale. Due to its widespread use of ethanol,

---

104. UNEP, "Movilidad Eléctrica," pp. 21–22.

105. Enerdata (2015), cited in Vergara et al., "Zero Carbon Latin America," p. 34.

106. USDA Foreign Agricultural Service, "Brazil Biofuels Annual—Annual Report 2016" (August 12, 2016), p. 16 https://gain.fas.usda.gov/Recent%20GAIN%20Publications/Biofuels%20Annual_Sao%20Paulo%20ATO_Brazil_8-12-2016.pdf (accessed July 25, 2017).

107. Ibid., p. 1.

Table 7: CO2 Emissions Factors by Fuel

Fuel	CO2 emissions factor
Gasoline "A" (27 percent anhydrous ethanol)	2.269 kg/L
Anhydrous ethanol	1.233 kg/L
Hydrous ethanol	1.178 kg/L
Diesel	2.671 kg/L
Natural gas	1.999 kg/m^3

Source: Ministério do Meio Ambiente (Brasil) - Secretaria de Mudanças Climáticas e Qualidade Ambiental, "1º Inventário Nacional de Emissões Atmosféricas por Veículos Automotores Rodoviários," (January 2011), p. 35 http://www.anp.gov.br/wwwanp/images/Emissoes-Atmosfericas-1Inventariodeemissoes.pdf (accessed July 24, 2017).

Brazil's oil demand is much lower than average for the size of its economy and population. Argentina, Colombia, Ecuador, Panama, Paraguay, and Peru also have ethanol blend mandates, biodiesel blend mandates or both. Other countries in the region, like Chile, have blending targets but not mandatory blending levels.

Biofuels provide reductions in vehicle emissions and resulting health benefits—a recent study by the Getulio Vargas Foundation estimates that biodiesel emits 57 percent less pollutants and a 5 percent biodiesel blend avoids about two thousand premature respiratory disease deaths per year.[108] Yet there is disagreement as to whether biofuels lower net GHG emissions. While emissions per liter of fuel are much lower (see Table 7), when emissions from land use change are taken into account some studies find that GHG emissions nearly double over thirty years from using corn-based ethanol.[109] Others find as much as a 48 percent reduction in lifecycle GHG emissions from corn-based ethanol.[110] Sugarcane and canola-based ethanol, more commonly used in Latin America, are much more efficient, offering greater emissions reductions. Cellulosic materials like switchgrass and agricultural waste offer even greater efficiency and lower emissions, though the process of converting them into fuel is more difficult and costly.

---

108. Danielle Nogueira, "Biodiesel emite 57% menos gases poluentes, diz FGV," O Globo, September 16, 2012 https://oglobo.globo.com/economia/biodiesel-emite-57-menos-gases-poluentes-diz-fgv-6096296 (accessed July 24, 2017).

109. Vergara et al., "Zero Carbon Latin America," p. 34.

110. "Ethanol Vehicle Emissions," Alternative Fuels Data Center, US Department of Energy (March 16, 2017) https://www.afdc.energy.gov/vehicles/flexible_fuel_emissions.html (accessed July 24, 2017).

Natural Gas Vehicles

Natural gas vehicles also offer significant CO_2 reductions, though they may result in a net increase if fugitive emissions (leaks) are significant. Compared to gasoline, estimates indicate that natural gas offers 6-11 percent lower lifecycle GHG emissions.[111] GHG emissions from CNG and LNG are very similar, but CNG offers a slight benefit in terms of emissions reductions as its production uses less petroleum.

In Latin America, natural gas represents just 2 percent of transport sector fuels, though Argentina and Brazil have sizable fleets and Bolivia's fleet is growing rapidly.[112] Argentina has about 1.7 million natural gas vehicles in circulation with approximately 2,500 natural gas service stations and an average of 15,000 vehicles per year are converted from gasoline to compressed natural gas (CNG).[113] As Argentina has reduced longstanding fossil fuel subsidies and the gap between natural gas and gasoline prices has narrowed, the country has seen a drop-off in vehicle conversions. To compete, natural gas prices need to be about one third the price of gasoline as they require more frequent fueling and an upfront investment for conversion.[114] Further scheduled natural gas price increases in Argentina leave little room for this market to expand in the near term. Although Bolivia's fleet remains small, its free natural gas conversion program has led to rapid growth. Between 2006 and 2016, the country's fleet grew to 350,000 vehicles using CNG as a primary fuel—a 722 percent increase.[115]

Conclusion

Providing adequate transportation is one of the greatest policy challenges facing most Latin American countries. Transportation — from individuals commuting to work to trucks carrying goods across the country for export—

---

111. "Natural Gas Vehicle Emissions," *Alternative Fuels Data Center, US Department of Energy* (April 12, 2017) https://www.afdc.energy.gov/vehicles/natural_gas_emissions.html (accessed July 24, 2017).

112. Enerdata (2015), cited in Vergara et al., "Zero Carbon Latin America," p. 34.

113. Carlos Arbia, "Posible quita de subsidios pone en riesgo la continuidad del GNC para autos particulares," *Infobae*, May 10, 2017 http://www.infobae.com/economia/2017/05/10/el-gobierno-eliminaria-la-utlizacion-de-gnc-en-los-autos-particualres/ (accessed July 25, 2017).

114. Ibid.

115. "EEC-GNV Reports Continued Success with Bolivia's CNG Vehicle Conversions," NGV Global News, May 3, 2016 http://www.ngvglobal.com/blog/eec-gnv-reports-continued-success-with-bolivias-cng-vehicle-conversions-0503 (accessed July 25, 2017).

underpins economic growth across the region. Yet transportation systems in Latin America are increasingly inadequate for the region's growing economies. Booming demand for transportation from private citizens, the public sector, and industry is currently on track to generate a significant increase in GHG emissions. Thus, establishing policies that encourage low-carbon transportation is critical to ensuring green growth in Latin America.

The most important area for expansion is in electric mobility, as it offers the only viable pathway to zero emissions. Natural gas vehicles lower emissions in the short term but still rely on fossil fuel energy. Biofuels for transport also generate emissions and are not viable on a large scale in most Latin American countries outside of Brazil. Improving fuel efficiency and expanding mass public transportation also help reduce CO_2 and local air pollutants but cannot alone achieve zero emissions.

In the near-term, Latin American countries should significantly increase their efforts to electrify high-use vehicles such as taxis, buses, and metros. The benefits of electrifying high-use vehicles are twofold: this approach has a greater impact on emissions because the vehicles travel many kilometers throughout the day while private cars sit idle the vast majority of the time. At the same time, electrifying high-use vehicles provides exposure for many people to the unfamiliar technology. While prioritizing high-use vehicles, governments also need to develop plans and establish specific targets for mass use of private electric vehicles in order to move towards zero emissions. Policies to promote electric mobility should be coupled with efforts to encourage electricity generation from renewable sources. This approach alone will ensure that Latin American countries achieve the goals of the Paris climate accord to which every country in the region has signed on.

Chapter Five

Prospects for Decarbonizing Transport in Africa

Roger Gorham

In 2014, Africa was responsible for only 3% of world's total CO_2 emissions, and only 4% of world's *transport-related* CO_2 emissions. CO_2 emissions from transport in Africa are quite low by world standards, but are nonetheless an important cause for concern for those interested in stemming the onset of global warming, for several reasons. First, the intensity of transport-related CO_2 emissions in Africa relative to economic output is high by world standards; as African economies grow, therefore, CO_2 emissions from transport will grow relatively faster in Africa than in other world regions. Second, the proportion of CO_2 emissions that comes from transport is higher in Africa than almost all other regions. On a per-capita basis, transport CO_2 emissions are already growing faster than any other source of energy-related CO_2 emissions across the continent.[1] Third, notwithstanding this already high growth, most of Africa's growth trajectory in transport has yet to occur. Africa is the fastest urbanizing region in the world, and with urbanization comes motorization—that is, the adoption and use of motor vehicles. Exacerbating this situation is that, for the foreseeable future, most of this added vehicle stock, particularly among light-duty vehicles, will come from importation of second-hand vehicles from other world regions, meaning that—all else being equal—other regions will benefit from efficiency and carbon-reducing technologies before Africa.

In this context, then, a key question will be what are the prospects for African transport to decarbonize. This chapter provides a brief, qualitative survey of the prospects for decarbonization of the transport sector in Africa. It relies on the EASI conceptual framework, put forward by the Africa Transport Policy Program to structure the discussion.[2] This framework allows for a policy-based decomposition of the sources of CO_2 growth. The analytical components of the EASI framework are shown in Figure 1.

---

1. International Energy Agency, "Per capita CO2 emissions by sector," IEA CO2 Emissions from Fuel Combustion Statistics online database (by subscription), (Paris, IEA, 2017).

2. M. Stucki, *Policies for Sustainable Accessibility and Mobility in Urban Areas of Africa* (Washington, DC, Africa Transport Policy Program (SSATP), 2015).

Figure 1. EASI Conceptual Framework

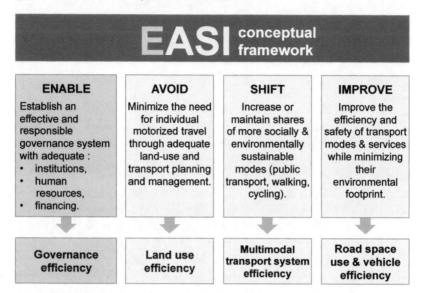

Source: M. Stucki, *Policies for Sustainable Accessibility and Mobility in Urban Areas of Africa* (Washington, DC, Africa Transport Policy Program (SSATP), 2015).

In this framework, each of the elements above can be understood to contribute to potential CO_2 emissions reduction from the sector, when considered against a hypothetical business-as-usual case. *Enable* as a category contributes only indirectly; the ability of governments and governance systems to organize themselves in a manner that can generate CO_2 emissions savings through *Avoid*, *Shift*, or *Improve* methods depends on the governance and institutional aspects of the Enable pillar.

Avoid refers to the minimization of the need for individual motorized travel, generally through adequate land-use and transport planning, consistent implementation of plans, and effective management of land-development processes. *Shift* refers to shifting *over time* the per unit carbon intensity of the modal mix of travel. This generally means reducing the amount of vehicle kilometers of travel by migrating the toward higher numbers of higher-capacity vehicles and improving utilization rates. *Improve* refers to minimizing the per kilometer CO_2 emissions of vehicles by a combination of better vehicles, better drivers, better road conditions, and the decarbonization of fuels and drive-trains themselves.

The remainder of this chapter examines the prospects for each of these approaches in the decarbonization of transportation in the African context.

Avoid: Heading Off the Need for Motorized Transport

Idealized Solution: Urban Context

In most world regions, a conventionally effective way to reduce energy consumption—and with it, GHG-related emissions—on an urban and metropolitan level is to develop and implement mutually supportive land-use and transport plans in a way that avoids the need for motorized transportation demand (current and/or future). The ideal approach would take advantage of highly-populated urban settings which are both compact and dense. Land areas in such an urban space would be developed in a way to facilitate mixed primary uses, and would be easily walkable and cyclable.

African Reality: Urban Context

In Africa, however, the notion of avoiding motorized travel through development of compact, dense cities is challenged by two phenomena: developing compact, dense cities in Africa is actually quite difficult, and if it is done well, in the short run, it is likely to—and should—generate *more*, not less, motorized travel.

Several factors make development of compact and dense cities difficult in the African context. The first is time itself. Compact cities require planning and infrastructure investment to nurture their harmonious growth. But the rate of urban growth is so rapid that both planning and infrastructure investment are swamped by it. Cities in Africa are growing so fast that by 2035, the urban population in sub-Saharan Africa (SSA) will be equal to the *total* population of Africa in 2005. In 1990, Africa as a whole had only one urban agglomeration larger than 5 million people; by 2030, it will have 18. By 2050, over 750 million more people will live in sub-Saharan African cities than in 2015.[3]

If Africa's cities are growing at unprecedented rates in terms of population, they are growing even faster in terms of land consumed. A recent compilation of data from 119 cities found that the built-up area of cities in Africa grew at 2.5 times the rate of population growth from 1990 to 2000 (as shown in

---

3. United Nations, *World Urbanization Prospects: The 2014 Revision* (New York, UN Department of Economic and Social Affairs, Population Division, 2014), CD-ROM Edition.

Figure 2. African Cities' Expansion of Built-up Areas and Population growth, 1990-2000

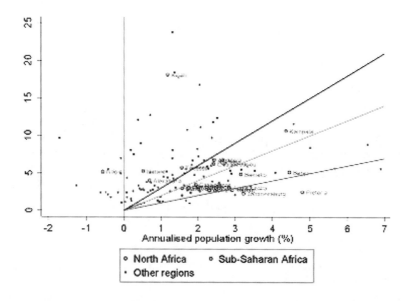

Source: African Development Bank, OECD Development Centre and United Nations Development Program, *African Economic Outlook 2016: Sustainable Cities and Structural Transformation*. African Economic Outlook. (Abidjan, Paris, New York, 2016).

Figure 2).[4] This means that population densities in African cities are declining over time.

A second key constraint is that land markets do not function as well as they do in other world regions.[5] The traditional focus of development institutions in this respect is on developing those aspects of the land-market that are within the purview of the public sector—cadasters, taxation, business processes, etc. But even private sector roles within land markets, such as titling, insurance, appraisal, and brokerage, are poorly developed in Africa. This is important, because creating compact, dense cities means creating nodes where accessibility value is captured into land transactions. But if the

4. African Development Bank, OECD Development Centre and United Nations Development Program, *African Economic Outlook 2016: Sustainable Cities and Structural Transformation*. African Economic Outlook. (Abidjan, Paris, New York, 2016).

5. Urban LandMark, *Africa's Urban Land Markets: Piecing Together an Economic Puzzle* (Nairobi, UN Habitat, 2013).

services which should work to do that are dysfunctional, then the market response to accessibility value—density—will also be muted.

A third key constraint results from the second. African cities do not aggregate opportunities effectively. Capital investment is not keeping up with population influx. For example, Lall et al. have noted that the share of land devoted to street space is higher in eight representative cities than in comparable cities than in other cities in the world.[6] They also show that during a period of rapid urbanization, African countries have had annual capital investments of about 20 percent of GDP, while those figures were over 40 percent for Asian countries on average during a similar period of urban growth. They show that the value of building stock in four representative cities of Africa (using several different indicators) is markedly lower than for Central American cities, as a benchmark. In short, they conclude, capital influx has not followed population growth in sub-Saharan African cities, which has led to urban sprawl and population density declines.[7]

In the African cities they examine, Lall et al. argue that these factors contribute not only to sprawl and low densities (which are, after all, phenomena observed in many world regions) but, in the case of sub-Saharan Africa, also to spatially fragmented and dysfunctional cities. Using a tripartite index of spatial fragmentation, they conclude that urban Africans have less potential for interaction than urban dwellers in other world regions, and that cities in Africa are becoming more fragmented over time. This means that people in African cities are not as connected to jobs as they are in other regions' cities.

Finally, because of this historical challenge in aggregating opportunities effectively, even if African cities could be transformed magically such that they start creating articulated density with the development of mixed-use, compact, high-intensity urban villages, the economic and development needs of the region are such that avoidance of growth of motorized travel would be neither feasible nor desirable. As Lall et al. argue, the very point of facilitating articulated density in land-development patterns is to enable land-uses to sort themselves in an economically efficient manner, and therefore to draw from a broad labor pool made increasingly viable through improvements in transportation.[8] Indeed, this is the very matchmaker function—of linking labor to jobs—which is the *raison d'être* of cities in the first place.

---

6. J. V. Lall, S. Henderson and A. Venables (2017). *Africa's Cities: Opening Doors to the World* (Washington, DC, World Bank, 2017).

7. Ibid.

8. Ibid.

In the context of African cities, then, motorized transport needs to be *facilitated*, not avoided, in order for cities to play their potential roles in leading to economic development.

Shift: Re-Orient Toward High-Capacity Vehicles

Given the need for more motorized travel in African cities for economic development as just discussed above, there is even more need for emphasis on the second of the three broad strategies for de-carbonization of the sector, namely shifting toward high-capacity vehicles that reduce the growth in the total number of vehicle kilometers of travel needed to deliver this higher level of motorized travel.

Shift as a concept—generally reducing the number of vehicle kilometers by better vehicle utilization—has a number of applications in passenger and freight transport. These will be discussed in turn.

Urban Bus Reform

Idealized Solution

The premise of urban bus reform is to facilitate the development of a business model for delivery of urban bus services that improves client orientation of the services, while facilitating professionalization of and capital accumulation for operators. Improvement in client orientation means addressing frequency, comfort and affordability of services, thereby retaining passengers on public transport longer as incomes increase than would be the case in the absence of reform. At the same time, professionalization and capitalization of operators, enables them to invest in larger capacity and higher quality vehicles than they would otherwise be able to afford, thereby increasing vehicle occupancy.

African Reality

In most cities in Africa, public transport services are dominated by small, artisanal operators using small vehicles or mini-buses, referred to here generically as *paratransit* following Behrens, McCormick et al.,[9] though they are often referred to by place-specific colloquial names (e.g., *danfo* in Lagos,

---

9. R. Behrens, D. McCormick and D. MFinanga, "An Introduction to Paratransit in African Cities" in R. Behrens, D. McCormick and D. MFinanga, *Paratransit in African Cities: Operations, Regulation, and Reform* (New York, Routledge, 2016) pp. 1-25.

matatu in Nairobi, etc.). A 2008 survey of 14 African cities found that, on average, minibuses dominated motorized transport service, with an average of 41 percent mode share. Conventional buses averaged only 10 percent of motorized mode share across the cities. (Kumar and Barrett 2009). A more recent compilation of available data from over 20 African cities found that the share of road-based transport carried by paratransit ranged from 36 to nearly 100 percent, with a median of 86 percent.[10]

Paratransit operations are characterized by a very large number of very small-scale owners and operators (typically one or two vehicles per owner), a range of operating models (e.g., daily rental to drivers, owner-operation, and driver-owner employee models, etc.), and a weak governmental regulatory system.[11] Such characteristics do not necessarily mean that paratransit operations are always unregulated, small in scale, and informal—indeed, there are examples of large-scale and formal mini-bus operations throughout the continent—but on balance, regulation is as likely to occur through bottom-up operator associations as through top-down governmental permitting. The result, however, is competition for passengers on the street, slim operating margins, and poor quality of services reflecting operators' objectives to minimize operating costs, rather than provide responsive service.[12]

Because of these pressures, paratransit-based public transport services tend to be more VKT-intensive (that is, a substantial number of vehicle kilometers of travel are required to deliver a given number of, say, 5-kilometer passenger trips) than would a conventional public transport structure, both because paratransit operators use almost exclusively small vehicles, and because the absence of fare integration means that there is substantial duplication of services. In addition, the operational model provides little opportunity or incentive for investment in vehicle equipment improvements. The survey of 14 cities cited above found that the average age of the paratransit fleet across all the cities was 14 years.[13] Since it is well known that fuel economy deteriorates with vehicle age, it is likely that the vehicles used for public transport in most African cities are relatively fuel intensive. Africa's paratransit-based public transport systems, therefore, have substantial scope

---

10. Ibid.

11. A. Kumar and F. Barrett (2009). "Stuck in Traffic: Urban Transport in Africa," in V. Foster, *Africa Infrastructure Country Diagnostic*, (Washington, DC, World Bank, 2009); and Behrens and McCormick et al., op. cit.

12. Behrens and McCormick et al., op. cit.

13. Kumar and Barrett, 2009, op. cit.

for CO_2 emissions reductions through paratransit reform, which can both reduce VKT and improve fuel economy.

Mass Transport Development

Idealized Solution

A related strategy to affect a shift in the kinds of public transport movements occurring in African cities is to foster creation of mass transport systems, which channel movements into corridors of peak movements between 25 to 50 thousand passengers per hour per direction, usually through a combination of feeder services and high intensity development at nodes along the service. By structuring a hierarchy of services orientated to these high-capacity corridors, cost-effective operations can be deployed across a range of neighborhood types and densities that further avoids duplication of services and VKT. Depending on the structure of the city, the availability of street space, and the final design flow capacity needed, such corridors could be developed underground, above-ground, or at-grade, and could be either rail or road-based.

African Reality

Surprisingly few sub-Saharan African cities have functioning mass transport services, and even for those that do, they are relatively recent developments. With the exception of commuter rail services in several South African cities, almost all of the region's extant mass transport systems—the Bus Rapid Transit systems (BRTs) in Lagos, Dar es Salaam, Cape Town, and Johannesburg, the light rail in Addis Ababa, and the metropolitan rail system in Gauteng Province of South Africa were all developed within the last 10 years, and are so new that they are comprised of individual lines, rather than being networks.[14] A number of other cities are either planning or constructing mass transit lines, including Dakar, Accra, Nairobi, Abuja, and Durban, but it remains to be seen how rapidly or successfully they will be developed.

One of the key challenges for the development of mass transport has been shortcomings in the decision- and project-management-support structures of municipal, and often even national, governments.[15] Often investment decisions are made in response to politically mandated timelines, without

---

14. There are a handful of other commuter rail services operating in sub-Saharan Africa, but the passenger volumes on these services are such that they cannot be classified as 'mass transport' in any meaningful way.

15. Stucki, 2015, op. cit.

adequate consideration to design, cost, or other aspects of the development, in part because the institutions which should be responsible for studies underlying such decisions are inadequately staffed or lack technical capacity. Even in instances where studies are done, they are often sequenced improperly, again because of lack of technical know-how and processes. For example, for a number of the recent African mass transport systems that have opened or are near to opening, civil engineering designs were commissioned and completed even before the operational needs of the system were understood, and in a number of cases, construction proceeded on the basis of these designs. Examples include the Addis Ababa light rail, the Blue line rail system in Lagos, and the Dar es Salaam BRT.

A second challenge in addition to that of planning and decision-support is in the capacity to manage mass transport development generally.[16] The challenge in managing that development is not necessarily related to management of civil works; indeed, civil works project management is often the least problematic aspect of these types of projects. Rather, the challenge is that mass transport development projects are often treated by political decision-makers, transport authorities, and the press, as *purely* civil works projects. Very challenging and complex issues such as who will operate the system (and how will the operator be selected), who will provide operating subsidies, or how will the services be integrated with other urban transport services, are not addressed until very late in the project development process. For example, in Dar es Salaam, the question of who would operate the BRT service was not addressed in earnest until very late in the construction of the BRT infrastructure, necessitating the use of an interim service provider until a more permanent selection process of the service provider could be arranged.[17]

Finally, lack of investment finance capacity in African cities is a substantial constraint to mass transport development. The viable sources of such investment funds vary substantially from country-to-country, and even within a given country, but the finance challenges often relate to lack of local government capacity to adequately source local revenues (such as property taxes, household taxes, and fees), competing priorities for use of whatever local and intergovernmental resources are available, and inability (for various reasons) to access local or international capital markets.[18] Multi-lateral

16. Ibid.

17. World Bank, *Tanzania: Second Central Corridor Improvement Project Implementation Completion Report* (Washington, DC, World Bank, forthcoming, 2017)

18. World Bank, *Planning, Connecting & Financing Cities Now: Priorities for City Leaders* (Washington, DC, 2013).

Development Banks can sometimes be a source for such financing (for example, in Dar es Salaam), but the slow speed of delivery, the need for sovereign guarantees or intermediary lending, and the relative dearth of such finance limit the role that it can play in the long run. Increasingly, MDBs such as the World Bank are looking for ways to use their finance more strategically to 'crowd-in' private capital financing that would not be available otherwise (the so-called 'cascade' approach), but such efforts are just in their infancy.[19]

Last-Mile Connectivity

Idealized Solution

Another key component in effecting a shift in urban transport is to address the challenge of last-mile connectivity. Although the objective of the *avoid* approach is to limit the necessity of as many people as possible to need to use motorized transport for first- or last-segments (indeed, or any other segment of the trip), in practice there will continue to be a large number of people whose origin or destinations will not be within a comfortable walking distance of mass transport. Enticing these people to use mass transport for their trip, therefore, will depend on the attractiveness of the last-mile options. Cities have seen an explosion of options in the last ten years, often enabled by ICT. These include bike-sharing, car-sharing, van-sharing, taxis and shared-taxis, and ICT-enabled paratransit.

African Reality

The elements for good last-mile connectivity are already present and relatively strong in sub-Saharan African cities. Paratransit is omnipresent, including not only mini-bus operations, but also commercial motorized two and three wheelers. Bike-sharing has yet to make a strong penetration in sub-Saharan African cities, but new technologies enabling pod-less bike sharing are likely to bring down the operational costs, such that introduction in the African context may be imminent. Many of these technologies can be facilitated through the use of ICT-enablers, for example, to use smart phones to facilitate access and increase convenience. Smart-phone penetration is already fairly high in sub-Saharan Africa. The industry reports that unique mobile subscribers in SSA are already at about 420 million, of which 27

---

19. World Bank Group Development Committee (2017). "Forward Look—A Vision for the World Bank Group in 2030 Progress and Challenges" from the World Bank and International Monetary Fund Spring Meetings (Washington, DC, World Bank, 2017).

percent are smartphone connections. Smartphone penetration rate is growing at 26.6 percent per year, meaning that by 2020, there will be an estimated 54 percent penetration rate of smartphone. This means that in just a few years' time, just under one in three Africans will have a smartphone. Use of mobile money applications in Africa is also among the most advanced in the world; according to the industry, over 40 percent of the adult population in seven SSA countries use mobile money regularly.[20]

The elements are in place for effective last-mile connectivity in African cities. The challenge for the region, however, is to find the way to utilize these pieces to connect the first and last segments of urban trips, rather than use them for the *entire* trip. Used as a means to ensure last-segment connectivity to efficient transport services, ICT-enabled paratransit such as discussed above has the potential to enhance mobility and reduce transport-related emissions in SSA cities.

Truck Shipment Consolidation

Idealized Solution

The discussion about *Shift* approaches in the *Enable-Avoid-Shift-Improve* framework has until now focused uniquely on cities. But a *Shift* strategy can also be applied to the freight sub-sector as well. One key way is to engage in cargo consolidation processes to facilitate trucking shipment consolidation earlier in the logistics chain than might otherwise occur, and to minimize empty backhauling. The objective is to improve vehicle loading factors and to reduce the total amount of truck VKT.

African Reality

The need for improved logistics in SSA is well documented, not only as an explicit means of reducing truck VKT and reducing CO_2 emissions, but also, and more importantly, as a way of bringing down the logistics costs generally, and enhancing access to markets.[21] Africa regularly scores the lowest of any region in the World Bank's Logistics Performance Index (LPI) global rankings, as shown in Figure 3. However, there are some profound structural challenges to improving freight logistics in Africa. First among

---

20. GSMA, "The Mobile Economy: Sub-Saharan Africa 2017" (London, GSM Association, 2017) http://www.gsma.com/mobileeconomy (accessed September 27, 2017.)

21. See S. Teravaninthorn and G. Raballand, "Transport Prices and Costs in Africa: A Review of International Corridors" in *Directions in Development*. (Washington, DC, World Bank, 2009); and African Development Bank, *African Development Report 2010: Ports, Logistics and Trade in Africa* (Oxford, African Development Bank, 2010)

Figure 3. World Map of Logistics Performance Index, 2016

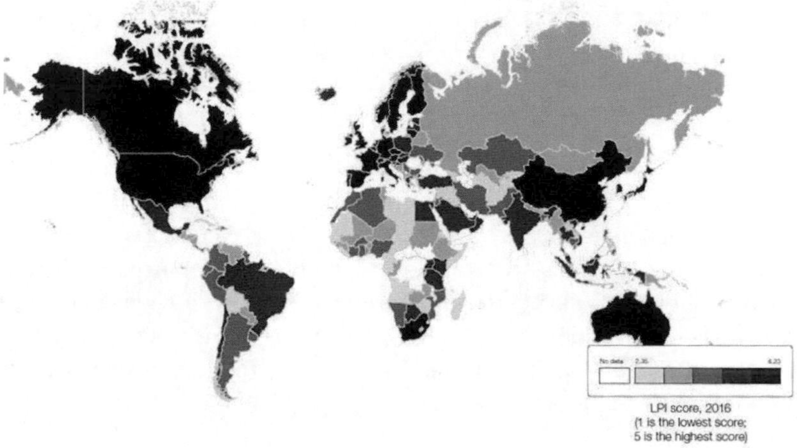

LPI score, 2016
(1 is the lowest score;
5 is the highest score)

Source: J.F. Arvis, D. Saslavsky, L. Ojala, B. Shepherd, C. Busch and A. Raj (2016). "Connecting to Compete 2016: Trade Logistics in the Global Economy. The Logistics Performance Index and Its Indicators" (Washington, DC, World Bank, 2016).

these are the relatively low rural densities and sparseness of road networks across Africa.

A 2008 survey from the World Bank found that Africa's road network is the sparsest in the world, when measured both by population and by land area (see Figures 4 and 5.) The sparsity of this network makes the need for logistics consolidation all the more pressing for Africa, but it makes the opportunities to do so quite limited.

A second structural impediment to improved logistics management of freight enabling lower VKT and GHG emissions in Africa is the imbalance of trade flows prominent throughout the continent. In many parts of the continent, the directionality of the volume of goods being shipped is highly imbalanced. Figure 6 shows the volume of freight shipments to and from Chad through the port of Douala for the period 2002 through 2016. The figure shows that the volume of imports to Chad are orders of magnitude higher than exports, particularly in the early part of the current decade. Clearly, with such an imbalance, there is little opportunity to reduce the number of empty backhauls by truck.

Figure 4. Spatial Density of Road Networks in World Regions

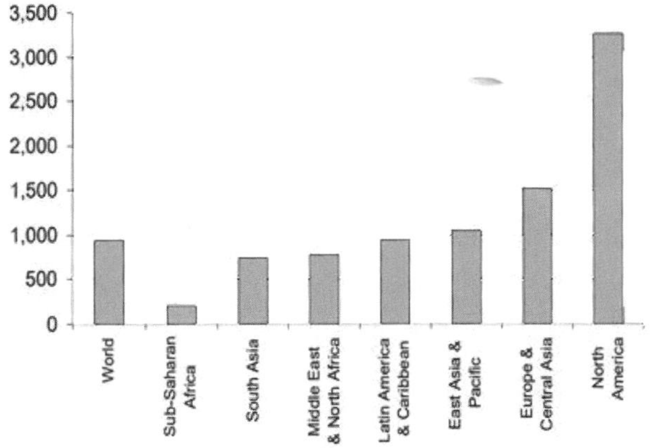

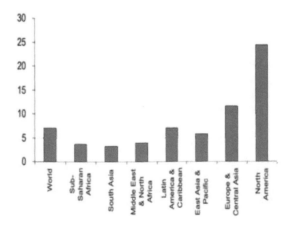

K. Gwilliam, V. Foster, R. Archondo-Callao, C. Briceño-Garmendia, A. Nogales and K. Sethi (2008). "Roads in Sub-Saharan Africa" in V. Foster, *Africa Infrastructure Country Diagnostic* (Washington, DC, World Bank, 2008).

Figure 5. Total Road Network per Capita in World Regions

Source: Gwilliam, Foster et al., 2008.

Figure 6. Trade imbalance in Chad and Cameroun

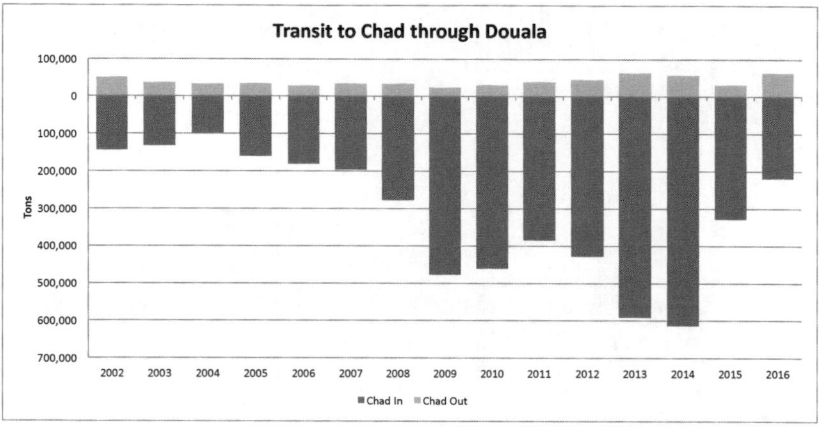

Source: World Bank.

Freight Mode Shift to Rail

Idealized Solution

A second way that a *Shift* strategy might be applied to freight logistics would be to try to affect a mode shift toward rail over time. One of the most ambitious examples of undertaking such a strategy is the multi-billion-dollar investment by the Indian government in dedicated freight rail corridors (Figure 7). A study looking at the Western dedicated freight corridor from Delhi to Mumbai estimated that the corridor could result in cumulative savings in CO_2 emissions of 170.5 million tons of CO_2eq, over the 30-year period between 2016 and 2046. 87 percent of this change was assessed to be due to modal shift from road to rail, with the remaining 13 percent resulting from switch to fully electric traction and energy efficiency improvements over time.[22]

African Reality

For Africa, it is unlikely that efforts to shift toward freight rail would be successful in generating substantial CO_2 emissions savings on the order of those calculated for India. First, the extent of the rail network in Africa is

---

22. P. Pangotra and P. R. Shukla, Promoting Low-Carbon Transport in India: A Case Study of the Delhi-Mumbai Dedicated Freight Corridor (Riso, UNEP Riso Centre, 2012).

Figure 7. Proposed and in-Construction Dedicated Freight Rail Corridors in India

Source: Pangotra and Shukla, 2012.

quite limited. Most existing rail facilities are from the colonial-era, oriented toward moving bulk goods from sites of extraction to ports. The network of rail lines is not only sparse, but it also does not serve many of the key intra-African origin and destination pairs, as shown in Figure 8.

Second, and related, traffic volumes in sub-Saharan Africa are very low by world standards. Even before the dedicated rail corridor project in India, traffic volumes on rail were high—nearly 7 billion tons shipped by rail in 2007-2008 alone. In South Africa, which has the highest levels of rail traffic in sub-Saharan Africa by far, annual volume in 2014 was only about 2 million tons. Relative density can be measured by traffic units (in tons) per kilometer of track. Figure 9 shows that SSA (except for South Africa) has a rail density orders of magnitude lower than the other world regions.

Figure 8. Rail Network in Africa in 2008

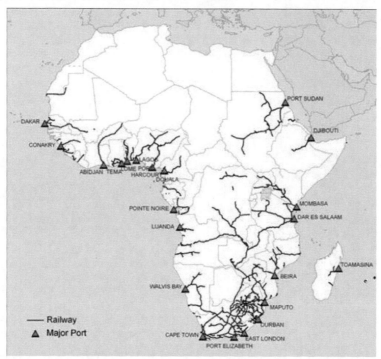

Source: Africa Infrastructure Country Diagnostic, World Bank, 2008.[23]

Figure 10 shows how rail traffic density affects costs, with average revenue as a proxy. The five services on the left of the graph are SSA concessions. The figure shows that rail operators' cost structure is uncompetitive with such low volumes of traffic. It should be reiterated that rail operators are also subject to the same traffic flow imbalance pressures as truck operators (discussed in the previous section). For these reasons, prospects to use mode shift to rail as a mechanism to restrain the growth of CO_2 emissions in the transport sector in Africa are limited for the foreseeable future.

Improve: Characteristics of Vehicles and Systems They Operate On

For the most part, the two strategies to reduce transport-sector associated GHG emissions discussed so far in this chapter have focused on reducing the

23. Gwilliam, et al., op. cit.

Figure 9. Rail Traffic Density Comparison of Select Countries, Regions (traffic units/km of track)

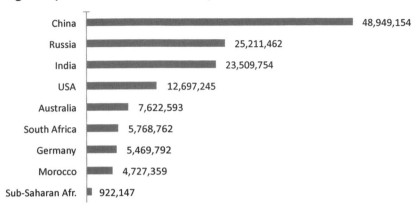

Source: V. N. Olievschi, *Framework for improving railway sector performance in Sub-Saharan Africa* (Washington, DC, SSATP, 2013).

number of vehicle-kilometers traveled (VKT), either by encouraging less motorized travel, or by facilitating the efficiency of the services by which they occur. Reducing transport-related GHGs can also involve a third strategy, namely modifying the characteristics of the vehicles themselves and the networks on which they operate, in an effort to reduce the specific GHG emissions of each VKT. Broadly, there are three sub-strategies that tend to be followed in this respect: (1) efforts to improve the energy efficiency of vehicles; (2) efforts to reduce the carbon content of fuels and drive-trains; and (3) efforts to improve networks and / or behavior of operators so as to minimize the number of and intensity of accelerations per vehicle kilometer. This section discusses the first two of these sub-strategies collectively, in the context of motorization management. The third, improvement of networks and driver behavior, will not be discussed because of space constraints.

Motorization Management:
A Neglected Area of African Transport Policy

Africa currently hosts the smallest proportion of the vehicle fleet (only 42.5 million in-use vehicles), and has the lowest vehicle penetration rate (44 vehicles per 1000 population)[24] of any region in the world, but this fleet has

---

24. Deloitte Consulting, "Navigating the African Automotive Sector: Ethiopia and Nigeria" *Deloitte Africa Automotive Insights*, 2016, pp. 4.

Figure 10. Rail Traffic Density and Costs

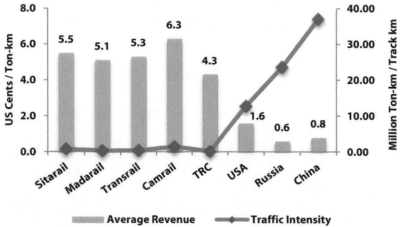

Source: Olievschi, 2013.

been forecast to grow by at least 4 percent per year between 2012 and 2040.[25] The current profile of the fleet in many African countries reflects the fact that the continent has, to some degree, served as a dumping ground for old, obsolete vehicles from much of the rest of the world. Most countries on the continent are primarily import-driven in their automotive industries, with only two (South Africa and Nigeria) currently having any vehicle emissions standards. In addition, a high percentage of imported vehicles are second-hand—85 per cent in Ethiopia, 80 per cent in Kenya and 90 per cent in Nigeria in 2015[26]—many of which are more than 10 years old. This is mainly a result of the low capacity of local vehicle assembly and manufacturing, and the limited disposable income to purchase brand new vehicles (burdened with high tariffs and other taxes).

Two aspects of motorization characterize the developing world in general and Africa in particular, and make it distinct from the developed world and perhaps other parts of the Atlantic Basin as well: (1) very high rates of growth in motorized two-wheelers—either primarily for commercial purposes or as a household's *first* vehicle—combined with (2) the predominance

25. International Energy Agency, *Africa Energy Outlook: A Focus on Energy Prospects in Sub-Saharan Africa*. World Energy Outlook Special Report (Paris, 2014), pp. 89.

26. Deloitte Consulting, op. cit.

of imported, second-hand cars as the main source of light-duty, four-wheel vehicle fleet growth.

Worldwide, the volumes and flows of trade in second hand, four-wheeled vehicles are poorly understood. Fuse et al. surveyed the reasons that good quantitative estimates of second-hand vehicle flows are difficult to develop, and proposed a triangulating methodology, based on information partially available from different sources. They estimated a worldwide volume of about 5.65 million units in 2005.[27] Sakai et al., using a methodology based on observed differences between expected and actual scrapping volumes, estimated a volume of about 18.6 million units in 2012.[28] Using Fuse et al.'s 2009 estimate as a base, and applying Kenya's used-car import growth rate of 8 percent per year as a representative low-end benchmark of the worldwide growth in used vehicle flows, Gorham and Qiu have estimated that the current international flows of used cars could be on the order of 14 to 15 million units per year.[29]

Because of the prevalence of two-wheelers and second-hand cars in the growth of the sub-Saharan Africa vehicle fleets, fleet growth management requires a different approach than models available in, for example, OECD countries, and even a different approach than that utilized in many sub-Saharan African countries (based on a perceived need to limit the *age* of vehicles coming into the country). African vehicles, particularly in the light duty fleet, tend to be old. Indeed, average vehicle age in Kenya and Ethiopia in 2016 was 11.7 and 15.6 years, respectively. In 2015, 96 and 73 percent of Kenyan and Ethiopian car imports respectively were older than 5 years at the time of import. Indeed, Kenya would have a substantially older car fleet profile but for the prohibition against importation of cars 8 years or older.

The concern about vehicle age—and the justification for import restrictions based on it—is the presumed link between age and vehicle performance, not only with respect to fuel economy, but also in relation to pollution emis-

27. M. Fuse, H. Kosaka and S. Kashima, "Estimation of world trade for used automobiles" *Journal of Material Cycles and Waste Management* 11(4), 2009, pp. 348-357.

28. S. I. Sakai, H. Yoshida, J. Hiratsuka, C. Vandecasteele, R. Kohlmeyer, V. S. Rotter, F. Passarini, A. Santini, M. Peeler, J. Li, G.-J. Oh, N. K. Chi, L. Bastian, S. Moore, N. Kajiwara, H. Takigami, T. Itai, S. Takahashi, S. Tanabe, K. Tomoda, T. Hirakawa, Y. Hirai, M. Asari and J. Yano, "An international comparative study of end-of-life vehicle (ELV) recycling systems" *Journal of Material Cycles and Waste Management* 16(1), 2014, pp. 1-20.

29. R. Gorham, O. Hartmann, Y. Qiu, D. Bose, H. Kamau, J. Akumu, R. Kaenzig, R. Krishnan, A. Kelly and F. Kamakaté, *Motorization Management in Kenya* (Washington, DC, World Bank, 2017)..

Figure 11. Age Profile of Motor Vehicle Stock in Kenya, 2016

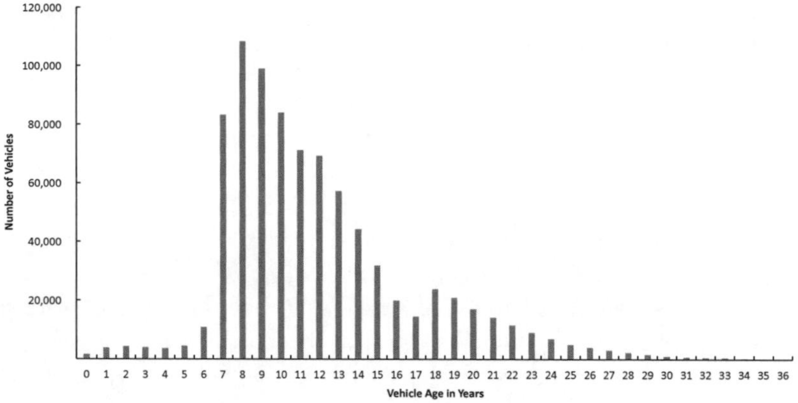

Source: R. Gorham, O. Hartmann, Y. Qiu, D. Bose, H. Kamau, J. Akumu, R. Kaenzig, R. Krishnan, A. Kelly and F. Kamakaté, *Motorization Management in Kenya* (Washington, DC, World Bank, 2017). Based on registration data provided by Kenyan National Transportation Safety Authority.

sions and road-worthiness. Age is a quick and dirty proxy for these other characteristics, one which is relatively easy to monitor in an import regime.

In the African context, however, Gorham and Qiu (2018) argue that for a number of reasons vehicle age may not be a particularly effective lever to improve vehicle fleets at all—at least not as a stand-alone criterion. First, there is enormous variance in the fuel economy of cars across the world. While it may be true that, all else held equal, newer models of a given car may be more fuel efficient than older models (both because of the technology available in the car and because fuel economy deteriorates with age), it would be more effective as a fuel economy policy to influence the specific kinds of vehicles imported rather than their age *per se*. Second, with respect to vehicle emissions, newer vehicles may have more sophisticated emissions control technology, but without an adequate fuel and maintenance 'eco-system,' such technology would be useless anyway. Third, with respect to road-worthiness, age may indeed be associated with dilapidation, but nothing inherently guarantees that newer models will be more road worthy than older models; this is rather a function of maintenance and upkeep, which can only be verified through an inspection regime, rather than through age checks. Further, there is also little correlation between the age of the vehicle and its crash-worthiness; automobile manufacturers regularly market dif-

Figure 12. Age Profile of Motor Vehicle Stock in Ethiopia, 2016

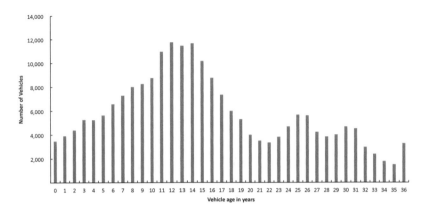

Source: R. Gorham, O. Hartmann, Y. Qiu, D. Bose, H. Kamau, J. Akumu, R. Kaenzig, R. Krishnan, A. Kelly and F. Kamakaté, *Motorization Management in Ethiopia* (Washington, DC, World Bank, 2017). Based on registration data provided by Ethiopian Federal Transport Authority.

ferent brand-new vehicles of the same model to different world regions, with very different empirically tested crash-worthiness characteristics.[30]

For these reasons, a recent World Bank assessment recommended that Ethiopia and Kenya (and governments in Africa more generally) should adopt more comprehensive practices toward management of vehicle fleets than simply age restrictions.[31] These practices (referred to collectively as *motorization management*) are understood as the deliberate process of shaping, through public policies and programs, the profile, quality and quantity of the motor vehicle fleet as motorization occurs. It requires an integrated approach, simultaneously considering different policy objectives that can be addressed by and through the vehicle fleet. In that respect, it is concerned with fuel efficiency, safety (both crash avoidance and crash worthiness), pollution emissions characteristics of the fleet, and potentially even the speed with which the fleet grows.

A fundamental tenet of the motorization management concept is based on the premise that policies alone will not affect an improvement in safety, emissions, or fuel efficiency characteristics of vehicle fleets; what is needed is a more comprehensive set of enabling measures, whose design recognizes

---

30. Ibid.
31. Ibid.

the fundamental importance of the second-hand vehicle market in fleet growth in these countries. The World Bank team identified 10 such implementation programs plus one or two policy *processes* whose implementation would likely lead to more effective control of the evolution of safety, emissions, and fuel efficiency characteristics of the vehicle fleet itself. These are:

- Motor Vehicle Information Management Systems
- Public engagement to reach citizens at all phases of the vehicle life-cycle
- Import certification process for vehicle imports
- Inspection and maintenance of in-use vehicles
- National protocols for visual and instrumented enforcement
- Mechanics' training and certification
- Quality assurance program for vehicle parts
- Performance standards for vehicle body construction and modification
- Fuel quality testing
- End-of-Life Vehicle management.

In addition, the World Bank team recommended that governments at the national—or even regional—level undertake policy processes to define Dynamic Profiles of Standards for tailpipe emissions, fuel quality, vehicle safety, and fuel economy expected for all vehicles entering the country or region over a foreseeable period.

The World Bank team modeled the potential impacts of these measures on a range of attributes in the motor vehicle fleets in Kenya and Ethiopia. They found that implementing these kinds of measures could lead to a reduction on the order of 4 to 8 percent in overall fuel consumption by 2040, compared to a business-as-usual case for the motor vehicle fleet as a whole, but a 6 to 12 percent reduction for the private car fleet. Such results, while modest, reflect only a portion of the larger benefits that can come from a motorization management approach, which would also include safer vehicles, improved emissions performance, and, potentially, a shift in drivetrain and propulsion technology.[32]

---

32. Ibid.

Conclusion

This chapter has tried to provide a brief survey of the various mechanisms available to reduce or head off the growth of CO_2 emissions and energy consumption from the transport sector, with a particular focus on such challenges in sub-Saharan Africa. The picture that emerges is a complex one, but several broad observations can be made.

First, the objective of managing energy consumption in the African transport sector is closely tied to the most basic development objectives: increasing access, improving affordability, and making transport and land-markets function. For this reason, efforts to separate energy management objectives in Africa's transport sector from core development objectives are likely to fail. Second, no single strategic approach to managing energy from the sector is likely to be successful; rather, a combination of aggressive Avoid, Shift, and Improve measures will be necessary to keep transportation energy consumption and GHG emissions from growing unsustainably.

Third, as daunting as the challenges are, there are some sources for optimism in the region's potential to manage its transport energy consumption growth. The strong potential in African cities to use ICT to facilitate a shift to more efficient vehicles and modes has already been discussed above. In addition, if motorization management measures are adopted, there is tremendous potential for African countries to leapfrog technologies, particularly since, unlike most other world regions, the large part of motorization in Africa—in terms of vehicle penetration—has yet to occur. There is, therefore, a window of opportunity to orient the profile of the vehicle fleets and affect fairly rapid change. Another potential source of optimism is that growing incomes and the emergence of a vibrant middle class may create opportunities for motor vehicle manufacturers that could drive improvements in the quality of vehicles on offer. Finally, though perhaps too soon to tell, it is also possible that Africa's imminent motorization may be interrupted by disruptive technology in a (positive) way that has not affected other regions. For now, Uber-like services do not seem to be affecting fundamental car ownership decisions in developing countries like Ethiopia or Kenya, but it is possible that niched service delivery models for the growing middle classes will emerge that do.

Part III

**Energy and Transportation in the
Maritime Realm of the Atlantic Basin**

Chapter Six

Atlantic Maritime Transportation and Trade: Impacts on Shipping Transport Emissions and International Regulation

Jordi Bacaria and Natalia Soler-Huici

The chapter analyzes the expanding maritime transport in the Atlantic Basin (stimulated by the evolution of global value chains and logistics) and the massive growth of the shipping industry in recent decades. Since the mid-1990s, however, the development of regulation to address shipping's environmental impact and to restrict the sector's atmospheric emissions has been slow. This chapter reviews the role of the International Maritime Organization (IMO) and its current regulatory framework, assesses the difficulties and complexities associated with it, and evaluates IMO regulatory efforts to date. It also proposes a strategic line of action for the EU: to push forward with the regulation of maritime emissions unilaterally—faster than the US or the IMO seem inclined to move—and then partnering with interested collaborators in the Southern Atlantic, in Africa and Latin America.

Emissions from intercontinental maritime transport are significant, and are currently linked to industrial emissions through international trade. More specifically, trade in raw materials and manufactured goods have seen spectacular increases in the last decade because of the logistics and container transportation revolutions. Over 90 percent of physical merchandise traded by volume takes place via maritime transport along the world's sea lanes, which include two-thirds of the global oil trade, one-third of the gas trade, and the large majority of other global material flows.[1] Manufactured goods are not the most important part of maritime transport, but they are relevant in terms of value and their contributions to the world fragmentation of production.

As the transport revolution has reduced unit costs and increased volumes of transported freight, it has also facilitated, and been fed by, one of the central phenomenon of contemporary globalization: the fragmentation of production

---

1. Paul Isbell, "The Emergence of the Atlantic Energy Seascape: Implications for Global Energy and Geopolitical Maps" in *The Future of Energy in the Atlantic Basin*, eds. Paul Isbell and Eloy Alvarez Pelegry (Washington, DC, 2015), pp. 259-267.

and the emergence and continuing evolution of global value chains (GVCs). This phenomenon creates a feedback effect: to take advantage of wage differences and shifting global demand, GVCs stretch across the globe and reach into all continents; however, the result is that more transportation is required in all its varieties—maritime, terrestrial and air—which in turn promotes intermodality. The ultimate consequence is that—in spite of the greater and rising efficiency of transportation and a reduction of emissions per unit transported— the significant marginal increase of transported freight volumes stemming from such efficiencies actually raises the absolute levels carbonization and GHG emissions. Indeed, the reduction of such transport costs implies an externalized cost in the form of CO_2 emissions, in terms of both path (direct) and derivative (indirect) emissions (i.e., construction, ports, etc.).

The solution is to establish regulatory instruments targeting the emissions of maritime transport in the same way that such instruments have been established to reduce the emissions of terrestrially (or land-based) transport. In this sense, the Atlantic Basin has two advantages. First, the volume of Atlantic Basin maritime transport is much lower than that of the world's other ocean basins connecting Asia and the Americas (the Pacific Basin) and Europe and Africa with Asia (the Indian Ocean Basin). Second, the European Union (EU), together with the countries of the Atlantic Basin, could lead this regulatory effort to reduce maritime transport emissions even in the face of US isolationism vis-a-vis the Paris Agreement. Just as the economic crisis of 2008-2010 negatively affected the demand for transportation and caused a supply crisis which provoked the failure of a few shipping companies, the renegotiation or suspension of free trade agreements (e.g. NAFTA or the TPP) could stall the expansion of GVCs, or even bring them to an irreversible halt. Although this would bring a reduction of transport demand and attendant emissions, it would not be a desirable solution, given the negative consequences on economic growth, the development of the emerging economies, and levels of global welfare. We need a balanced solution, one that allows economic growth and trade to be compatible with maritime emissions reductions.

The first sections of this chapter analyze the evolution of maritime transport in the aftermath of significant growth in both international trade and GVCs—two of the principal vectors of contemporary globalization—and concludes with a discussion of possible regulatory solutions in the Atlantic Basin. These sections also analyze the container revolution in transportation, the evolution of Atlantic Basin maritime transport, recent improvements in logistics, the expansion of GVCs, as well as key determinants of maritime transport like investment requirements and energy costs. The later sections of the chapter address themselves to: (1) current and potential future regulatory efforts to reduce maritime emissions; (2) the difficulties faced by the maritime industry in this regard; and (3) the different positions of the various maritime industry pressure groups.

The Container Revolution and the Decline in the Cost of Maritime Transport

Ever since containerized freight began in the late 1950s—with the introduction of the first container (which we could call a humble steel box) transported by ship in 1956—international trade in manufactured goods has continued to grow, dominating shipping in terms of value. Since 1968, container-carrying capacity has increased 1,200 percent: from the first vessel's capacity of 1,530 TEU[2] to the latest generation vessels of 19,000 TEU or higher.

Since the first container's voyage, this method of freight transport grew steadily; five decades later container ships would carry about 60 percent of the value of goods shipped via sea.[3] The capacity of container ships has also increased, along with their efficiency. Today there are nearly 5,000 container ships in the global fleet—most of which are operated by members of the World Shipping Council—and there are 445 new vessels on order.[4] As result, container ships have grown in size from just 1,500 TEU in 1976 to capacities in excess of 12,000 TEU today, while some ships currently on order will be capable of carrying 18,000 TEU.

Not only are today's ships able to carry more goods in one voyage than in the past; they are also much more fuel-efficient. The fuel efficiency of container ships (with 4,500 TEU capacity on average) improved 35 percent between 1985 and 2008. It is estimated that, on average, a container ship emits around 40 times less CO_2 than a large freight aircraft, and over three

---

2. Twenty-foot equivalent unit or TEU.

3. World Shipping Council, "About the Industry. History of Containerization," 2017, http://www.worldshipping.org/about-the-industry/history-of-containerization (accessed June 23, 2017).

4. World Shipping Council, "About the Industry. Liner Ships," 2017, from *Alphaliner - Cellular Fleet July 2013,* http://www.worldshipping.org/about-the-industry/liner-ships (accessed July 5, 2017).

times less than a heavy truck. Container shipping is estimated to be two and a half times more energy efficient than rail and 7 times more so than road.[5]

In any case, despite the overall conclusion that fuel price is an important driver of design efficiency there are differences between the types of maritime transport in the historical trends of ship design efficiency. For bulk carriers, design efficiency has improved considerably. Such efficiency increased 28 percent in 10 years during the 1980s; however, beginning in 1990, design efficiency gradually deteriorated until 2013. Such changes stem from the evolution of: (1) the main engine power; (2) capacity; or (3) the speed of ships. By contrast, for tankers this efficiency improvement has been lower: 22 percent over the same 10 years. After 1988, however, there was a gradual deterioration in efficiency, which lasted until around 2008, after which efficiency improvements in tankers again became apparent.

The efficiency of container ships depends on both ship size and the year. Comparison is difficult over time because of the dramatic increase in the size of container ships. The largest container ship in the 1970s carried 50,000 dead-weight tonnage (dwt); in the 1980s, 60,000 dwt; in the 1990s, 82,000 dwt; and in the 2000s, 165,000 dwt. There were large swings in the average efficiency of new constructions in the 1970s, a marked decline to the mid-1980s, when it rebounded. From 2000, however, the design efficiency of new container ships deteriorated steadily. But then, in 2006, the fastest container ships ever built entered the fleet.[6] In any case, the largest container ships were built before the last economic crisis. In 2010, the South Korean shipping company was the first to introduce a 10,000 TEU class carrier ship, travelling between Asia and Europe. But the aftermath the crisis saw a decline in transport demand and led to the bankruptcy of some companies owning these new large ships, as occurred with the Hanjin shipping line in 2016. Such bankruptcies caused turbulence in global shipping and the shipping price of a 40-foot container from China to the US rose to 50 percent in a single day.[7]

---

5. World Shipping Council, "About the Industry. Container Ship Design," 2017, http://www.worldshipping.org/about-the-industry/liner-ships/container-ship-design (accessed June 23, 2017).

6. Jasper Faber, Maarten 't Hoen, "Historical trends in ship design efficiency," Delft, CE Delft (March, 2015)http://www.cleanshipping.org/download/CE_Delft_7E50_Historical_trends_in_ship_design_efficiency_DEF.pdf (accessed June 28, 2017).

7. The Guardian, https://www.theguardian.com/business/2016/sep/02/hanjin-shipping-bankruptcy-causes-turmoil-in-global-sea-freight (accessed September 17, 2017).

According to the current global data, there are 5,985 active ships (including 5,131 which are fully cellular)[8] annually transporting 20,894,673 TEU (of which over 98 percent is transported in fully cellular ships) and 257,805,686 DWT (deadweight tonnage). From the regional perspective, weekly capacities are now 135,501 TEUs in the Transatlantic Region, 442,261 TEUs in the Trans-Pacific and 397,435 TEUs in FEAST-Europe. Therefore, the Atlantic region is the least important in terms of container trade, relative to other major sea lane regions.[9]

Some studies conclude that the introduction of containers has been more important for international trade than free trade agreements (FTAs). In a group of 22 industrialized countries, containerization explains a 320 percent rise in bilateral trade over the first five years after adoption and a 790 percent increase over 20 years. By comparison, a bilateral free-trade agreement raises trade by 45 percent over 20 years, while GATT membership adds 285 percent.[10] In any case, the more recent bilateral and regional agreements, including the NAFTA, have played only a minor role in the growth of world trade. Reforms in emerging market economies, for example, have contributed much more to the expansion of trade than FTAs.[11]

The economic effects of containerization are clear. From a transportation technology perspective, containerization resulted in the introduction of intermodal freight transport. This is because the shipment of a container can travel along multiple modes of transportation—ship, rail or truck—without any freight handling required when changing modes. By eliminating sometimes as many as a dozen separate handlings of the cargo, the container resulted in a tighter linking of the producer to the customer. Since containerization resulted in a reduction of the total resource costs of shipping a good from the (inland) manufacturer to the (inland) customer, its impact is not adequately captured by looking only at changes in port-to-port freight costs.[12]

---

8. Ship fitted throughout with fixed or portable cell guides for the carriage of containers. OECD Glossary of Statistical Terms https://stats.oecd.org/glossary/detail.asp?ID=4244 (accessed September 18, 2017).

9. ALPHALINER TOP 100, 2017 https://alphaliner.axsmarine.com/PublicTop100/index.php (accessed June 22, 2017).

10. Daniel M.Bernhofen D., El-Sahli Z., Kneller R., "Estimating the Effects of the Container Revolution on World Trade," Lund University, Working Paper (February 13, 2013), p.19. http://www.lunduniversity.lu.se/lup/publication/704527ec-23e1-4561-a611-a582cffefb4c (accessed June 18, 2017).

11. Gene Grossman, "What trade deals are good for," *Harvard Business Review*, (May 24, 2016) https://hbr.org/2016/05/what-trade-deals-are-good-for (accessed June 26, 2017).

12. Ibid. p.4.

On the other hand, with the blockade of the Suez Canal (as a consequence of the Six Day War in 1967), large oil tankers were introduced (at the same time as liquefied natural gas). This development, however, only partially replaced the transport of energy by land-based intercontinental pipelines (i.e., the gas pipelines between Algeria and Europe, Russia and Europe, and the Persian Gulf and China by way of Iran); despite the increasing transport capacity of gas pipeline flows, due to long sea distance and the flexibility offered by maritime transport to purchase oil in transit, transatlantic maritime energy transport flows continued to be more difficult to replace with other transport systems.

This container revolution—along with innovations in transport logistics, new port infrastructures, intermodality and information and communications technology (ICT)—has led to a reduction in shipping costs. This reduction in costs has, in turn, stimulated the displacement and fragmentation of production, and the emergence of global value chains. Even more important than costs have been the knock-on effects on efficiency. In 1965, dock labor could move only 1.7 tons per hour onto a cargo ship; five years later a container crew could load 30 tons per hour.[13]

However, this reduction in transport costs fails to reflect the increase in external costs (or externalities) arising from CO_2 emissions, both those generated by maritime transport and those produced by the construction of large transport ships. The internalization of such externalities through the regulation of emissions is one of the solutions currently being worked on at the international level by the International Maritime Organization (IMO) and will be analyzed in the second part of this chapter.

Maritime Transportation and Trade in the Atlantic Basin

Data on the volumes of maritime trade routes indicate that the Atlantic Basin is less traversed when compared to the main routes between Asia and Europe (across the Indian Ocean Basin) and between Asia and North America (across the Pacific Basin). Among the Atlantic Basin trade routes, the North Atlantic route between Europe and North America is currently the most important (see Table 1).

---

13. Richard Baldwin, "Trade and Industrialisation After Globalisation's 2nd Unbundling: How Building and Joining a Supply Chain are Different and Why It Matters," NBER Working Paper 17716, (December, 2011) http://www.nber.org/papers/w17716 (accessed June 18, 2017).

Table 1. Leading Global Maritime Trade Routes, TEU, 2013

Atlantic Basin Routes	West Bound	East Bound	North Bound	South Bound	Total
North Europe-North America	2,636,000	2,074,000			4,710,000
North Europe/Mediterranean-East			795,000	885,000	1,680,000
North America-East Coast South			656,000	650,000	1,306,000
Other top routes					
Asia-North America	7,739,000	15,386,00			23,125,00
Asia-North Europe	9,187,000	4,519,000			13,706,00

Source: Adapted from "World Shipping Council" http://www.worldshipping.org/about-the-industry/global-trade/trade-routes. Note: Trade between an origin group of countries and a destination group of countries is referred to as a trade route. The figure presents the top maritime trade routes in terms of TEU shipped in 2013.

The Inter-American Development Bank (IDB) analyzed the effects of the economic crisis on maritime transport and the consequences on supply due to the bankruptcy of some shipping companies. The effects of this new supply and demand scenario are even more remarkable in Latin America and the Caribbean (LAC), where connectivity limitations and below-average logistics performance are considerable barriers to integration and growth in maritime trade. Infrastructure shortcomings, operational inefficiencies, high port costs, lack of integration in logistics platforms (e.g. electronic single windows) result in higher regional maritime transport costs.[14] In the case of LAC countries, therefore, there is space to increase efficiency through investments without significantly increasing emissions.

As we will see below, connections between ports and liners are important to maintain high efficiency and lower transportation costs. Reviewing the most important ports listed in the "Top 100,"[15] one finds that the first Atlantic port in terms of total cargo traffic (both in total volume and number of containers handled) is Rotterdam. In terms of container traffic, among the first 30 world ports, six are European—Rotterdam (11), Antwerp (14), Hamburg

14. Erick Feijóo, Iván Corbacho, Krista Lucenti, and Sergio Deambrosi, "Staying afloat? Opportunities in the maritime transport sector in the Americas," Inter-American Development Bank blogs, June 13, 2017, https://blogs.iadb.org/integration-trade/2017/06/13/staying-afloat-opportunities-in-the-maritime-transport-sector-in-the-americas/ (accessed July 9, 2017).

15. The American Association of Port Authorities, "World Port Rankings 2015," Alexandria, Va., 2015, http://www.aapa-ports.org/unifying/content.aspx?ItemNumber=21048 and http://aapa.files.cms-plus.com/Statistics/WORLD%20PORT%20RANKINGS%202015.xlsx (accessed July 12, 2017).

Table 2. Top 100 Ports, Cargo Volume (metric tons) and Container Traffic (TEUs), 2015

TOTAL CARGO VOLUME TONS, 000s					CONTAINER TRAFFIC TEUs (Twenty-Foot Equivalent Units), 000s			
RANK	PORT	COUNTRY	MEASURE	TONS	RANK	PORT	COUNTRY	TEUs
5	Rotterdam	Netherlands	Metric Tons	466,363				
					11	Rotterdam	Netherlands	12,235
14	South Louisiana	United States	Metric Tons	235,058	14	Antwerp	Belgium	9,654
16	Houston	United States	Metric Tons	218,575				
					17	Hamburg	Germany	8,821
					23	New York / New Jersey	United States	6,372
					24	Bremen/Bremerhaven	Germany	5,547
27	Itaqui	Brazil	Metric Tons	146,647				
28	Metro Vancouver	Canada	Metric Tons	138,228	28	Valencia	Spain	4,615
29	Hamburg	Germany	Metric Tons	137,824	29	Algeciras - La Linea	Spain	4,516
32	Santos	Brazil	Metric Tons	119,932	32			
34	New York/New Jersey	United States	Metric Tons	114,933	34	Santos	Brazil	3,780
					35	Savannah	United States	3,737
					36	Felixstowe	United Kingdom	3,676
37	Itaguai	Brazil	Metric Tons	110,362				
					38	Gioia Tauro	Italy	3,512
					39	Piraeus	Greece	3,360
					40	Balboa	Panama	3,078
41	Amsterdam Ports	Netherlands	Metric Tons	98,776			Turkey	3,062
44	Algeciras - La Linea	Spain	Metric Tons	91,950	44	Tanger	Morocco	2,971
46	Marseilles	France	Metric Tons	81,920	46			
					47	Colon	Panamá	2,765
48	New Orleans	United States	Metric Tons	79,661				
49	Beaumont	United States	Metric Tons	79,081				
51	Corpus Christi	United States	Metric Tons	77,724				
					52	Cartagena	Colombia	2,607
						Le Havre	France	2,556
55	Bremen/Bremerhaven	Germany	Metric Tons	73,447	55	Virginia	United States	2,549
					58	Southampton	United Kingdom	2,349
59	Long Beach	United States	Metric Tons	70,911				
60	Valencia	Spain	Metric Tons	69,601				
62	Le Havre	France	Metric Tons	68,289	62	Genoa	Italy	2,243
					63	Dublin	Ireland	2,217
					64	Houston	United States	2,131
						Charleston	United States	1,973
68	Baton Rouge	United States	Metric Tons	62,399	68	Barcelona	Spain	1,965
71	Grimsby and Immingham	United Kingdom	Metric Tons	59,103				
					72	Manzanillo	Panama	1,821
73	Trieste	Italy	Metric Tons	57,161				
79	Virginia	United States	Metric Tons	52,402	79	Chennai	India	1,571
					80	Zeebrugge	Belgium	1,569
81	Lake Charles	United States	Metric Tons	51,431				
					83	Montreal	Canada	1,446
84	Genoa	Italy	Metric Tons	51,299	84			
85					85	Buenos Aires (incl. Exolgen)	Argentina	1,428
86					86	Freeport	Bahamas	1,400
87					87	Sines	Portugal	1,332
88	Sao Sebastiao	Brazil	Metric Tons	49,539				
					90	La Spezia	Italy	1,300
					91	Marseilles	France	1,220
92	Plaquemines	United States	Metric Tons	48,541				
93	Dunkirk	France	Metric Tons	46,592				
94	Barcelona	Spain	Metric Tons	45,921	94	San Juan	Puerto Rico	1,211
95	London	United Kingdom	Metric Tons	45,430				
					96	London	United Kingdom	1,185
98	Bergen	Norway	Metric Tons	43,591				
100	Paranagua	Brazil	Metric Tons	43,275	100	Limon/Moin	Costa Rica	1,106

NOTE: The cargo rankings based on tonnage should be interpreted with caution since these measures are not directly comparable and cannot be converted to a single, standardized unit.
Sources: Agência Nacional de Transportes Aquaviários - ANTAQ(Brazil), Institute of Shipping Economics & Logistics ; U.S. Army Corps of Engineers' Waterborne Commerce Statistics Center, Secretariat of Communications and Transport (Mexico), Waterborne Transport Institute (China); AAPA Surveys; various port internet sites.

Elaborated by the authors for the Atlantic case. Source: The American Association of Port Authorities, "World Port Rankings 2015 ," Alexandria, Va, 2015, http://www.aapa-ports.org/unifying/content.aspx?ItemNumber=21048 and http://aapa.files.cms-plus.com/Statistics/WORLD%20PORT%20RANKINGS%202015.xlsx (accessed July 12, 2017).

(17), Bremen/Bremerhaven (24), Valencia (28), Algeciras-La Linea (29)[16] — and one is in the US—New York/New Jersey (23).

Logistics Improvement and the Expansion of Global Value Chains (GVCs)

When considering international trade, the traditional view is that each country is producing finished products that are exported to consumers in another country. This type of trade represents only one quarter of the total trade in goods and services. Today, three quarters of international trade consists of firms buying inputs and investment goods or services that contribute to the production process.[17]

What is more, international production, trade and investment are increasingly organized within so-called global value chains (GVCs) in which the different stages of the production process are dispersed across different countries. Globalization motivates companies to restructure their operations internationally through outsourcing and offshoring of activities.[18]

Global Value Chains

The development of GVCs is associated with the decline in the cost of shipping and its rising efficiency. This is particularly true of the intercontinental transport of manufactures between Asia, Europe and Latin America. Furthermore, technological advances—especially in the realm of information and communications technology—have also reduced trade and coordination costs. On the other hand, foreign direct investment (FDI) has also been a major driver of the growth of GVCs.[19]

In short, the emergence of GVCs continues to change the conditions of trade, and the international relations associated with it. These GVCs are

---

16. Algeciras-La Linea is a hub for distributing containers.

17. OCDE Trade and Agriculture Directorate, "Trade policy implications of GVC," November 2015 http://www.oecd.org/tad/trade-policy-implications-gvc.pdf (accessed July 5, 2017).

18. OCDE "Global Value Chains," http://www.oecd.org/sti/ind/global-value-chains.htm (accessed July 5, 2017).

19. OCDE-WTO-UNCTAD, *Report to G-20 on Implications of Global Value Chains for Trade, Investment, Development and Jobs. Prepared for the G-20 Leaders Summit Saint Petersburg (Russian Federation)*, August 6, 2013, p.9 http://www.oecd.org/trade/G20-Global-Value-Chains-2013.pdf, (accessed July 28, 2014).

detected by observing how countries increasingly need foreign inputs for exports from their own firms that in turn can be reprocessed in partner countries.

Between 30 percent and 60 percent of G20 exports consist of intermediate inputs traded within GVCs. Compared 2009 with 1995, GVC participation has increased in almost all G20 economies, and particularly in China, India, Japan and Korea.[20]

For the European countries of the G20, like Germany and France, this share has also increased, (although less for Italy), as a result of the GVCs connecting these countries to Asia and Latin America. In Latin America, Mexico has the highest share of imported inputs used for exports (30 percent), mainly because of its strong trade ties with US. However, this share is somewhat lower for both Argentina and Brazil (around 10 percent in 2009). This implies that the exports originating in Asia and the EU use more intensively imported intermediate inputs than do the exports of the LAC region. Indeed, the exports of Asia and the EU incorporate 12 and 15 percentage points more foreign value-added, respectively, than the exports of Latin America. This suggests that the countries from these two regions are more involved in sequentially linked production processes than the countries in the LAC region.[21]

Global Value Chains, Maritime Security and International Relations

The significance of GVCs to international relations can found in the relationship between countries' participation in GVCs and their overall strategic approaches to certain aspects of foreign policy.

An empirical observation of G20 countries allows us to focus on this relationship. Between 30 percent and 60 percent of the exports of G20 countries in 2009 consisted of intermediate inputs traded within GVCs. It should be noted that of these countries, Saudi Arabia had the lowest share of imported inputs used to produce exports (around 1 percent in 2009), followed by Russia (5 percent), Brazil (9.5 percent) and United States (10 percent). By contrast, Canada, China, France, Germany, India, Italy, Korea, Mexico and Turkey all exceed 20 percent.[22]

---

20. Ibid. p .8.

21. Juan S. Blyde, ed., *Synchronized Factories. Latin America and the Caribbean in the Era of Global Value Chains* (New York, 2014), p.17 https://link.springer.com/book/10.1007%2F978-3-319-09991-0 (accessed July 2, 2017).

22. OCDE-WTO-UNCTAD, ibid. pp. 8-9.

However, we should distinguish *backward* participation within GVCs—
that is, the foreign value- added content of exports (also referred to as vertical
specialization)—from *forward* participation in GVCs (the percentage share
of a country's exports that are destined to be used as inputs other countries'
exports).

Backward GVC participation corresponds to the value added of inputs
that were imported to produce intermediate or final goods/services to be
exported. The countries with the highest backward participation in 2011
were China, Korea, Mexico and Italy. Those with the lowest were Saudi
Arabia, Brazil, Indonesia and Russia (see Table 3).

Backward GVC participation could be seen as proxy indicator for a country's broad strategic tendencies in foreign policy because countries that have
strong backward GVCs have a greater strategic need for relative stability in
the realm of maritime transport than those countries with less. This is because
products exported from countries with strong backward GVC linkages are
mostly parts or components with high value added coming from non-con-
tinental partners countries, which are assembled and re-exported.

This is the case for Korea and China, countries with the highest backward
participation (see Table 3) and both highly dependent on the world's sea
lanes. The case of Mexico is somewhat different due to the large amount of
land transported trans-border trade with US. Although Mexico does not use
maritime transport for trade with the US, the need for stability of land transportation becomes even more important in its case.

On the other hand, *forward* participation in GVCs represents the percentage of a country's exports used as inputs in the exports of third countries.
Among the countries with the highest forward participation in 2011 were
Saudi Arabia, Russia, Japan and Indonesia; among those with the lowest
were China, Mexico, Turkey and Argentina (see Table 3).

This suggests that Saudi Arabia, Brazil, Indonesia and Russia—countries
with relatively high forward participation (see Table 3)—participate more,
on average, than Asian or European countries do as a supplier of value
added to those farther downstream in the chain. On average, countries with
highest levels of forward GVC participate more than Europe and Asia in
international value chains as suppliers of primary inputs, while Europe and
Asia participate more than the exporters of primary products as suppliers
of manufacturing inputs.

Table 3. G20 Countries, GVC Participation, Total, Backward and Forward, % of Exports, 2011

Country	Total GVC participation	Backward	Forward
G20 Countries with the Lowest Levels of Backward GVC Participation			
Saudi Arabia	45.3	3.3	42
Brazil	35.2	10.7	24.5
Indonesia	43.5	12	31
Russia	51.8	13.7	38.1
Argentina	30.5	14.1	16.4
Australia	43.6	14.1	29.5
Japan	48.6	14.6	32.8
United States	39.8	15	24.9
G20 Countries with the Highest Levels of Backward GVC Participation			
Korea	62.1	41.6	20.5
China	47.7	32.1	15.6
Mexico	46.8	31.7	15.1
Italy	47.5	26.4	21.1
Turkey	41	25.7	15.3
Germany	49.6	25.5	24.1
India	43.1	24	19.1
Canada	42.4	23.4	19
UK	47.6	22.9	24.7

Source: Elaborated from OECD/WTO (2016), "Trade in value added (Edition 2016)," OECD-WTO: Statistics on Trade in Value Added (database). http://dx.doi.org/10.1787/2644abe4-en (Accessed on 02 July 2, 2017).

Maritime transport is also very important for these countries with high forward participation. However, because they are exporters of primary products the value added is lower. Such countries are also more flexible in their response (either using alternative routes or oil tankers and bulk carriers) than the countries with backward links that need more secure and stable maritime routes for liner vessels.

There is also an interesting relationship between the *total participation* (i.e., backward *plus* forward) in GVCs and the armed forces per capita (see Figure 1). G20 Countries that have a strong total participation in GVCs tend to have less armed forces per capita. On the contrary, countries (G20) that have less participation in GVCs tend to have more armed forces per capita. Korea is an exception given the long and permanent confrontation on its peninsula. As an outlier, Korea is the G20 country with more participation in the GVCs and with more armed forces per capita.

Figure 1. Total GVC Participation and Armed Forces (as % of population), G20 Countries, 2015

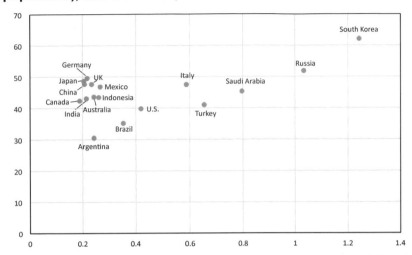

Elaborated by the authors. Source: Table 3 and armed personnel, https://data.worldbank.org/indicator/ MS.MIL.TOTL.P1 (accessed September 22, 2017), population https://data.worldbank.org/indicator/ SP.POP.TOTL?view=chart (accessed September 22, 2017).

One could posit that countries that are less integrated into GVCs tend to follow more isolationist and unilateral strategies, and countries that are most highly integrated into GVCs tend to pursue more co-operative strategies with their neighbors and trading partners. As a result, such countries would be more open to multilateral strategies.

In the case of the Atlantic Basin, however, following the United States' renunciation of multilateralism and that country's recently announced departure from the Paris agreement, the EU (with a relatively high level of backward GVC participation) might seek to contribute to the stability of the maritime realm by forging some Atlantic Basin agreements on carbon emissions in the maritime industries.

Intermodal Interdependence between Maritime and Terrestrial Transportation

The efficiency of maritime transport and supply chains is based on the ability to arrive in the minimum time and at the minimum cost from the point of production to the point of distribution and sale. However, in a world in which international supply chains are no longer the relatively simple port-to-port affair that they once were, the overall effectiveness of international supply chains is also linked to—and dependent on—the efficiency of the inland distribution of international cargo arriving to a country by sea.

Contemporary international supply chains require an intermodal transportation network. An intermodal network consists of ships, trains, airplanes, trucks or even bicycles in cities (the latter closely linked to increasingly rapid and non-polluting distribution systems and e-commerce). The connections or transfer points between modes are called intermodal connectors. Service interruption or capacity failure anywhere on the network could lead to delays in shipments and increased costs. A failure in one mode is effectively a failure of the entire chain. Sufficient land-side capacity to keep cargo moving is essential for liner vessels to maintain their schedules.

To achieve maximum efficiency, investment in ports, containers, roads, trains, different types of vehicles, Wi-Fi and smartphones become necessary. These investments in turn benefit from the GVCs since the imported inputs are the basis for the value added of the goods and services that are exported.

There are some notable differences between U.S. and EU in transport connections and intermodal networks. The U.S. is the largest trading nation in the world and as such represents one of the largest markets for shipping liner companies and their customers. This makes the efficiency of the U.S. intermodal network very important to the efficiency of the global shipping liner network and to global supply chains. The Marine Transportation System National Advisory Council (MTSNAC) is a chartered federal body tasked with advising the Secretary of Transportation about matters related to the US intermodal network and its connections to maritime transport. The MTSNAC has been a World Shipping Council member since 2000.[23] In 2009, MTSNAC completed a report[24] that provided the Secretary with a series of recommendations to improve the marine transportation system, with a particular emphasis on intermodal freight movement.

Europe is another very large and important market. However, the European intermodal network poses unique challenges because many countries are land-locked, or do not have deep-water ports that can accommodate liner vessels. This means cargo often must transit long distances by truck, rail or barge, often through several countries, between the actual origin or desti-

---

23. World Shipping Council, http://www.worldshipping.org/industry-issues/transportation-infrastructure/u-s-intermodal-network.

24. Marine Transportation System. National Advisory Council, "2009 Report to Secretary of Transportation ," Washington D.C. January 2009 www.worldshipping.org/pdf/MTSNAC_Report_2009_FINAL.pdf (accessed July 3, 2017).

nation and the port served by the liner vessel.[25] To close the gaps between member States, the EU adopted a new transport infrastructure policy in January 2014 that connects the continent from East to West, and North to South.[26] European Coordinators — high level personalities with long standing experience in transport, finance and European politics — are leading the drive to build the core network corridors, which represent the strategic heart of the trans-European transport network (TEN-T) and therefore deserve a concentrated amount of effort and attention for their financing, required cooperation, efficiency and quality. Core network corridors[27] were introduced to facilitate the coordinated implementation of the core network. They bring together public and private resources and concentrate EU support from the Connecting Europe Facility (CEF)[28] particularly to: remove bottlenecks, build missing cross-border connections and promote modal integration and interoperability.

The second generation of the work plans of the 11 European Coordinators (as approved in December 2016) establish the basis for action until 2030.[29] The links among different corridors such as the Atlantic and the Mediterranean will improve the intermodal network in Europe and tighten European connections with the Atlantic Basin.

Despite this deficit of corridors in Europe, there are isolated examples that reflect the existence of GVCs involving companies from both regions, in particular within the car industry (for the production and sales of parts and finished cars). Volkswagen has plants in both Latin America (Argentina, Brazil and Mexico) and Central and Eastern European (CEE) countries (Poland, Hungary, Czech Republic and Slovakia). Audi AG belongs to the Volkswagen group producing in Hungary, and has close intra-firm relations with Volkswagen do Brazil, Volkswagen de Mexico and Volkswagen Argentina. Renault's Slovenian subsidiary exports models to France, where

25. World Shipping Council, http://www.worldshipping.org/industry-issues/transportation-infrastructure/europe-intermodal-network (accessed June 25, 2017).

26. European Commission, Mobility and Transport, https://ec.europa.eu/transport/themes/infrastructure_en (accessed July 9, 2017).

27. European Commission, Mobility and Transport, https://ec.europa.eu/transport/themes/infrastructure/ten-t-guidelines/corridors_en (accessed July 9, 2017).

28. The Connecting Europe Facility (CEF) is a key EU funding instrument to promote growth, jobs and competitiveness through targeted infrastructure investment at European level https://ec.europa.eu/inea/en/connecting-europe-facility (accessed September 24, 2017)

29. European Commission, Mobility and Transport, Transport Infrastructure: Second Generation of the Work Plans https://ec.europa.eu/transport/node/4876 (accessed July 9, 2017).

they are finished and re-exported as French cars to subsidiaries in Latin America.[30]

Therefore, with better infrastructure in Latin America and better corridors in Europe, an improvement of the GVCs between the two regions can be expected and, consequently, an increase of maritime transportation. However, infrastructure is a necessary but not a sufficient condition; often it is growth in GVCs which creates pressures for better infrastructure (as has been the case with the transport corridor plans in Europe).

Trade in the Face of GHG Emissions from the Maritime Industry

Shipping is the least environmentally damaging mode of transport when its productive value is taken into consideration.[31] For example, international shipping accounts for 2.2 percent of the global emissions of carbon dioxide (CO_2). However, air-borne CO2 emissions from the shipping industry are a growing source of the overall greenhouse gas (GHG) emissions.[32] Together with combustion emissions of nitrogen oxides (NOx), sulfur oxides (SOx), particulate matter (PM) and non-methane volatile organic compounds (NMVOC), the CO_2 emissions of the world's commercial shipping fleet contribute to environmental problems that include global warming, sea level rise, ocean acidification and eutrophication,[33] as well as adverse effects on public health.[34]

---

30. EU-LAC Foundation, *Latin America, the Caribbean and Central and Eastern Europe: Potential for the economic Exchange*, (Hamburg, May 2014) https://eulacfoundation.org/en/documents/latin-america-caribbean-and-central-and-eastern-europe-potential-economic-exchange (accessed August 20, 2017).

31. IMO, http://www.imo.org/en/OurWork/Environment/Pages/Default.aspx (accessed July 8, 2017).

32. EMSA, http://www.emsa.europa.eu/main/air-pollution/greenhouse-gases.html (accessed July 8, 2017).

33. Ocean acidity is an indicator of the amount of carbon dioxide dissolved in water. Increased atmospheric CO_2 concentrations lower oceanic pH and carbonated ion concentrations rendering the oceans much less hospitable to many forms of marine life. Eutrophication is a process driven by the enrichment of water by nutrients. Phosphorus and compounds of nitrogen are responsible for the increased growth, primary production and biomass of algae that lead to degradation of ecosystem health and biodiversity. Nitrogen oxides from ships contribute to eutrophication as they are transferred via the atmosphere through precipitation.

34. Cullinane K and Cullinane S, "Atmospheric Emissions from Shipping: The Need for Regulation and Approaches to Compliance" (2013) 33 Transport Reviews, p. 377.

Maritime transport is not immune to the effects of climate change. Sea level rise is a major concern for coastal communities.[35] Adaptation plans for these regions are of paramount importance to the availability of maritime transport. Clearance under bridges near coasts will be reduced and port infrastructure will be threatened by changed sea level conditions. Other climate factors related to global warming involve more frequent and intense extreme weather conditions that will entail longer waiting times and less reliable shipments that directly translate into sizable losses of gains from trade.[36]

These prospective changes have led the IMO to regulate the contribution to atmospheric pollution of the shipping industry. However, it was not until 1988 that the issue was included in the work program of the IMO's Marine Environment Protection Committee (MEPC).

The contribution of the shipping industry to climate change was put forth in the Third IMO Greenhouse Gas Study.[37] For the period 2007-2012, the annual average CO_2 emissions for international shipping accounted for 2.6 percent of the global total. However, total GHG emissions from shipping accounted for 3.1 percent of the global total. Nitrogen oxides (NOx) and sulfur oxides (SOx) are responsible for indirect formation of ozone and aerosol warming at the regional scale. For the same period, NOx and SOx emissions from international shipping represented 13 percent and 12 percent of global NOx and SOx from anthropogenic sources, respectively.[38] International shipping is the dominant source of the total shipping emissions of CO_2 and other GHGs.[39] CO_2, other GHGs, and combustion emissions of NOx, SOx, PM and NMVOC correlate with fuel consumption. Fuel is consumed for propulsion power, electrical production and auxiliary systems

---

35. The Washington Post, https://www.washingtonpost.com/news/energy-environment/wp/2017/06/26/sea-level-rise-isnt-just-happening-its-getting-faster/?utm_term=.de827243819f (accessed July 8,2017).

36. An increase in transport costs of 10 percent would decrease trade by 20 percent. Andreas Kopp, "Transport costs, trade and climate change," in Regina Asariotis and Hassiba Benamara (eds), *Maritime Transport and the Climate Change Challenge* (Earthscan 2012).

37. IMO, "Third IMO GHG Study 2014, Reduction of GHG from ships," MEPC at its 67th session.

38. IPCC Fifth Assessment Report, IPCC, 2014: Climate Change 2014: Synthesis Report. Contribution of Working Groups I, II and III to the Fifth Assessment Report of the Intergovernmental Panel on Climate Change [Core Writing Team, R.K. Pachauri and L.A. Meyer (eds.)]. IPCC, Geneva, Switzerland, 151 pp.

39. Third IMO GHG Study 2014: "nitrous oxide (N_2O) emissions from international shipping account for the majority (approximately 85 percent) of total shipping N_2O emissions, and methane (CH_4) emissions from international ships account for nearly all (approximately 99 percent) of total shipping emissions of CH_4."

Table 4. Bottom-up CO2 Emissions from International Shipping, by Ship Type, in 2012

Ship Type	Fuel Consumption ('000 tons of oil eq)	CO2 emissions (million tons)
Vehicle*	7,900	25
Ro-Ro**	9,300	29
Refrigerated bulk	5,700	18
Other liquid tankers	300	1
Oil tanker	39,700	124
Liquefied gas tanker	15,700	46
General cargo	21,700	68
Ferry-RoPax***	9,900	27
Ferry-pax only****	3,700	1
Cruise	11,100	35
Container	66,000	205
Chemical tanker	17,500	55
Bulk carrier	53,400	166

* cargo-carrying transport ships whose capacity is measured in vehicle units.

** Ro-ro (roll-on/roll-off): wheeled cargo carrier.

*** Ro-pax: vehicle-and-passenger ferry.

**** Pax-only: passenger-only ferry.

Source: Elaborated from IMO, "Third IMO GHG Study 2014, Reduction of GHG from ships," MEPC at its 67th session p.6.

and mainly by three types of ships: oil tankers, container ships and bulk carriers. For all ship types, the main engines (propulsion) are the dominant fuel consumers.[40]

Airborne emissions from shipping can be reduced by improving fuel efficiency, that is, reducing fuel consumption. Better fuel efficiency implies reduced fuel costs. However, the interest of the maritime industry in taking unilateral action to maximize fuel efficiency is diminishing as the "growth in the sheer volume of shipping has far outweighed any fuel efficiency savings."[41]

---

40. IMO, "Third IMO GHG Study 2014, Reduction of GHG from ships," MEPC at its 67th session p.3.

41. Cullinane K and Cullinane S, "Atmospheric Emissions from Shipping: The Need for Regulation and Approaches to Compliance," (2013) 33 Transport Reviews, p. 377.

Operational measures such as developing better logistics, port efficiency and avoiding less than full back-hauls or ballast voyages entail bigger profits as they positively affect productivity. The industry has already taken advantage of these operational measures. Technical measures such improving engines for better fuel efficiency or improving the hull design require research investments that the industry is not willing to assume. There are no incentives left to the industry to offset environmental externalities relating to air emissions.

Tellingly, the Third IMO GHG study also concludes that:

> Emissions projections demonstrate that improvements in efficiency are important in mitigating emissions increase. However, even modeled improvements with the greatest energy savings could not yield a downward trend. Compared to regulatory or market-driven improvements in efficiency, changes in the fuel mix have a limited impact on GHG emissions, *assuming that fossil fuels remain dominant.* (Authors' emphasis)

According to the United Nations Conference on Trade and Development (UNCTAD) Review of Maritime Transport in 2016: "The world fleet grew by 3.5 percent in the 12 months to 1 January 2016 (in terms of dead-weight tons (dwt)). This is the lowest growth rate since 2003, yet still higher than the 2.1 percent growth in demand, leading to a continued situation of global overcapacity."[42] Nevertheless, this is clearly only a cyclical phenomenon: projections of maritime transport demand foresee a rapid increase in future demand for unitized cargo transport.

Indeed, maritime CO_2 emissions are projected to increase significantly in the coming decades. The Third IMO GHG Study projects an increase of anywhere between 50 percent and 250 percent during the period to 2050.[43] Although CO_2 emissions from shipping industry have accounted for anywhere from 2 percent to 3 percent of the global totals, without any further action, such maritime emissions are expected to rise to 5 percent by 2050.[44] Furthermore, methane (CH_4) emissions are also expected to increase rapidly as the share of LNG in the fuel mix increases.[45]

---

42. UNCTAD Review of Maritime Transport 2016, http://unctad.org/en/PublicationsLibrary/rmt2016_en.pdf (accessed July 8, 2017).

43. IMO, "Third IMO GHG Study 2014, Reduction of GHG from ships," MEPC at its 67th session p. 20.

44. EMSA, http://www.emsa.europa.eu/main/air-pollution/greenhouse-gases.html (accessed July 20, 2017).

45. On the other hand, as a result of Tier II and III engines entering the fleet, NOx emissions are projected to increase at a lower rate than CO2 emissions. Particulate matter

This increase in emissions is not compatible with the Paris Agreement's central aim of keeping a global temperature rise this century well below 2 degrees Celsius above pre-Industrial levels and to pursue efforts to limit the temperature increase even further to 1.5 degrees Celsius. The IMO, as the international organization entrusted with the prevention of pollution by ships, is bound by the Kyoto Protocol to pursue limitation or reduction of GHG emissions from marine bunker fuels. However, the IMO's regulatory efforts to date are far from achieving a reduction in emissions in line with the goals set forth in the Paris Agreement.

International Regulation of Maritime Industry Emissions

Part XII of the Law of the Sea Convention (LOSC) on the Protection and Preservation of the Marine Environment is an essential component of the Convention and serves as the framework for the regulation of marine pollution carried out by the IMO. The negotiation of this part of the LOSC played an important role at United Nations Convention of the Law of the Sea (UNCLOS) III.[46]

Prior to the adoption of the LOSC, states were merely empowered to regulate marine pollution,[47] but not obliged to do so. Coastal states had no prescriptive power beyond the territorial sea to regulate operations of ships, while flag states had an ill-defined duty to regulate marine pollution. Indeed, there was no definition of the prescriptive jurisdiction, rendering it not protective enough of the interests of coastal states. There was also no requirement to comply with international standards, and a number of important flag states were not a part of the International Convention for the Prevention of Pollution from Ships (MARPOL) or other international instruments regulating vessel-source pollution.

The adoption of the LOSC entailed the introduction of a general duty on states to protect and preserve the marine environment[48] and a redefined framework for regulation of marine pollution. The LOSC also specifies that rules and standards regarding vessel-source pollution shall be established

(PM) is also expected to experience an absolute decline, at least up to 2020, while SOx emissions are projected to decline through 2050 as the result of the imposition of sulfur caps.

46. M.H. Nordquist and others, *United Nations Convention on the Law of the Sea, 1982: a commentary* (Martinus Nijhoff 1991).

47. A.E. Boyle, 'Marine Pollution Under the Law of the Sea Convention' (1985) 79 The American Journal of International Law 347, p. 347.

48. Article 192 of the Law of the Sea Convention (LOSC).

through the competent international organization—that is, the IMO. The MARPOL Convention is the response of states to that obligation. The regulation of air pollution from ships in MARPOL is constructed upon the framework for jurisdiction set up in the LOSC.[49]

The LOSC framework for vessel-source pollution establishes the extent to which states may regulate this type of pollution. While elaborating Part XII of the LOSC on Protection and Preservation of the Marine Environment, difficulties arose when it came to creating a regime for vessel source pollution.[50] Maritime states had an interest in making the regime of flag state jurisdiction prevail over the jurisdiction regime of coastal states. They feared that unilateral regulation of vessel-source pollution by coastal states would hinder their navigational freedom and increase their operating costs. A coalition of developed and developing coastal states with no shipping interests fought this position at UNCLOS III but maritime states were able to limit any effort of expanding coastal state jurisdiction over vessels.[51]

Flag States

The resulting regulation of vessel-source pollution in the LOSC reflects the pressure displayed by maritime interests, given that flag states bear the primary responsibility of prescribing and enforcing rules on vessel-source pollution. The obligations of flag states with respect to vessels flying their flag (art. 94 LOSC) include maintaining a register of the ships and assuming jurisdiction under its internal law over each ship sailing with respect to administrative, technical and social matters. This provision also establishes that flag states shall adopt measures on matters relating to, among others, the construction (relevant for controlling air pollution from ships) and manning of the ship, the use of signals, the surveillance of the ship, the qualifications of the masters and officers, the training of the crew and acquaintance of the crew with the applicable international regulations concerning the safety of life at sea and prevention of marine pollution. In taking measures to prevent marine pollution, flag states must conform to generally accepted international regulations, procedures and practices. By means of this provision, the LOSC makes international standards compulsory for all ships through the 'rule of reference.'

---

49. MARPOL, article 9.3: "the term 'jurisdiction' shall be construed in light of international law in force at the time of application or interpretation of the present Convention."

50. Tan AKJ, *Vessel-Source Marine Pollution*, p. 199.

51. Ibid.

It is important to note, however, that while the top five ship-owning economies are Greece, Japan, China, Germany and Singapore, the top five economies by flag registration are Panama, Liberia, the Marshall Islands, Hong Kong and the Republic of Korea.[52] As a general trend, ship-owners began to flag their vessels in foreign registries during the 1970s (and even earlier) with the objective of being subject to less stringent safety and environmental regulation.

The registries of developed states have traditionally required that the vessels registered in their registries be owned and flagged by the flag state nationals. These are closed registries which traditionally have required vessels to comply with stricter regulations, entailing added costs to the operation of the ship. Registering a ship in an open registry—rather than in one's own national (closed) registry—is a practice with significance for the ratification and implementation of relevant conventions dealing with vessel-source pollution.

Coastal States

Coastal states are empowered to adopt laws and regulations for the prevention, reduction and control of vessel-source pollution—but they are not bound to do so. The measures that a coastal state can prescribe over vessel-source marine pollution vary according to the distinct ocean zones. They include discharge standards, CDEM standards[53] and navigational standards.

Deriving from national and international standards (including CDEM and general navigational standards), coastal states enjoy unlimited prescriptive and enforcement authority—within both its ports and internal waters—for the prevention and reduction of marine pollution, and for the control of the marine environment. However, a coastal state's authority could be limited by bilateral treaties of friendship, commerce or navigation that guarantee port access.

Within its territorial sea, a coastal state is sovereign, although its authority is circumscribed by the interests of maritime states in free navigation. The laws and regulations that the coastal states can adopt for vessels in their territorial sea shall not apply to the design construction, or to the manning and/or equipping of foreign ships unless they are giving effect to generally accepted international rules and standards. Therefore, coastal states can pre-

---

52. UNCTAD, http://unctad.org/en/pages/PublicationWebflyer.aspx?publicationid=1650 (accessed July 25, 2017).

53. Construction, design, equipment and manning.

scribe national discharge standards (and national navigation standards) but not national CDEM standards. Enforcement of these standards consists in undertaking physical inspections and instituting proceedings against a vessel in violation of those standards.

On the other hand, the jurisdiction of coastal states within their respective exclusive economic zone (EEZ) is highly circumscribed. This jurisdiction is limited to adopting regulations that give effect to generally accepted international rules and standards established by the IMO. This provision leaves no room for states to adopt national discharge, CDEM or navigation standards unless they are prescribed for special[54] or ice-covered areas.

IMO Action on Maritime Emissions

It is to this jurisdictional framework (i.e., EEZs) that the international rules on air-borne emissions from ships established by the IMO need to respond. MARPOL is the IMO's instrument dealing with operational discharges from ships, that is, discharges stemming the normal operation of a vessel.[55] It was in the late 1980s that the IMO started work on the prevention of air pollution from ships.[56] In the early stages, the IMO had recognized the scientific evidence of the negative effects on the environment and human health of emissions to the atmosphere from numerous sources. Ships were regarded as co-responsible for this type of pollution, as one of the sources that generates air pollution.

The international rules on air-borne emissions from ships were added to MARPOL by the means of a Protocol adopted at a Conference of the Parties held in London in 1997. The Protocol of 1997 added Annex VI to MARPOL and it was entitled Regulations for the Prevention of Air Pollution from Ships. The Conference also adopted the Technical Code on Control of Emissions of Nitrogen Oxides from Marine Diesel Engines (NOx Technical Code). Annex VI entered into force in 2005.

Annex VI of MARPOL limits the main pollutants in a ship's exhaust gas (SOx and NOx), prohibits deliberate emissions of ozone depleting substances, regulates shipboard incineration and emissions of volatile organic

---

54. The IMO shall determine whether an area requires special measures for recognized technical reasons in relation to its oceanographical and ecological conditions.

55. Otherwise known as the 1973 International Convention for the Prevention of Pollution from ships.

56. IMO, *MARPOL: Annex VI and NTC 2008 with Guidelines for Interpretation* (2013), p. 1.

compounds from tankers. Annex VI also contains CDEM standards concerned with the replacement or modification of diesel engines, exhaust gas cleaning systems and shipboard incinerators.

Amendments to MARPOL adopted in 2011 added a chapter to Annex VI on Regulations on Energy Efficiency for Ships. These amendments responded to the aforementioned mandate of the Kyoto Protocol according to which a number of steps were to be taken in order to tackle GHG emissions from shipping. A first step consisted in assessing GHG emissions from ships. Once a study was issued, the IMO Assembly urged the MEPC to "identify and develop the mechanism or mechanisms needed to achieve the limitation or reduction of GHG emissions from international shipping."[57] This provision also urged the MEPC to give priority to the establishment of a GHG emission baseline, the development of a methodology to describe the GHG efficiency of a ship in terms of a GHG emission index for that ship, the development of guidelines by which the GHG emission indexing scheme may be applied in practice and the evaluation of technical, operational and market-based solutions.

The amendments to Annex VI introduced the regulation of GHG emissions from ships into MARPOL. This regulation establishes different degrees of obligations for ship-owners. It applies to all ships of 400 gross tonnage and above. All ships with these characteristics must keep on board a ship-specific Ship Energy Efficiency Management Plan (SEEMP). The MEPC adopted guidelines for the development of the SEEMP in which it recognizes that "there are a variety of options to improve efficiency—speed optimization, weather routing and hull maintenance, for example—and that the best package of measures for a ship to improve efficiency differs to a great extent depending upon ship type, cargoes, routes and other factors."[58] Because of this, ship-owners have discretion to adopt the energy efficiency measures that they consider appropriate and the goal they aim at achieving. The guidelines emphasize that the goal setting is voluntary. The purpose of this Plan is to provide "a possible approach for monitoring ship and fleet efficiency performance over time."[59] Thus, what will move ship-owners to adopt energy efficiency measures is economic gain rather than a prescriptive requirement.

---

57. Resolution A.963(23) of 5 December 2003 para. 1.
58. Resolution MEPC.213(63) 2 March 2012 para. 4.1.2.
59. Ibid.

There are binding obligations in Annex VI to limit GHG emissions from ships. These, however, apply only to newly constructed ships or ships that have undergone major conversion. Ship-owners shall meet the required Energy Efficient Design Index (EEDI). The EEDI is determined by a formula that varies according to the ship's size and type. The requirements of the EEDI are to be attained over time. They are applied in four phases, each with a higher rate for reduction of emissions. The reason for the progressively stringent targets is the expectancy that technology advancements will allow for ships with lower GHG emissions. In order to improve technology so that it is possible for ships to comply with the required EEDI, Annex VI establishes that parties shall promote the development of technology. The IMO is obliged to review the targets set in each phase in order to evaluate if they are attainable given the status of the technological developments. In the case where the technology allows for more stringent targets, these should be reviewed. In the same way, if technology has not improved as expected, the targets will need to be review if they are unattainable.

Amendments to MARPOL adopted in 2016 will require that all ships of 5,000 tonnage and above record and report their fuel oil consumption. The data collection will be reported to the flag states which then will transfer it to an IMO Ship Fuel Consumption Database. These amendments are another step into the IMO's three-step approach to reduce GHG emissions. The step following the data collection is analysis. Such analysis will determine what further measures shall be required.[60]

The IMO's regulations on GHG emissions are widely regarded as insufficient to address the expected increase in shipping emissions. They are far from achieving a reduction in emissions that is line with the goals of the Paris Agreement. For this reason, action in this regard might arrive in the form of a unilateral, regional response.

Unilateral EU Action instead of Multilateralism

The first instrument to ever regulate sulfur oxides and nitrogen oxides from the burning of fossil fuel is the 1979 Convention on Long-Range Transboundary Air Pollution. This instrument provided a regional response to sulfur and nitrogen oxide emissions for North America and Europe. The 1985 Protocol on the Reduction of Sulfur Emissions or their Transboundary Fluxes

---

60. IMO, http://www.imo.org/en/OurWork/Environment/PollutionPrevention/AirPollution/Pages/Data-Collection-System.aspx (accessed August 10, 2017).

to the Convention did not specify its scope, resulting in the potential inclusion of emissions from ships. However, when the time came to further the reduction of sulfur emissions with a new protocol, the parties to the Convention agreed not to tackle emissions from ships under this regime and instead to pursue emissions reductions within the context of IMO in order to generate a global response to the issue. Similarly, another protocol to this Convention established a series of targets to reduce national annual nitrogen oxide emissions. Because the scope of this Protocol referred to stationary *and* mobile sources of nitrogen oxides, ships are included in the definition of mobile sources. Nevertheless, the parties to this Convention never directly addressed emissions from shipping because they already agreed that such emissions would be better regulated at the global level through the IMO.

The IMO began work on air pollution from ships in 1988 following a submission from Norway. At the same time, the Second International Conference on the Protection of the North Sea issued a declaration from the ministers of North Sea states that compelled them to initiate actions to improve quality standards of heavy fuel oil and reduce marine and atmospheric pollution at the IMO. After further submissions by Norway in 1990, which included an overview on air pollution from ships, the MEPC developed a draft Annex to MARPOL over the course of six years. The draft was adopted in 1997 and it added Annex VI to MARPOL, which set the standards for the sulfur content of fuel oil used on board ships, established standards for the construction and design of ship engines allowing a maximum of nitrogen oxide emissions at a given speed and prohibited deliberate emissions of ozone depleting substances.

Regional initiatives have proven to be very important for the global regulation of sulfur and nitrogen oxides. In the same way, the lack of a global regulation providing an effective response to reducing shipping emissions has lead the EU to consider including maritime CO_2 emissions in its Emission Trading Scheme (ETS). Indeed, the EU institutions are currently conducting a revision of the ETS Directive for the period 2021–2030 in which maritime emissions are included in the ETS in the absence of an agreement at the IMO. In 2015, the European Parliament submitted a legislative proposal aiming at achieving at least a 43 percent reduction in GHG by 2030 in comparison with 2005 levels. To this end, in the adoption of its first reading position it was agreed that maritime CO_2 emissions should be accounted for in EU ports and during voyages to and from them. These measures would also imply the creation of a maritime climate fund to offset shipping emissions, improve energy efficiency and encourage investment in technologies cutting CO_2 emissions from the sector.[61]

The EU's first step towards cutting domestic GHG emissions from shipping is the Regulation 2015/757 on the Monitoring, Reporting and Verification of Carbon Dioxide emissions from Maritime Transport.[62] This regulation amends Directive 2009/16/EC and from 2018 it will apply to all ships above 5,000 tonnage voyaging to, from and between ports under the jurisdiction of EU member states.

Ship-owners have expressed their discontent with the inclusion of shipping emissions in the EU ETS as they will be charged for carbon pollution in EU waters. They have argued through the International Chamber of Shipping and the European Community Shipowners' Association that this will put unrealistic pressure on the IMO that will hurt a global sector.[63] However, cargo owners and European ports have supported the initiative as they are willing to commit to the challenge.[64]

Conclusion

In maritime transport, energy commerce occupies the first place in terms of volume. The volume of manufactured products has been traditional lower, although since the 'container revolution' there has been a steady increase in container volumes. An analysis of the container category of maritime transport reveals that: a) the Atlantic basin is relatively less important in container transportation than other ocean basins despite the tight and dense connection between Europe and America; b) intermodality in maritime and land transport is the central axis of development of GVCs; c) the EU has an intermodal network that poses unique challenges because many countries are landlocked, or they do not have deep-water ports to accommodate liner vessels;

---

61. European Parliament, http://www.europarl.europa.eu/legislative-train/theme-resilient-energy-union-with-a-climate-change-policy/file-revision-of-the-eu-ets-2021-2030 (accessed August 20, 2017).

62. Regulation (EU) 2015/757 of the European Parliament and of the Council of 29 April 2015 on the monitoring, reporting and verification of carbon dioxide emissions from maritime transport, and amending Directive 2009/16/EC.

63. Ship and Bunker, https://shipandbunker.com/news/emea/113801-european-parliament-approves-inclusion-of-shipping-in-european-ets (accessed August 20, 2017).

64. Transport and Environment, https://www.transportenvironment.org/news/shipowners-isolated-maritime-industry-supports-eu's-'first-move'-regulate-co2 (accessed August 20, 2017).

and d) the increase in container transportation, associated with its efficiency and lower costs, has implications for the increase of CO_2 emissions that must be resolved within a global governance framework.

The regulation of emissions from shipping is still in its early stages. While developments at the IMO are slow, action is increasingly required to offset the impact of increasing GHG emissions from shipping. Because of this, the EU has stepped in to develop a regional regime as the framework for the regulation of these emissions, as the LOSC allows for such a regime. The EU's work on shipping emissions has received strong support from EU institutions as well as from European ports and cargo owners.

The Atlantic Basin is, despite being less important than other basins in terms of maritime volume transported, capable of driving such global environmental policies. The EU should incorporate maritime emissions into its overall regional emissions regime and into its emissions trading system. The EU's heavy weight in global trade will draw much of global transportation within its regulatory reach. The EU should then also attempt to engage in Atlantic Basin collaboration on investment in maritime transport infrastructure and maritime emissions reduction with other partners in the Atlantic Basin, particularly in Africa and Latin America, but also in North America, despite current US reticence toward international energy and climate cooperation (possibly even through an extension to the maritime realm of the existing 1979 Convention on Long-Range Transboundary Air Pollution). Finally, as has been highlighted by the Atlantic Future research project, experiences in the Atlantic Space provide case studies that together may be considered a laboratory for multilateralism at global level.[65]

---

65. Jordi Bacaria and Laia Tarragona, eds., *Atlantic Future. Shaping a New Hemisphere for the 21st century: Africa, Europe and the Americas* (Barcelona, 2016). https://www.cidob.org/es/publicaciones/serie_de_publicacion/monografias/monografias/at-lantic_future_shaping_a_new_hemisphere_for_the_21st_century_africa_europe_and_the_ame ricas (accessed August 22, 2017).

Chapter Seven

The Greening of Maritime Transportation, Energy and Climate Infrastructures: Role of Atlantic Port-Cities

João Fonseca Ribeiro

The best approach for Atlantic countries to maritime energy and transportation—and for related climate change and other marine environmental issues—would focus on the wider Atlantic Basin. Although individual countries have their own responsibility—and their own incentives—to limit emissions as much as possible, the pursuit of coherent action within their regional economic communities (RECs)—for example the European Union, the African Union, Mercosur, CARICOM, etc.—and coordinated at the ocean basin scale would be far more effective.[1]

A basin approach would maximize the results of measures taken through the achievement of economies of scale—lowering costs and minimizing trade disruption—and by addressing the various transformational processes—in energy, transportation, and maritime and port governance— along the logistics chain in an integrated fashion to efficiently achieve decarbonization and continued smart growth (including the sustainable development of the emerging blue economy).

This ocean basin approach would more effectively cut greenhouse gases (GHG) and air pollutants emitted along the major maritime routes and more efficiently stimulate access to and use of new energy sources (marine or otherwise) across the broader Atlantic space. Transnational cooperation among Atlantic actors could catalyze new low carbon industries and facilitate the greening of Atlantic marine exploitation zones and of maritime transportation and trade.

Such a basin focus would also allow the Atlantic Basin's port cities to respond appropriately to the emerging energy, transportation and climate challenges. The envisaged hub capacity of the port-cities of the Atlantic could convert them into major assets supporting this transformation, not just in the use of new energy resources in the maritime activities, but also in a

---

1. For a list of regional economic communities and organizations to which Atlantic countries belong can be found in Table 8 in the Annex.

myriad of other associated activities. Because of their key locations at the geographic interfaces between land and sea, port-cities represent the nexus of the Atlantic Basin's maritime and terrestrial transportation systems. Along with their other unique characteristics, this strategic positioning—in both spatial and policy terms—lends port-cities the potential to be the facilitators of the low-carbon energy and multimodal transportation co-transformations not only in the maritime realm (not yet incorporated into the global climate agreements) but also in their coastal areas and continental hinterlands. Leveraging upon this capacity, and with effective pan-Atlantic transnational cooperation among port-cities and their various relevant actors, the port-cities of the Atlantic could become key enablers for most of what can be designated as "continental desired effects."

Harnessing integrated maritime policies and other relevant regional strategies to pursue a cooperative Atlantic Basin approach on energy, transportation and climate change action would bring to light a much broader geopolitical dimension within the maritime realm—that of the blue economy and its sustainable development—and convert maritime activity into a strategic driver for economic growth. The economic value of the Atlantic Ocean is enormous for the countries located on its shores; the basin provides economic opportunities not only to its approximately 80 coastal states and relevant territories, but also to any national or transnational actors with the capacity to accede to spaces outside their national jurisdictions.

Convergence with the regions of great development potential in the two Atlantic continents of the Southern Hemisphere will be a major challenge, but ultimately could enable the maritime governance of the Atlantic Basin to be tackled with the appropriate instruments. This would allow sustainable development in the Atlantic Ocean and its coastal zones to be leveraged to an unprecedented level.

The Atlantic Basin is a shared resource and a unified marine system linking Europe with Africa and the Americas. All Atlantic coastal states have a responsibility—and an interest—to ensure good ocean governance—building upon the United Nations Convention on the Law of the Sea (UNCLOS), the International Maritime Organization (IMO) (including MARPOL[2] which remains relevant for limiting maritime air emissions and water discharges),

---

2. Many actions have been undertaken in recent years to significantly reduce air emissions from ships. Most of these actions have been taken through Annexes IV and VI of MARPOL, an international instrument developed through the IMO that establishes legally-binding international standards to regulate specific emissions and discharges generated by ships.

and the International Seabed Authority (ISA)—but also to promote the blue economy and its sustainable growth by engaging their RECs and private players in this strategic effort.

A strategic and policy focus on the port-cities of the Atlantic Basin, and a coordinated effort at pan-Atlantic cooperation between them in the areas of energy, transportation and marine environment, could build upon and integrate these existing maritime regulatory efforts and, as such, constitute an important step towards good ocean governance across the Atlantic space.

The first part of the chapter analyzes the nature, characteristics and synergistic potentials of port-cities, along with the changing dynamics of energy, transportation, trade and other forces of global competition that constrain or otherwise impact upon them. Part Two presents the European Union's integrated strategic approach to energy, transportation, climate and maritime challenges and analyzes the policy-relevance and potential of the port-cities of Europe and the broader Atlantic to such integrated strategies. The third section focuses in a similar way upon African development and the continent's transportation and maritime strategies, along with the nascent role for port-cities these strategies envision. Part Four proposes a new monitoring tool for port-cities to be used in their transformations into agents of maritime greening and good ocean governance and, possibly, as a best practices anchor for a new collaborative forum for Atlantic Basin port-cities, which this chapter concludes by proposing.

Port-Cities: The Strategic Levers of Maritime Energy and Transportation Transformation

Port-Cities: Interfaces Between Land and Sea

Port-cities are unique in the way they concentrate many specialized human resources, scientific and technological research centers, and energy and transportation capital equipment and infrastructure. Port-cities also tend to be large and densely populated zones, and in many Southern Atlantic countries they are often the largest population centers. Most importantly, port-cities are the geographic, economic and human interfaces between land and sea. As such, port-cities constitute the key investment and planning platform for both the projection of the blue economy and its progressive decarbonization (including that of shipping) and for the development of transportation multi-modality.

Port-cities and their collective resources also represent vulnerable ecosystems under heavy anthropogenic pressure and domination: marine and coastal air quality are deteriorating from the burning of oil as a shipping fuel and the discharge of wastes, while sea levels and increasingly frequent extreme weather events are threatening to damage assets in ports and city coastlines, in part due to the continued and increased use of fossil fuels to power transportation, including maritime shipping.

Nevertheless, port-cities are emerging as the major enablers for transformation towards sustainable development of blue economy activities, including the decarbonization of maritime energy and transportation. This critical mass of human, capital and technological resources could project the blue economy in way that responds to major societal challenges in a smart and sustainable fashion.

Future green port-cities should be, and could be, facilitators of trade; creators of value- added through local port services and port-related industries and clusters; generators of specialized local employment; end-users of local research and innovation; champions of climate change mitigation and adaptation; guarantors of local air quality and stewards of ecosystem preservation.

A desired model for port-city transformation would: (1) accommodate the main challenges of growing ports and growing population, including the coherent development of new port sites, while (2) minimizing the mismatches in port capacity, urban development and infrastructure investments (including in passenger mobility and multimodal freight transport) that often come with relocation of port sites, (3) transforming land abandoned by port relocation into new housing or mixed urban development, and (4) valuing and protecting air quality for the benefit of their citizens and the local marine ecosystem itself.

However, reality is not always so easy. A combination of varying factors currently shapes the economic environment of port-cities. There are wealthy ports experiencing at least moderate growth, but many are also suffering from a decline in port activity, city population, or both. The nature and capacities of port-city hubs are also very much dependent on the geography and infrastructure of the land-based transport corridors which connect the hinterland with the port-city. This link to the realities of land transportation is likely to become the principal factor shaping the possibilities for development of blue economically-competitive, low carbon and climate resilient Atlantic port-cities.

Table1. Atlantic Basin Port-City Typologies

Rim Area	Typology
Atlantic's Europe	Inland urban/commercial concentration and coastal gateways
Atlantic's Africa	Inland urban/commercial concentration and coastal gateways
	Coastal urban/commercial concentration and land bridge connection also in the Southern region between West and East
Atlantic's North America	Coastal urban/commercial concentration with land bridge connection between East and West
Atlantic's Central America	Coastal urban/commercial concentration and land bridge connection between East and West
Caribbean	Coastal urban/commercial concentration and low hinterland coverage
Atlantic's South America	Coastal urban/commercial concentration and low hinterland coverage
	Inland urban/commercial concentration and coastal gateways in the Northern part

Source: Own elaboration.

Different port and urban growth patterns lead to distinctly different impacts and policy challenges. Taking such variables into consideration when observing the Atlantic Basin, it is possible to identify patterns which articulate different port-city typologies, as seen in Table 1.

In summary, the policy, innovation and competitiveness efforts of port-cities should pursue:

- Low-carbon strategies, including energy and sustainable mobility (both maritime and terrestrial) in and around port-cities;
- Climate change adaptation strategies and risk management for the protection of port-city assets;
- Development of appropriate maritime and other industrial clusters;
- Sustainable protection of the health of the marine ecosystem where port-cities are located;

- Smart Cities policies which reflect their maritime nature of coastal cities and their ports.

Economic Perspectives of Port-Cities

Economic Decline

The operational context of shipping has changed dramatically over the last decades, producing significant impacts on port-cities. Many ports have suffered losses due to the significant reduction of port taxes, the shrinking of the fleets (although not necessarily the size of the vessels), including fishing fleets, and the competitive pressures stemming from the expansion of air and railway passenger transportation (at the expense of passenger ferries). Lasting labor conflicts at ports have also caused profound impacts on their operations, leading to the loss of commercial relevance for some ports.

Moreover, working within international networks open to intense competitive pressures driven by technological and other economic, environmental and demographic changes, ports can no longer remain based on a set of infrastructures developed to respond to heavy industrial production in the regions where they are located and oriented towards exports to foreign markets. On the other hand, new export products have different characteristics from the so-called traditional heavy industries and outputs, and are increasingly specific.

Today, the competitiveness of port-cities (which continue to sustainably innovate) requires:

- creation of an adequate port-city operational and governance interface;
- analysis and monitoring of both the city and the port in terms of (changing) functional composition;
- elaboration of a development model based on a balance between building on existing strengths and the acquisition of new assets and capabilities;
- the integration and complementarity of public policies promoting maritime links and routes, the effectiveness of port operations, their hinterland penetration, heightened local awareness and mobilization of their communities (including actions to address safety issues), and
- environmental impact mitigation measures which take into consideration the significant combined effect of the many influences generating pressures on urban air quality.

However, new trends in maritime traffic — affecting the size and design of bulk carriers, maritime transport of energy (particularly rising quantities of LNG), the use of containerized cargo on short-sea-shipping routes and the growth in cruise tourism, together with the increased cooperation at the level of logistic platforms — are lending new momentum to the port sector. Consequently, in many cases, the relationship between the port and the city is undergoing a transformation.

Port Relocation and Port-City Renewal

Because of the increasing size of freight vessels, the relocation of terminals to deep-water ports is becoming a necessity. Such relocation of port facilities typically leaves behind an economic void in and around the heart of the old port. In the worst cases, the footprint of such social degradation and economic decline will involve large areas of land, buildings and abandoned infrastructures in the heart of the old, traditional areas of port-cities. The functional relationships of such spaces, including the public transportation networks associated with the old business, begin to lose relevance and priority, and to pose barriers to any local economic revival.

As part of port modernization, the re-location to new port sites is to some extent inevitable, if both the city and the port are growing. If this is the case, at some point both the port and the city have an interest in relocating (at least part of) the port to another site that has less opportunity costs and that provides the port more possibilities for expansion.

However, the socio-economic degradation of the populations directly involved (resulting from the decline in traditional activities) can be offset by the potential development of green spaces that can fill such voids.

Alignment of Port-City Planning and Policy

Alignment of port and city planning — and of land and maritime spatial planning, including integrated coastal zone management — is essential to the resolution of the port-city mismatch (both landward and seaward) often produced by port modernization, relocation and rehabilitation. Such an alignment should guarantee that the port and city mutually reinforce — rather than oppose — each other, and that sea and land use planning are also aligned, if not actually integrated. Such a port and city planning policy alignment is dependent on many different variables. The most important and visibly identifiable include: (1) the role of the national government, (2) the role of port authorities, (3) the functions of cities, (4) the level of involvement of cities

Table 2. Policy Aims for Archetypal Ports-Cities

	Port	City	Port-City
Economic	Port volumes	Value added, diversification	Smart port growth strategies, maritime clusters
Transportation	Freight	Passengers	Integration of smart co-existence of freight and passenger traffic
Labor	Efficiency	Employment	High value-added port-related employment
Environment	Limit impacts	Quality of life	Green growth
Land use	Cargo handling industry	Urban waterfront as opportunities for housing	Mixed development, with role for port functions
Structural logic	Closed industrial cluster	Open network with pure agglomeration effects	Mix

Source: The Competitiveness of Global Port-Cities: Synthesis Report (OECD, 2014)

in their ports, (5) the involvement of the port in urban development, and finally (6) the way strategic planning is harnessed (or not) as mechanism to engage and involve stakeholders.[3]

At present, such constraints and potential adaptations are subject to increasing attention. This intensifying spotlight is due to the range of new opportunities on offer within the context of port-city rehabilitation—whether to diversify the activities of the ports themselves, or in the planning of their relocation in a way that does not lose sight of the increased availability of land to develop new poles of attraction at the seaside, through requalification and reuse of public heritage and infrastructure in an innovative way and by bringing, for example, nautical leisure and maritime tourism activities into the heart of the old port.

Such a focus raises fundamental questions regarding the links between ports and cities:

---

3. Olaf Merk, ed., *The Competitiveness of Global Port-Cities: Synthesis Report*, (Paris, OECD Publishing, 2014) http://dx.doi.org/10.1787/9789264205277-en.

- What factors may contribute to the evolution, or the inhibition, of greater urban sustainability in port-cities?
- How might these cities continue to deal with major demographic changes and challenges, globalization and climate change?

Port-City Competitiveness and Clusters

From the perspective of port-city competitiveness, freight volumes will double by 2050, and the diversification of activity will continue, particularly regarding passenger transportation and multimodality. With the potential relocation of freight terminals, the links between cities and ports must be reinforced, especially in the areas of spatial planning stewardship, research and innovation, and new added-value services.

To move towards cluster creation, strong control measures to cope with environment and climate change issues will become essential. In fact, a recent ESPO study on European port governance shows that of the main industrial sectors associated with a sample of port clusters, ship building and repair is strongly present at ports (found in 63 percent of them), followed by chemicals (54 percent), the food industry (51 percent), electrical power (49 percent), petroleum (49 percent), construction (49 percent), steel (40 percent), the fishing industry (35 percent), the automotive industry (23 percent), and many others (35 percent),[4] including the manning and training of seafarers, the management of maritime services, and ship registry.

These plants and business services benefit from their location in a port because they provide ease of access both for the import of raw material and for the export of finished goods, due to the shortening of the transport leg (or last mile connectivity). To this end, synergistic clusters should be also created in the ports, where they generate even more advantages when, for example, they are associated with new energy access and circular economy activities (including ecofriendly dismantling of ships), etc.

Marine Environment, Maritime Transport and Port-Cities

Maritime Emissions and Port-Cities

The anticipated effects of projected air quality point to a need to control such pollution impacts in ports, if the quality of life of the citizens in the cities is not to deteriorate further. Furthermore, by promoting and sustaining

---

4. "Trends in EU ports governance," https://www.espo.be/media/Trends_in_EU_ports_governance_2016_FINAL_VERSION.pdf (accessed August 19, 2017).

a high level of air quality, port-cities can generate the conditions for green growth within an expanding blue economy.[5]

Maritime shipping is the most carbon-efficient form of transport in terms of grams of carbon dioxide emissions per cargo ton compared to other modes such as rail, road or air transport.[6] Nevertheless, as we have seen in Chapter Six, maritime GHG emissions are growing rapidly and will soon constitute 5% of the global total.[7]

Onboard combustion and energy transformation processes—mainly for propulsion and energy production onboard ships—are maritime sources of both GHGs and air pollutant emissions to the atmosphere. In addition to CO_2 emissions, sulfur oxides (SOx), nitrogen oxides (NOx), and particulate organic matter (PM) are also emitted into the atmosphere as a direct result of shipping transport and other maritime activities.

Epidemiological studies consistently link ambient concentrations of particulate organic matter (PM) to negative health impacts, including asthma, heart attacks, hospital admissions, and premature mortality.[8] Moreover, the simulation results of different scenarios of PM emissions indicate that marine shipping-related PM emissions contribute to approximately 60,000 deaths annually at the global scale, with impacts concentrated in coastal regions along major trade routes. Most mortality effects are seen in Asia and Europe where large and dense populations coincide with high levels of shipping-related PM concentration. These studies have also estimated that the large majority of these emissions (approximately 70 percent) occur within the Economic Exclusive Zones (EEZ) of coastal states (i.e., within 200 nautical miles of their coastal communities).

Meanwhile, current policy discussions aimed at reducing shipping emissions are focused on two concerns:

• The geospatial aspects of policy implementation and compliance (e.g., the desirability of uniform global standards versus requirements for designated regional control areas); and

---

5. Olaf Merk, ed. *The Competitiveness of Global Port-Cities: Synthesis Report* (OECD), op. cit.

6. Ibid. p. 116.

7. For a deeper discussion of maritime GHG emissions, see Chapter Six of this volume,

8. James J. Corbett, James J. Winebrake, Erin H. Green, Prasad kasibhatla Veronika Eyring, and Axel Lauer, "Mortality from Ship Emissions: A Global Assessment," *Environmental Science & Technology*, published online, May 11, 2007.

- The costs and benefits of various emissions-reduction strategies (e.g., fuel switching versus treatment technologies or operational changes).

Emissions Control Areas (ECAs)

Emission Control Areas (ECAs) are sea areas in which stricter controls have been established by the International Maritime Organization (IMO) to minimize airborne emissions (SOx, NOx, ozone depleting substances (ODS), and volatile organic compounds (VOC)) generated by ships.[9] These regulations resulted from concerns about the contribution of the shipping industry to local and global air pollution and other environmental problems.

The SOx rules apply to all vessels, irrespective of date of construction. Although the SOx requirements can be met by using a low-sulfur fuels, regulations allow alternative methods to reduce the emissions of SOx to an equivalent level, namely, through the use of scrubbers, at least during a transition period. However, scrubbers are not capable of comprehensively addressing the problem: they do nothing to contribute to a more pragmatic approach towards LNG (or other alternative maritime fuels) or to the adoption and installation of electrical shore connections (to be used when ships are in port)—both major aspects of a potential integrated solution.[10]

To support EU measures on SOx, in accordance with the EU's marine fuel Sulphur Directive,[11] the sulfur content in marine fuels within the territorial waters of an EU Member State may not exceed 0.1 percent by weight. This applies to all ships regardless of flag. Table 3 presents the authorized sulfur content limits—in effect from January 1, 2015 through to January 1, 2020—that apply to the marine fuels used by ships operating within the North European Emission Control Areas (i.e., Baltic Sea and North Sea ECAs), compared with fuels used by ships operating outside these ECAs .

On the other hand, the 2015 projections of Ivan Komar and Branko Lalić for SOx and NOx emissions up to 2030 indicate that maritime activities around Europe will continue to steadily increase emissions. They anticipate that such maritime emissions will surpass land-based emissions by 2020.[12]

---

9. As defined by Annex VI of the MARPOL 73/78 of the IMO.

10. The environmental benefits of scrubbers can be debated. Current scrubber technology can cut only one exhaust at a time (i.e. SOx or NOx). Consequently, it must be emphasized that scrubbers will not be able to match long term MARPOL VI deadlines, which require a drastic reduction of both SOx and NOx. Also, if the sulfur content in the fuel is more than 3.5 percent then the required reduction of SOx is not fully 100 percent. Finally, scrubbers cannot cut the emission of CO_2 and they reduce the PM only by 60 percent.

11. 1999/32/EG, Article 4 with amendment as per directive 2005/33/EC.

12. Ivan Komar and Branko Lalić, "Sea Transport Air Pollution," *Environmental Sciences—Current Air Quality Issues*, Chapter 8, (accessed July 18, 2017).

Table 3. Sulfur Content Limits, EU ECAs, 2015-20

	Inside EU ECA	Outside EU ECA
At berth/anchor	0.1 percent	0.1 percent (not if < 2hrs or with shore-side electricity)
Passenger ships on regular services	0.1 percent	1.5 percent
Other ships	0.1 percent	3.5 percent

Source: Own elaboration.

With respect to air pollution and climate impacts stemming from shipping, according to James Corbett,[13] there are two reasons to reduce vessel emissions. First, vessels contribute to these problems today, and the estimated growth in shipping will make such problems worse in the future (see Chapter Six). Second, maritime transport controls are more cost-effective than the regulation of other transportation modes, but impact mitigation may be asymmetric across transport modes (as shipping is also more heterogeneous than other transport modes).

Among other things, Corbett suggests that the future of transportation should become increasingly multimodal at the global systemic level. Irrespective of the technologies applied in vessel retrofits or in new constructions, or of the cost differences between alternative fuels, the likely short-term pattern would be characterized by multimodal logistics effects producing reductions in all emissions and pollutants.

Perhaps even more relevant would be the suggestion that an extension of sulfur emission-controlled areas may be justified across large regions. Independent of the possible beneficial health effects in the confined coastal areas of the port-cities, SOx control benefits appear to be greater than control costs. Furthermore, reducing SOx, NOx, and particulate emissions simultaneously would allow for a modification of climate assessments (particularly given that these pollutants often combine to form ozone, a highly heat-trapping GHG).

Because of their position at the border between terrestrial and maritime realms, and their role as the interfaces between distinct transportation modes,

---

13. James Corbett, P.E., Ph.D. Presentation to OECD/ECMT JTRC WG on Transport GHG Reduction Strategies May 21-22, 2007.

Figure 1. Existing and Possible Future Sulfur Emission Control Areas

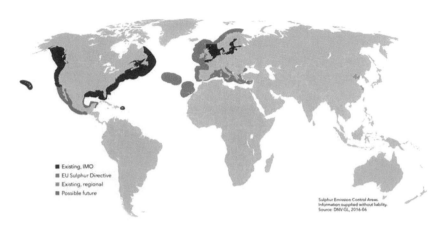

Source: DMV-GL, 2016-06. Note: ECAs, as defined by MARPOL Annex VI, the scope of the EU Sulphur Directive, and other regionally controlled areas.

it is important to understand, explore and develop the leveraging support than can be provided by port-cities in the Atlantic Basin in the effort to reach such emissions and pollution reduction goals.

ECAs in the Atlantic Basin

Meanwhile, the United States and Canada have also implemented ECAs within their respective EEZs. Furthermore, a possible future IMO ECA might be created within the Atlantic Basin in the Gulf of Mexico (see Figure 1 below). In contrast with the EU, the RECs of the Americas are not yet engaged at such a level. Nevertheless, for the case of the United States, Canada, and Mexico, their national and state policies have shown boldness in moving ahead to implement ECAs to a scale that is not so evident in Europe. Finally, African RECs are appointed to be the drivers for transformation of the transport system and environmental policies, but still fall short in reflecting these in their recent programs.

In this context, the wider Atlantic Basin suffers from an unbalanced implementation of IMO ECAs, given that they are still virtually absent in the Southern Atlantic. This imbalance represents a clear vulnerability for air quality in a significant number of port-cities which are currently struggling to maintain the air quality of their urban zones. In contrast to the current situation in the North Sea and Baltic Sea areas, unless vessels are in port or at anchor (inside territorial waters) in the port-cities of the European Atlantic littoral and the Mediterranean Sea, passenger ships are allowed to generate 15 times more sulfur emissions than the limits authorized inside the European ECAs of the North and Baltic Seas; freight ships operating outside of EU ECAs are allowed to emit 35 times more SOx emissions while they are sailing in territorial waters and the EEZ (refer back to Table 3). Finally, despite the stringent restrictions applied to ships when in port (which limit SOx emissions to 0.1 percent) high levels of emissions continue to persist within the EEZs of the coastal countries and are subject to airstreams which ultimately bring organic particulate matter to the coastal zones, including to their port-cities. As a result, even very focused local measures are not sufficient and, in the cases of existing systematic winds, can be even unrealistic.

According to health studies and other scientific data, there is an increasing likelihood of anthropogenic pressure continuing to mount upon European port-cities located outside the EU's ECAs and beyond the coastal urban façade of this Atlantic Region (particularly in the Southern Atlantic), implying a degradation of air quality that could be avoided if ECAs were implemented in the other European geographies where marine traffic is rather high and projected to continue growing (i.e., within member-states EEZ limits), according to the consensus of estimates.

Ports As the Key Lever for Reducing Maritime Emissions

Port-cities are not only, de facto, at the forefront of strategies to implement international emissions reductions regulations, but they are also themselves the originators and enablers of emissions reduction policies. The first and most fundamental step that a port authority should take is to conduct a thorough port emissions inventory.[14] Moreover, port-cities can logically become the root source for the energy and transportation transformation process if their clusters embrace not just the port activities and infrastructures, which provide the interfaces between land and sea, but also the core of the shipping industry, including shipbuilding, management, and operations. These are the segments of the shipping industry which drive maritime trends and, consequently, shape the way fleets will operate in the future.

Climate Change Adaptation and Port-Cities

Strategies for adapting to the potential consequences of climate change are increasingly important as ports remain at the forefront of the phenomenon.

------

14. Olaf Merk, ed., op. cit., p. 118.

Due to their coastal locations, ports can be particularly affected by rising sea levels, floods, storm surges and strong winds. Assuming a sea level rise of half a meter by 2050,[15] it is estimated that the value of exposed assets in 136 port megacities may be as high as US$28 trillion. Rising port awareness and policy consideration is a function of both economic and ecological drivers. Modeling and simulation of different scenarios reveal a level of uncertainty inherent in the development of adaptation measures such that it is likely that decision-makers will act only upon foreseeable conditions — which will not necessarily address the major problems. On the other hand, implementation of adaptation strategies will suffer from the discrepancy between the current planning frameworks of port authorities and the time span of climate change impacts (with an unfolding time span of up to 100 years, about double the typical lifespan of major port infrastructure).[16] In general, adaptation measures may feature a mixture of protection, adaptation, or retreat. Likewise, a comprehensive vision which would integrate land, water and air quality and their interlocking issues, should not be disregarded when addressing climate adaptation options for port-cities.

Maritime LNG and Port-Cities

Meanwhile, liquefied natural gas (LNG) systems have already been installed on several vessels, although these are still isolated cases. Consequently, there is a need to add considerable value by contributing to the removal of major existing barriers (which currently obstruct a broader uptake of new technologies and their proper introduction at ports) and by providing unbiased assessment, based on data, of environmental, safety, and supply chain concerns and claims. Another important goal is to render this cryogenic fuel technology accessible to small and medium enterprises (SME) across the coastal regions of the Atlantic Basin, especially those SMEs addressing unattended areas of intervention and which sail inland waterways, coastal zones (including fishing zones) and short sea shipping routes. At the same time, there is a need to demonstrate that the new technologies, once introduced, will reduce not only GHGs and other pollutant emissions, but also the overall costs for ship owners and operators.

---

15. Lenton T, A. Footitt and A. Dlugolecki, "Major Tipping Points in the Earth's Climate System and Consequences for the Insurance Sector," 2009, p. 89, cited in The United Nations Conference on Trade and Development, Ad Hoc Expert meeting on Climate Change Impacts and Adaptation: a Challenge for Global Ports, Geneva, September, 29-30 2011.

16. Olaf Merk, ed., op. cit., p. 118.

However, for both the technical community and civil society, the safe use of LNG must become verifiable in an explicit fashion—not through applying prescriptive regulations, but through proper assessment tools and methods.

It is worth noting that some of the work on engine design, for instance, is oriented towards enabling their improvement by optimizing natural gas and dual-fuel engines for natural gas operation. For coastal zones, and in particular for port-cities, these technologies represent both a smart technological application in different vessel fleets and a response to today's urgent need to reduce GHGs and other pollutant emissions which continue to degrade the air quality in their urban zones. In this context, the pre-requisites for introducing LNG for shipping on a wide scale, and therefore for exploiting its promise of improved efficiency and reduced engine emissions, can be summarized as follows:

- Verifiable tools for assessing the true environmental performance of LNG and CNG to be provided to the regulatory bodies;
- Assessment methods and tools to be made widely available to all interested parties;
- Communication and dissemination aimed at civil society, expert engineers, and policy makers to assure broader acceptance by both the technical and nontechnical communities.

In conclusion, there is the general need to address these challenges by providing methods and tools for an unambiguous and verifiable assessment of the effectiveness of waterborne alternative fuels with respect to the socioeconomic, environment and safety domains.

Therefore, analyses of the viability of cryogenic gases as fuel (with respect to both emissions reduction and consequently cost) must establish a baseline against which most of the required technologies should be developed, innovated and applied, and by addressing their social, economic and environmental dimensions. Detailed analyses of the consequences of an incident versus the likelihood of an unintentional event are essential for full social acceptance of new fuel technologies such as for LNG in maritime activities, including their effects within port-cities. The latter is perhaps one of the most relevant challenges to overcoming safety dilemmas and concerns throughout this transformation process.

A common option pursued currently is the design, construction and testing of prototype demonstrators using LNG technologies close to the market. However, it is also important to not disregard the availability of innovative tools and methods for assessing socioeconomic, environmental and safety performance of LNG, for example, and making them available to authorities and industry stakeholders to ensure that port-cities are effectively able to engage in the process and respond to the needs of their citizens.

Transportation Intermodality and Port-Cities

But transformation is not about doing individual things better—it is about doing better things. Therefore, the greening of maritime activities with respect to energy, transportation and climate adaptation infrastructures in Atlantic Basin port-cities must be addressed through a broader and integrated approach, in a more holistic and eco-systemic fashion.

By focusing on transportation inter-modality, ports can encourage modal shifts and consequently port operations can reduce emissions related to the maritime transport sector. This can also apply to the inter-port transportation of empty containers. On the other hand, the emissions generated by rail transport are roughly equivalent to a third of those generated by road haulage, and many port authorities are thus encouraging switches to rail as a form of hinterland transport, often through targeted tax reductions and subsidies.[17]

Green Investment and Port-Cities

Investment into clean in-port technologies is an increasingly effective way of both ensuring environmental compliance and making the port more attractive to shipping operators. Because shipping companies must also comply with increasingly stringent regulations concerning the types of fuels they use, ports that can offer green services have become more attractive. For example, some ports located near ECAs have been able to leverage their position to become key suppliers of low-sulfur fuel.

Another clean technology strategy involves supplementing traditional energy sources with renewable energies. In some ports, this includes the purchase of power from companies specialized in renewable energy production. Until recently, the use of renewable energy in ports still was perceived as marginal, too expensive, or unreliable. However, given recent and future project renewable energy cost reductions, and the potential large-scale expansion of renewable energy production on all the continents of the Atlantic Basin, the outlook for the future is changing.

---

17. Olaf Merk, ed., The Competitiveness of Global Port-Cities, op.cit., p. 122.

There are a number of ways in which renewable energy could be increasingly relevant for port-city planning and transformation. The first would be the provision of on-shore electricity access to ships in port which, over time could be increasingly supplied by renewably-generated electricity (either by the national grid or from a port-dedicated micro-grid). Second, there is an increasing trend, particularly in Europe, to develop offshore wind energy capacity, which could be supported, in terms of maintenance, component storage and other related services, by the port-city. Such offshore wind farms could also provide the port-city with clean electricity, including in the port for ships at shore side. Third, the port-city could also encourage sectorial cluster development in wind energy manufacturing (for domestic use or for export), and research and development, or in other renewable energy spheres in the future, like ocean energy or even offshore solar farms. Some port-cities can plan to be renewable energy hubs, possibly embracing all of the functions above, providing locational, infrastructure, service and qualified labor force advantages to agents in these sectors.

Europe's Integrated Approach to Continental and Maritime Energy and Transportation

Europe 2020, EU Maritime Strategy, and the Atlantic Basin

To achieve the goals of Europe 2020—the EU's Strategy for Smart, Sustainable and Inclusive Growth—the European Commission has adopted a series of measurable EU targets for 2020 to steer the implementation of the various European and national action plans. These plans have been aligned each other and transposed into national targets for employment, research and innovation, climate change and energy, education, and poverty reduction. Such targets mark off the strategic directions to be taken, and—with proper monitoring—provide a measurement of the strategy's success.

Chief among the headline targets of the Europe 2020 strategy are those of the *Climate and Energy Package*, a set of binding legislation (proposed in 2007 and adopted in 2009) to ensure the EU meets its well-known climate and energy targets for the year 2020:

- a 20 percent cut in greenhouse gas emissions (from 1990 levels, a commitment which increases to 30 percent if other developed countries commit to comparable cuts);
- 20 percent of EU energy from renewables; and

- a 20 percent improvement in energy efficiency. They also represent the headline targets of the Europe 2020 strategy for smart, sustainable and inclusive growth.

The EU is acting in several areas—including the maritime realm—to meet these targets. Europe's integrated maritime policies support the goals of Europe 2020 by setting major sectorial strategic objectives—in maritime industry (mobility, transport and raw materials), energy and the environment—and through the implementation of macro-regional and sea basin-oriented maritime strategy action plans.[18] These action plans are the EU's main tools for implementing an integrated maritime policy and for promoting EU-wide recognition of the realities of its various coastal macro-regions (see the section on Europe's integrated maritime strategy below).

The EU has taken such region wide actions to begin to embrace the Atlantic Basin because experience has taught it that regional economic communities (RECs) can influence global issues, including fight against climate change, much more effectively than can countries individually.

European Alternative Fuels Strategy

One of the principal thrusts to achieve the Europe 2020 goals in the realm of European transportation, the *European Alternative Fuels Strategy*,[19] approved in 2013, promotes the increasing use of alternative fuels[20] (like electricity, natural gas, liquefied petroleum gas, and hydrogen) in European transportation fleets and established the following main policy objectives for the sector:

---

18. Each sea region—the Baltic Sea, Black Sea, Mediterranean Sea, North Sea, the Atlantic and the Arctic Ocean—is unique and merits a tailor-made strategy. The maritime policy promotes growth and development strategies that exploit the strengths and address the weaknesses of each large sea region in the EU: from the Arctic's climate change to the Atlantic's renewable energy potential, from problems of sea and ocean pollution to maritime safety.

19. COM (2013) 17 final - Communication from the Commission to the European Parliament, the Council, the European Economic and Social Committee and the Committee of the Regions—Clean Power for Transport: A European alternative fuels strategy—{SWD (2013) 4 final}, Brussels, January 24, 2013.

20. Alternative fuels refers to fuels or power sources which serve, at least partly, as a substitute for fossil oil sources in the energy supply for transportation and which have the potential to contribute to its de-carbonization and enhance the environmental performance of the transport sector. These alternative fuels include, inter alia: electricity, hydrogen, biofuels as defined in point (i) of Article 2 of Directive 2009/28/EC, synthetic and paraffinic fuels, natural gas (including bio methane) in gaseous form—compressed natural gas (CNG)) and liquefied form (liquefied natural gas (LNG)—and liquefied petroleum gas (LPG).

- To reduce the EU transport systems dependence on oil, and to diversify and secure energy supply;
- To reduce EU greenhouse gas (GHG) emissions in line with the targets of the *Climate and Energy Package*[21] and the 2011 *White Paper on Transport*;
- To improve the air quality in urban areas to meet EU air quality mandates;
- To enhance the competitiveness of European industry, boost innovation and generate economic growth.

The challenges to achieving and sustaining such effects include the need to:

- Establish a coherent policy framework that meets the long-term energy needs of all transport modes by building on a comprehensive mix of alternative fuels;
- Support the market development of alternative fuels in a technologically neutral way by removing technical and regulatory barriers;
- Guide technological development and private investments in the deployment of alternative fuel vehicles, vessels and infrastructure to lend confidence to consumers;
- Ensure citizen awareness as to the safe use of these new technologies and fuels—particularly when located close to urban areas (such as in the case of port-cities).

To this end, the *European Directive 2014/94/EU*[22] on the deployment of alternative fuels infrastructure established the minimum requirements for alternative fuels infrastructure build-up, including common technical specifications for recharging points for electric vehicles, and refueling points for natural gas—both *liquefied natural gas* (LNG) and *compressed natural gas* (CNG)—and hydrogen, along with user information requirements. The so-called DAFI directive also set a timeline for adoption by the EU institutions and their Member States, through the implementation of their respective National Policy Frameworks (NPF).

LNG and Maritime Transport

Public attention is generally centered on road, rail and urban transport. However, as Chapter Six amply demonstrated, there is also a pressing need

---

21. See the second paragraph of this section above.

22. Directive 2014/94/EU of The European Parliament and of the Council of October 22, 2014 on the deployment of alternative fuels infrastructure.

to focus on the energy consumption and emissions of the maritime sector and to promote alternative fuels in shipping.

LNG stands out as the leading candidate to replace petroleum-based fuels in maritime transport. European Directive 2014/94/EU considers LNG an attractive alternative fuel for maritime vessels to meet requirements for decreasing the sulfur content in marine fuels within the emissions-controlled areas which, in this case, affect half of the ships sailing in European short sea shipping.

Once adopted widely, LNG (and hydrogen) have the potential—compared with conventional fossil-based bunker fuels—to make shipping cleaner and more efficient by improving air quality and reducing GHG emissions while at the same time reducing overall costs for maritime economic activities.

A network of refueling points for LNG[23] at maritime and inland ports is scheduled be available at least by the end of 2025 and 2030, respectively, implying a major impact on facilities at port-cities over the coming decade. Refueling points for LNG include, inter alia, LNG terminals, tanks, tank vehicles, mobile containers, bunker vessels and barges. The decision on the location of the LNG refueling points at ports should be based on a cost-benefit analysis including an examination of the environmental benefits. Applicable safety-related provisions should also be considered. The deployment of LNG infrastructure provided for in this Directive need not hamper the development of other potentially up-coming energy-efficient alternative fuels and their implications for bunkering.

When considering the respective European national policy frameworks (NPFs), market incentives for port transformation should be promoted at several levels. These could include, for example, the articulation of benefits for participation in shipping registries and tonnage taxes, and the promotion of green incentives, including those for green-shipbuilding, all aligned with interests and efforts promoted by the flag state fleet. In addition, port requalification and improvement would also benefit from a special green tax regime aligned with interests and efforts promoted by the port state authorities. Because this is a transformational process which requires decades to implement, only a coherent promotion of policy instruments, international cooperation and private sector engagement will be able to achieve such a goal.

---

23. Refueling point for LNG refers to a refueling facility for the provision of LNG, consisting of either a fixed or mobile facility, offshore facility, or other system.

Furthermore, shore-side electricity[24] facilities at ports can serve maritime and inland waterway transport—and maritime and inland ports (where air quality or noise levels are poor)—as a clean power supply. In fact, shore-side electricity can contribute significantly to reducing the environmental impact of sea-going ships and inland waterway vessels.

According to a European Sea Ports Organization (ESPO) study on European port governance, 62 percent of onshore power supply services are run by port authorities, 34 percent by private operators, while 4 percent are under other less relevant frameworks. These numbers reveal a significant level of heterogeneity in the provision of these services to fleets.[25]

EU Transportation Strategy

TEN-T, European Transport Network, Energy and Port-Cities

With respect to European ports, policy and investment priority goes to infrastructures that are part of the new Trans-European Transport Network (TEN-T).[26] TEN-T is an ambitious policy and action plan with a budget of €24.05 billion up to 2020. With this policy, "the blueprint for a new transport infrastructure network which incorporates all transport modes—railways, inland waterways, roads, ports, airports and other transport systems—as well as equipment for innovative alternative fuels and intelligent transport solutions has been reinforced considerably in the last years."[27]

The relevance of the diversity of management frameworks of the different modal activities is significant, but there is a strong emphasis on the role of the private sector. For example, according to the ESPO study on European port governance, at those interfaces, 8 percent of the rail operations are run

---

24. Shore-side electricity supply means the provision of shore-side electrical power through a standardized interface to seagoing ships or inland waterway vessels at berth.

25. "Trends in EU ports governance," op. cit.

26. EU has a new transport infrastructure policy that connects the continent both East and West, and North and South. This policy aims to close the gaps between Member States transport networks, remove bottlenecks that still hamper the smooth functioning of the internal market and overcome technical barriers such as incompatible standards for railway traffic. It aims to promote and strengthen seamless transport chains for passenger and freight, while keeping up with the latest technological trends.

27. COM(2017) 327 final—Report from the Commission to the European Parliament, the Council, the European Economic and Social Committee and the Committee of the Regions—Progress report on implementation of the TEN-T network in 2014-2015, Brussels, June 19, 2017.

Table 4. Alternative Fuels Infrastructure Build-up Requirements and Coherence within TEN-T

Alternative Fuels	Coverage	Timeframe
Electricity in urban/suburban and other densely populated areas	Appropriate number of publicly accessible points	By end 2020
CNG in urban/suburban and other densely populated areas	Appropriate number of points	By end 2020
CNG along the TEN-T core network	Appropriate number of points	By end 2025
Electricity at shore-side	Ports of TEN-T core network and other ports	By end 2025
Hydrogen in the Member-States who choose to develop it	Appropriate number of points	By end 2025
LNG at maritime ports	Ports of the TEN-T core network	By end 2025
LNG at inland ports	Ports of the TEN-T core network	By end 2030
LNG for heavy duty vehicles	Appropriate number of points along the TEN-T core network	By end 2025

Source: own elaboration.

by the port authority, 10 percent by government, and 74 percent by private operators.[28]

TEN-T places a strong emphasis on Europe's major global gateways for maritime and air transport to ensure that Europe's trade flows are not restricted. It involves a core network and a comprehensive network to be completed by 2030 and 2050, respectively, to promote and guarantee the accessibility of all regions to European and global markets, as well as to prioritize infrastructure of strategic relevance.

To drive the future of the European transport system, TEN-T focuses on modal integration, interoperability and on the coordinated development of infrastructure, particularly facilities that stimulate low-emission solutions,

---

28. "Trends in EU ports governance," https://www.espo.be/media/Trends_in_EU_ports_governance_2016_FINAL_VERSION.pdf (accessed August 19, 2017).

new-generation service concepts and other fields of operational and technological innovation.

TEN-T and the Promotion of LNG

Although the initial focus of the TEN-T is on the infrastructural availability and use of LNG in the maritime and inland ports of the TEN-T core network, we should not rule out the possibility of LNG also being made available, in the long run, at ports outside the core network—in particular, those ports that are important for vessels not engaged in transport operations, but rather in other expanding economic activities, like offshore exploitation and maritime construction services, maritime tourism, fisheries and aquaculture, as well as naval and coast-guard function operations and basing facilities.

But public awareness and policies aimed at the safety of LNG transport and bunkering—until recently a major citizen fear—need to be properly addressed to allow large-scale transport and usage of LNG in ports and waterways, and to reflect the concerns expressed in the European Agreement on International Carriage of Dangerous Goods by Inland Waterways.[29] Already, a number of the agreement's safeguard provisions have become obsolete in the face of technological solutions and civil society discussions that have already allowed Europeans to transcend such fears.

Within the EU (but this would also equally apply to the other regions of the Atlantic Basin), Member States should ensure an appropriate distribution system between LNG storage stations and refueling points. Within the European Economic Area (EEA),[30] the TEN-T Core Network should be the basis for the deployment of LNG infrastructure because it covers the main traffic flows in Europe and allows for network benefits. However, when establishing their networks for the supply of LNG, the deployment of refueling points (for both LNG and CNG) should not be disregarded. Indeed, they should be adequately coordinated with the implementation of this network, enlarging the scope of possibilities for economic use. According to the Commission, the foreseen impact on Member-State ports of the TEN-T core network is to build-up approximately 140 refueling points at a cost of € 2,085 million.

---

29. Concluded at Geneva on May 26, 2000.

30. The Agreement on the European Economic Area (EEA), which entered into force on January 1, 1994, brings together the EU Member States and the three EEA EFTA States—Iceland, Liechtenstein and Norway—in a single market, referred to as the Internal Market, governed by the same basic rules. These rules aim to enable goods, services, capital, and persons to move freely about the EEA in an open and competitive environment.

The *EU Directive 2014/94* also requires Member States to adopt their respective NPF which should include, inter alia, an assessment of the current and future development of the alternative fuel markets in the transport sector, along with national objectives and targets. Supporting measures for the deployment of alternative fuels should also be contained in the NPF. These would ideally put into place a minimum level of infrastructure: (1) refueling points for LNG at maritime and inland ports, (2) infrastructure for shore-side electricity supply in maritime and inland ports, as well as (3) other facilities addressing CNG and hydrogen.

Even though most R&D is still occurring in the northern regions of the Atlantic Basin, research and innovation projects elsewhere in the basin are also proceeding apace and promoting scientific advances, as well as the deployment of technologies needed to assess the technical viability of using these cryogenic fuels on a wide scale, by addressing the various economic sectors which can benefit from their use.

The design of several demonstrators (for example, the EU GAINN project series)[31] would fulfill the requirements of small- and medium-sized vessels engaged not only in shipping, but also in fishing and aquaculture, offshore services, maritime tourism, navy and coast guard fleets operating in offshore, coastal or inland waters. Therefore, one can anticipate the mixed service supply of LNG and CNG, as a potential combination to address this broader set of maritime activities, by adapting various technologies to the most adequate solutions. Moreover, the same applies to electric power for nautical tourism, for example, including the possible mandatory use of these options in near shore marine reserves.

EU Maritime Strategy

Action Plan for the Atlantic Area

Five Atlantic Member States of the EU (France, Ireland, Portugal, Spain and the United Kingdom), along with their respective regions, drafted an Action Plan for a Maritime Strategy in the Atlantic Area[32] to help create

---

31. GAINN4SHIP INNOVATION on LNG Technologies and Innovation for Maritime Transport for the Promotion of Sustainability, Multimodality and the Efficiency of the Network, and GAINN4AMOS on Sustainable LNG Operations for Ports and Shipping - Innovative Pilot Actions.

32. COM (2013) 279 final—Communication from the Commission to the European Parliament, the Council, the European Economic and Social Committee and the Committee of the Regions—Action Plan for a Maritime Strategy in the Atlantic area - Delivering smart, sustainable and inclusive growth, Brussels, May 1, 2013.

sustainable and inclusive growth in their coastal macro-region. The Action Plan builds on the Commission's Atlantic Strategy,[33] in line with *Europe 2020* strategy and the Common Strategic Framework for the *European Structural and Investment Funds* (ESIF) and their thematic objectives: (1) supporting the shift towards a low-carbon economy; (2) increasing the capacity for research and innovation through education and training, and bringing industry closer to research; and (3) enhancing the competitiveness of small and medium enterprises (SMEs). Apart from what is already being done by these countries individually, this Action Plan identifies areas where additional collective work is becoming possible, or even necessary. Addressing these areas under the principles of the integrated maritime policy can promote innovation, contribute to the protection and improvement of the Atlantic's marine and coastal environment, and create synergies for a socially inclusive and sustainable development model.

In this context, the improvement of so-called connectivity is an area in which a more structured vision of port-cities can be developed connecting the rim land-continents of the Atlantic Basin, North, South, East and West. The Action Plan's specific objectives, expressed in "Priority 3: Improve accessibility and connectivity" include the promotion of cooperation between ports and a vision to develop ports as hubs of the blue economy by:

- Upgrading of infrastructure to improve connectivity with the hinterland, enhance inter-modality and promote fast turnaround of ships through measures such as provision of shore side electricity, equipping ports with liquefied natural gas refueling capacity, and tackling administrative bottlenecks;
- Enabling ports to diversify into new business activities; and
- Analyzing and promoting port networks and short-sea shipping routes between European ports, within archipelagos and to the coast of Africa to increase seaborne traffic.

The Internationalization of the EU Maritime Strategy and the Role of Port-Cities

One of the most relevant aspects of this maritime strategy is related to its own internationalization. The Wider Atlantic is not limited to Europe, but it is the key field of action for maritime Europe, a shared resource and a unified marine system linking Europe with Africa and the Americas. All EU Coastal States have a common interest and responsibility not only to ensure good ocean governance—building upon the United Nations Convention on

---

33. COM 782/2011 of November 21, 2011.

the Law of the Sea (UNCLOS), the International Maritime Organization (IMO) (including MARPOL,[34] which remains relevant for limiting maritime air emissions and water discharges), and the International Seabed Authority (ISA)—but also to promote the blue economy and its growth by engaging all the EU sea basin macro-regional strategies.[35]

In this context, the envisaged hub capacity for the port-cities of the Atlantic Basin will convert them into major assets supporting this transformation, not just in the use of energy resources in the maritime activities, but also in a myriad of other associated activities. The economic value of the Atlantic Ocean is enormous for the countries located on its shores. Therefore, the Action Plan could create, from the European side, a solid foundation for cooperation among Atlantic Basin nations.

Pursuing an ocean-scale strategy—in the context of integrated maritime policies, along with all the other relevant regional strategies—would make visible a much broader geopolitical dimension within the maritime realm and convert maritime activity into a strategic driver for economic growth. The Atlantic Basin provides economic opportunities not only for the approximately 80 Atlantic coastal states but also for other countries with the capacity to accede to spaces outside their national jurisdiction. Convergence with the two Atlantic continents of the Southern Hemisphere will be one of the major challenges that, ultimately, will enable the governance of the basin to be tackled by adapting the proper instruments. This would allow sustainable development in the Atlantic Ocean and its coastal zones to be leveraged to an unprecedented level.

Other Regional Economic Communities in the Atlantic Basin: The Role of Atlantic Africa

The Atlantic African rim-land is strategic for energy and natural resources, mining, and agriculture. The cultural links among these African rim-land countries can reinforce their transatlantic relations, if African ambitions can move beyond a continental self-conception as the world's natural resources

---

34. Many actions have been undertaken in recent years to significantly reduce air emissions from ships. Most of these actions have been taken through Annexes IV and VI of MARPOL, an international instrument developed through the IMO that establishes legally-binding international standards to regulate specific emissions and discharges generated by ships.

35. Ibid., 1.

Figure 2. EU Maritime Strategy for the Atlantic Area, Scope of Intervention

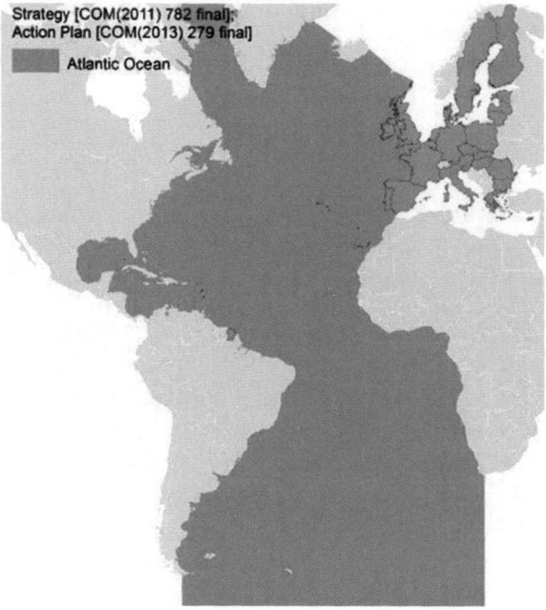

Source: GEOMAR Marine Plan

supplier and towards smart specialization and internationalization of economic power.

The African Union's Agenda 2063 and the 2050 Africa's Integrated Maritime Strategy

Despite many obstacles, the continent is moving in this direction. The African Union (AU) has created its *2050 Africa's Integrated Maritime Strategy* (2050 AIM Strategy).[36] Together with its Agenda 2063 strategic framework,[37] the 2050 AIM Strategy paves the way for the sustainable development of African coastal regions and waters.

---

36. 2050 Africa's Integrated Maritime Strategy (2050 AIM Strategy), AU, Version 1.0, 2012 https://au.int/en/documents/30928/2050-aim-strategy

37. Agenda 2063 Framework Document - The Africa We Want, September 2015 http://www.un.org/en/africa/osaa/pdf/au/agenda2063-framework.pdf)

Table 5. African Union Agenda 2063, Blue Economy and Climate Goals and Priority Areas

Aspirations	Goals	Priority Areas
#1: A prosperous Africa, based on inclusive growth and sustainable development	Blue/ocean economy for accelerated economic growth	• Marine resources and energy • Port operations and marine transport.
	Environmentally sustainable and climate resilient economies and communities	• Sustainable natural resource management • Biodiversity conservation, genetic resources and ecosystems • Sustainable consumption and production patterns • Water security • Climate resilience and natural disasters preparedness and prevention • Renewable energy.

Source: Agenda 2063 Framework Document—The Africa We Want, September 2015.

Given their various political, economic, technological, social and geographic divergences (and their internal and external disputes), African states tend to address their collective vision by eschewing declarations in which coastal and landlocked countries become isolated, opposed to, or disconnected from each other. Similarly, there is also a perceived need to avoid focusing of their uneven levels of development, natural resource endowments, infrastructure availability, and consistency of policy and robustness of their institutions. Nevertheless, African states recognize the role of the individual countries in tackling the different challenges.

With respect to the blue economy and climate change, Table 5 presents the related goals and priorities included in Aspiration 1 of the Agenda 2063.

With respect to port-cities, the AU's Agenda 2063 sets the following priority objectives:

- Implementation the AU 2050 AIM Strategy;
- Development and implementation policies for the growth of port operations and marine transport;
- Build-up of capacities for the growth of port operations and maritime transport;

- Intensification of research and development in support of the growth of marine transport businesses.

The AU 2050 AIM Strategy has emerged from a recognition that "the time has come for Africa to rethink how to manage her inland water ways, oceans and seas. The maritime areas are a key pillar for all AU Member States economic and social development, and are vital in the fight against poverty and unemployment."[38] The AU maritime strategy specifically aims to support the promotion of initiatives that improve citizen well-being while reducing marine environmental risks, and reversing ecological and biodiversity deterioration.

The 2050 AIM Strategy recognizes the importance of forging such a collective message and engagement, even if some of its concepts and definitions are not necessarily in line with those of international law (UNCLOS). They can nevertheless be used to leverage awareness and promote collective mobilization for major common objectives. One example is the project for a Combined Exclusive Maritime Zone of Africa (CEMZA)[39] — which would lend Africa the potential for cross-cutting geo-strategic, governance, economic, social, and environmental benefits. This is a challenging long-term strategic objective to achieve, mostly due to the inherent sovereign rights of individual coastal states. However, it can serve as a common basis for addressing some of the issues related to interoperability and cross-border coordination for a broad range of maritime activities. Such cross-border coordination and interoperability will be essential for the blue economy to support the required transformation needed in maritime governance, the shipbuilding and ship-repair industries, maritime transport, port and harbor management, maritime infrastructure development, and the promotion of a so-called pan African fleet.

Africa's Regional Economic Communities and Other Mechanisms for Maritime Strategy Implementation

At its 13th Ordinary Session, the AU Assembly decided to develop a comprehensive and coherent strategy and charged the Regional Economic

---

38. Ibid., p. 21.

39. CEMZE defines a common maritime zone of all AU Member States. It is to be a stable, secure and clean maritime zone in which common African maritime affairs policies for the management of African oceans, seas and inland waterways, along with their resources and multifaceted strategic benefits, can be developed and exploited. See *2050 Africa's Integrated Maritime Strategy* (2050 AIM Strategy) Annex B: Definitions, AU, Version 1.0, 2012 (https://au.int/en/documents/30928/2050-aim-strategy).

Communities (RECs) and other Regional Mechanisms (RM) of Africa to develop, coordinate, and harmonize policies and strategies, and to improve African maritime security and safety standards. The AU also agreed that African maritime economy should seek more wealth creation from its oceans and seas, so as to ensure the well-being of African people.

Africa's RECs are the building blocks of the African Economic Community (AEC), established by the 1991 Abuja Treaty to provide the overarching framework for continental economic integration. Within the Atlantic Basin, Africa's RECs include the Arab Maghreb Union (AMU), the Community of Sahel-Saharan States (CEN-SAD) in the North, the Economic Community of West African States (ECOWAS) in the West, the Economic Community of Central African States (ECCAS) in the center of the continent, and the Southern African Development Community (SADC) in the South.

These RECs will be essential and instrumental for the effective implementation, financing, monitoring and evaluation of Agenda 2063 and its flagship programs (including AIM), particularly at the regional levels. In addition, the monetary and special customs zones established in the RECs to date will continue to contribute to a more stable economic and business environment. This has been the case of the West African Economic and Monetary Union (WAEMU) and West African Monetary Zone (WAMZ) within ECOWAS, the Economic and Monetary Community of Central Africa (CEMAC) within ECCAS, and of the Southern African Customs Union (SACU) for the SADC.

Along with the RECs, the Gulf of Guinea Commission (GGC), for example, is a regional mechanism for harmonizing policies on the exploitation of natural resources (including the development of a framework for legal regulation of oil multinationals operating in the region), the protection of the region's environment and the provision of a framework for dialogue, prevention, management and settlement of conflicts between member states. Other African RMs—such as the New Partnership for Africa's Development (NEPAD) and the African Peer Review Mechanism (APRM)—incorporate global norms, standards, and structures within the overarching framework of African responsibility, and can assist maritime stakeholders. At the same time, the African Development Bank (AfDB) has a number of governance initiatives to assist member states implement resource governance mechanisms.

To this end, and as an umbrella, AU 2050 AIM Strategy goal iii aims to establish a common template—for the AU, the RECs/RMs, other relevant organizations, and member states—to guide maritime review, budgetary planning and effective allocation of resources, and to enhance maritime viability for an integrated and prosperous Africa. All of this can, ultimately, contribute to leveraging the transformation process by addressing the needs of the African shipping and maritime transportation sectors and their port-cities.

Africa at Multiple Crossroads: Maritime, Energy, Transportation, and Infrastructure

Atlantic African countries are often those with the least available resources to overcome the important upfront capital investment of the low-carbon transition. But many are also at a crossroads to change directions. By engaging in the same kind of technological leapfrogging that has already taken place in certain other African sectors (i.e., telecommunications and agriculture), African countries can still avoid, or even dislodge themselves from, the same fossil fuel-intensive development path followed by the advanced economies which have historically emitted the most GHGs.

Countries that have not irrevocably locked in a fossil fuel-focused centralized infrastructure could begin to cultivate a different energy model that would prioritize investment in and deployment of decentralized energy production and consumption systems.[40] Such a distinct possibility should be taken into serious consideration when approaching the proposed transformation of the African maritime sectors, including the future changes and adaptations.[41]

At present, Africa contributes less than 5% of global CO_2 emissions. Nevertheless, the continent bears the brunt of the impact of climate change. According to AU Agenda 2063, "Africa shall address the global challenge of climate change by prioritizing adaptation in all our actions, drawing upon skills of diverse disciplines and with adequate support (affordable technology development and transfer, capacity building, financial and technical resources) to ensure implementation of actions," and will participate in global efforts for climate change mitigation and adaptation that support and broaden the policy space for sustainable development on the continent while advancing its position and interests on climate change.[42]

---

40. "The Leapfrog Continent," The Economist, June 2015, http://www.economist.com/news/middle-east-and-africa/21653618GoGC-falling-cost-renewable-energy-may-allow-africa-bypass

41. For more on the potentials of the distributed energy model in Africa, particularly in relation to the energy cooperative movement, see Chapter Two.

42. Agenda 2063, op. cit. p. 22.

Currently, US$27.5 billion is being invested to develop ten key transport corridors within the sub-Saharan region including major port expansion projects now underway in more than 10 African countries. This is approximately the same amount of investment envisaged by the EU for the TEN-T but just until 2020. However, the scale and scope of this significant development will focus actions towards the elimination of infrastructure gaps, rather than to reorient existing infrastructure toward the use of alternative fuels. In addition, a broad range of development cooperation and investment sources are involved: from the World Bank, NEPAD, the African Development Bank (AfDB), and the Islamic Development Bank (IsDB) to China, the EU, and Japan.

Meanwhile, national development across Africa continues to support the commitment undertaken by the 54 members of the African Union to create a continent-wide free trade area. At the helm of this initiative is Africa's transport sector, taking continuous strides to unlock cross-border opportunities for intra-African trade and development. Intra-African trade is the lowest of any region in the world at a mere 10 percent of the total continent trade.[43] A properly crafted free trade area could change the African status quo and transform the continent. To this end, projects and initiatives in support of transport infrastructure development to boost intra-African trade continue to crop up across the continent under a vision of modernised transport and free trade for the region by expanding and modernizing ports, corridors and multi-modal connectivity.

Therefore, expansion and modernisation remain at the top of Africa's transport agenda as progressive development enables port connectivity and increases cargo throughput. Port and corridor expansion is not only creating new business opportunities for port-city development across the sub-Saharan region but also opening up new access to hinterland areas and strategic trade corridors.

With Africa's overall port utilisation capacity exceeding 70 percent, port authorities and terminal operators are actively calling for partners in development to help equip Africa's ports and harbours to respond to the new trade and shipping transportation requirements. Moreover, port authorities and rail operators across Africa—both instrumental for the required multi-modality—are actively seeking solutions to boost intra-African trade, reduce port congestion, increase port connectivity and throughput, and accommodate

---

43. 2050 Africa's Integrated Maritime Strategy (2050 AIM Strategy), AU, Version 1.0, 2012 https://au.int/en/documents/30928/2050-aim-strategy, op. cit. p. 27.

the next generation of ships being developed around the world in the wake of the latest Panama Canal upgrade and expansion. Of particular importance will be the opportunity to drive the development of transport infrastructure and vehicle and vessel fleets along a path that allows the continent to directly engage the maritime sector's energy transformation and its approach to climate change adaption. This integration of efforts would help green African ports and fleets and contribute to another technological leapfrogging in the realm of the blue economy and related maritime activity in Africa, as has already been occurring in the telecommunications and agricultural sectors.

Program for Infrastructure Development in Africa (PIDA)

Africa's Program for Infrastructure Development in Africa (PIDA) aims to develop a vision and strategic framework for the development of regional and continental infrastructure in the areas of energy, transport, information and communication technologies (ICT), and trans-boundary water resources.

The PIDA initiative is the successor to the NEPAD Medium to Long Term Strategic Framework (MLTSF), and is led by the African Union Commission (AUC), the NEPAD Secretariat and the AfDB.[44] PIDA is the key AU/NEPAD planning document and programming mechanism for guiding the continental infrastructure development agenda, along with its policies and investments priorities in transport, energy, ICT, and trans-boundary water sectors over the period 2011–2030. It will also provide the much-needed framework for engagement with development partners willing to support Africa's regional and continental infrastructure. Through the PIDA study, *Africa Transport Sector Outlook—2040*,[45] an African regional infrastructure development program was defined and underpinned by a strategic framework and implementation arrangements aiming to respond to the expected rising transportation demand resulting from continued economic growth on the African continent.

---

44. PIDA is managed through a governance structure that comprises a steering committee which is chaired by the AUC (charged with the role of providing program orientation and ultimate approval). The steering committee also includes the NEPAD Secretariat and engages the AfDB as the Executing Agency.

45. Programme for infrastructure Development in Africa (PIDA) - Africa Transport Sector Outlook—2040—produced by experts from AUC, the African Development Bank (AfDB), the NEPAD Planning and Coordinating Agency (NPCA), the United Nations Economic Commission for Africa (UNECA) and Development Partners (http://www.nepad.org/sites/default/files/documents/files/TOE-Transport-Outlook.pdf)

The PIDA analysis focuses on the major African freight corridors (as well as on the continent's international air transport system). Together these networks form the African Regional Transport Infrastructure Network (ARTIN). The ARTIN corridors carry 40% of international trade by African countries (and 90% of the trade of landlocked countries).[46] The 40 corridors selected for inclusion in the ARTIN (38 existing corridors and 2 new proposed corridors) are based on existing roads totaling some 63,000 km (out of a total of 2.3 million km in Africa). Of these ARTIN corridors, 16 also have competing or complementary railway lines (about 20,000 km). All of these corridors terminate at ports and/or link port-cities.

For the purpose of analyzing the transport infrastructure, the PIDA Study considers five RECs, four of them related to the Atlantic Basin, namely: AMU, ECOWAS, ECCAS, and SADC.

According to this study of the condition of the African Regional Transport Network (ARTIN):

- A quarter of the ARTIN roads are in poor condition with one tenth unpaved;
- Over half of the railways are in poor condition (including 100% in West and Central Africa);
- Most ports are in good condition but with little spare capacity in container terminals
- Lake and river transport offers good potential but is almost completely neglected.

There are more than 50 ports in Africa. Collectively, they handled more than 440 million tons of traffic in 2009 (excluding crude oil). All told, 19 ports are part of the ARTIN network. In their role as the entry gates and termination points of the corridors, these ports handle over 70 percent of Africa's foreign trade.[47] Most of these ARTIN ports are in good condition. However, the great majority are congested because port expansion, especially for container terminals, has been slow to respond to rising demand. The economic cost of ARTIN inefficiencies was estimated to US$172 billion in 2009. Suppressed freight demand accounted 38 percent of these losses, while another 43 percent were attributed to the inefficiencies of the corridors.

---

46. Not counting trade through non-corridor ports.

47. ARTIN also includes the major international airports (one per country), and the high-level air traffic control system. In total, ARTIN incorporates 53 airports which handle 90% of African air traffic.

Given the expected growth in economic output and international trade (6 to 8 percent per year), in 2014 a very large increase in demand for freight transport was projected up to 2040. The structure of African trade flows is also expected to change significantly over the next 30 years. Trade in ARTIN corridors is expected to grow faster than overall trade, as demand moves towards to the most efficient corridors.

In the future, containerized cargos will dominate port traffic and port traffic growth, while the importance of multimodal transport of containers will increase substantially along ARTIN corridors. Five countries (South Africa, Egypt, Algeria, Morocco, and Nigeria) account for more than half of total African trade, and they will continue to dominate in the future. Transit traffic from landlocked countries is expected to increase more than tenfold over the next 30 years, creating major infrastructure capacity problems. Planning to meet this demand should begin immediately.

Improved infrastructure would facilitate domestic and international trade, reduce the cost of doing business and enhance Africa's competitiveness both as an exporter and a destination for investors. Economists estimate that, overall, deficient infrastructure costs Africa 2 percent in reduced output each year.[48] Covering these infrastructure gaps ultimately will have a significant impact on major urban areas where intra-African consumption is likely to scale-up as welfare levels increase. This is expected to be higher in the port-cities where major hubs will be developed. On the other hand, the financial costs of closing Africa's infrastructure gap are vast. PIDA will cost around US$360 billion between 2011 and 2040,[49] with significant investments required by 2020. Such costs are beyond the financing capacities of governments or even donors. Attracting private sector participation through public-private partnerships (PPPs) is therefore essential for the delivery of various infrastructure projects envisioned under PIDA.

While many programs are in implementation across the continent—and some with significant relevance for the Atlantic Basin—there are two issues of note to consider in this analysis. First, the performance of cross-border transport needs to improve in order for the desired infrastructural effects to be achieved while minimizing bureaucratic red tape and other burdens. Cur-

---

48. Programme for Infrastructure Development in Africa (PIDA) - Africa Transport Sector Outlook—2040—produced by experts from AUC, the African Development Bank (AfDB), the NEPAD Planning and Coordinating Agency (NPCA), the United Nations Economic Commission for Africa (UNECA) and Development Partners (http://www.nepad.org/sites/default/files/documents/files/TOE-Transport-Outlook.pdf)

49. Ibid. p.83

Figure 3. ARTIN Transport Impact

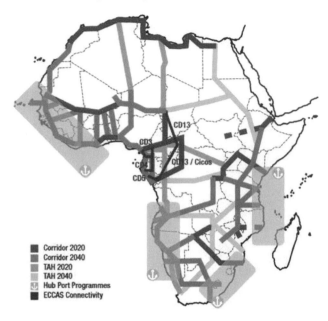

Source: PIDA, *Interconnecting, integrating and transforming a continent.*

rently, customs procedural constraints are still comparable to the current infrastructural gaps in posing real barriers to cross-border intra-African trade.

Second, although the objectives set in the Agenda 2063 treat climate change as a transversal policy theme that must be integrated into and across the different action plans, there are no specific references to the implementation of measures to address the use of alternative fuels in the future associated with the major PIDA programs.

But the projected growth of African urban areas and associated production clusters will demand the integration of policies—in particular, for the port-cities—in order to incorporate not just climate adaptation measures (which are driving investments towards renewable energy and hydropower), but also to include the use of the alternative fuels in the mobility vectors—including shipping fleets and the related logistics chain to be created in the ports—to further reduce GHG emissions and maintain air quality to acceptable levels.

Finally, as Chapter Two of this volume has revealed, the potential role of energy cooperatives in Africa and their capacity to provide renewable-based distributed power—for consumer and business use (lighting and machines), for home and industrial heating and cooling, for rural and urban mobility, and for low-carbon energy available for ports and ships at shore-side— should not be disregarded. Because the major energy programs in Africa are not necessarily the sole option for all purposes, smaller-scale cooperative projects can in fact contribute to a more decentralized response wherever it is required.

Monitoring the Transformation of the Port-Cities in the Atlantic Basin

Progressively greener Atlantic Basin port-cities (as presented in Part I) could act as facilitators of trade, stimulators of multi-modal transport transformation, generators of value added through the local port services and port-related industries and clusters, providers of specialized local employment, end-users of local research and innovation, protagonists of climate change mitigation and adaptation measures, and stewards of local air and water quality. But there will be no transformations of maritime fleets without a transformation in port planning logistics and this applies to the Atlantic Basin as a whole.

Much work has already been undertaken with respect to the key performance indicators informing the economic and social assessment of port-cities. However, not so much focus has been placed on their performance as environmental stewards, or as drivers of the transformation towards the use of alternative fuels. In order to generate a picture of the status and progress of such transformation, a monitoring process should be implemented—ideally through an Atlantic Basin Forum of Port-Cities—to track national policies, financial value chain support, and the implementation of appropriate infrastructure, equipment, and services in the port-cities themselves.

First-Level Monitoring

Linking National Policies and the Financial Value Chain to Support Transformation

Linking National Policy Frameworks (NPFs) with the financial value chain to reorient investments for the transformation towards a low-carbon, resilient blue economic model requires channeling financial flows to investments that are able to fulfill development objectives in all countries in a manner consistent and aligned with climate-related objectives. If climate change is addressed in terms of stovepipes (with efforts remaining isolated in silos), financial flows will not likely be sufficient to reach the scale of investment required to achieve long-term objectives. Therefore, such objectives (and the integrated process to avoid the stove-piping phenomenon) must be clearly considered when linking NPFs to the financial value chain by addressing financial instruments and other support mechanisms.[50]

Developing a comprehensive inter-sectorial approach is essential for this kind of reorientation of private investment and financial flows. This is essential if support for individual or isolated projects is to be shifted toward the support of the entire blue economy of countries, RECs and ocean basins.

To facilitate the implementation of effective NPFs and appropriately oriented financial instruments, a first level of monitoring indicators on the performance of this transformation process (and inspired by a study by Ian Cochran, Mariana Deheza, and Benoît Leguet on "The implications of 2015 for the Coming "Green Energy Revolution": Low-Carbon Climate Resilient Development"[51]) has been summarized in Table 6.

Second-Level Monitoring

Implementing Appropriate Infrastructure, Equipment, and Services to Support Port-City Transformation

A basic set of port information can be established for monitoring the performance of this transformation process across the entire Atlantic Basin. Such monitoring guidelines should take into consideration a selection of the most significant Atlantic Basin port-cities and involving all Atlantic coastal countries with very large and large ports. Despite the fact that smaller coastal countries are less relevant for the scale of the required greening contribution, inclusion of their medium and even small ports can help provide a coherent understanding as to how the respective infrastructures are being implemented to ensure connectivity at the basin scale. Table 7 in the Annex provides an example of a possible monitoring scorecard for Atlantic Port-Cities to be recurrently up-dated as part of the proposed Atlantic Basin Forum of Port-Cities.

---

50. Ian Cochran, Mariana Deheza, and Benoît Leguet,"The implications of 2015 for the Coming "Green Energy Revolution": Low-Carbon Climate Resilient Development," *Atlantic Currents: An Annual Report on Wider Atlantic Perspectives and Patterns*, The German Marshall Fund of the United States and OCP Policy Center, December 2016.

51. Ibid., p. 43.

Table 6. First Level Monitoring: Linking National Policies to the Financial Value Chain

Goal	Country Implementation of Specific Actions

#1: Economic environment creating demand for low-carbon maritime projects	• Establish NFP:
	  • to internalize externalities and overcome other general market barriers (i.e. carbon pricing, etc.)
	  • for regulatory and sectorial support frameworks
	  • for performance standards and regulations
	  • for subsidies to compensate for non-internalized externalities and other market failures and to foster development of new markets
	• Establish long-term price guarantees

#2: Incentives to project developers to build capacity and develop maritime projects in this area	• Cost reductions evident as project developers increase knowledge of financial models and prove investment bankability • Network of connections and specialized market players needed to catalyze shift in blue economy at the required scale, based upon port-cities clusters

#3: Foster the involvement of the entire financial value chain	• Government has signaled technological and investment priorities
	• Functioning of the blue economy financial value chain is properly ensured by supporting long-term investment and leveraging different capital sources
	• Programs by project type are targeted which:
	  • Improve capacity and knowledge of financial actors as to specific project and investment types.
	  • Reduce real and/or perceived risks to facilitate private-sector mobilization
	  • Overcome sector or project-specific obstacles to accessing the needed form of capital (volume, tenor, overly risk-adverse risk premium pricing, etc.)

Source: Inspired by and based on Ian Cochran, Mariana Deheza, and Benoît Leguet, "The implications of 2015 for the Coming Green Energy Revolution: Low-Carbon Climate Resilient Development" December 2016.

The Monitoring Network for the Atlantic Basin Port-Cities Transformation

In order to gain the broader picture of the process to be analyzed, and the challenges to be tackled collectively, a network of coastal countries needs to be established. To this end, coastal countries within the Atlantic Basin are shown in Table 8. For analytical purposes, they have been divided into four continental regional zones that involve Atlantic Basin coastal states (including all EU coastal member-states). Together with the coastal countries, a list of the most relevant RECs and other Regional Organizations (ROs)—assessed as important to both current and future stakeholders—to which they belong. As defended throughout this chapter, RECs are likely to be the major agents of change with the leverage to stimulate change which is beyond the reach of countries individually.

Conclusion

The sustainable development of the wider Atlantic—embracing the broad Atlantic basin and its coastal zones—requires a holistic approach. Such an approach should integrate, under a strong international governance platform, economic, social, and environmental pillars, as the foundation for a vibrant, growing blue economy.

To this end, the EU has developed a broad scope of strategic and governance mechanisms driving the process in favor of their Member States. This applies not just to the sectorial instruments but also to the integration of maritime policies, which should promote internationalization and establish coherent cooperation bridges across Atlantic RECs and UN organizations, agencies and authorities. Moreover, these RECs are likely to be the optimal driver for implementing this major transformational enterprise pivoting upon port-cities.

The African Union has also taken up the initiative in developing an integrated strategic framework adapted to the implementation principles of the African Economic Community. Investments in transport infrastructure and energy via the PIDA are significant. Other international development funds are associating themselves with this effort to provide an even larger scale response. Although the implementation of the PIDA programs could allow African capacity in this domain to leapfrog ahead—as it already has in the realm of IT infrastructure—the integration of climate change measures (particularly those necessary to address the use of alternative fuels in shipping and its associated logistics chain) is missing in current implementation, namely, for the targeted port-cities.

On the contrary, the RECs of the Americas are not yet engaged at such a level. Nevertheless, for the case of the United States, Canada, and Mexico, their national and state policies have shown boldness in moving ahead to implement ECAs to a scale that is not so evident in Europe. Control measures, addressing either air or water quality, are bound to expand their scope of intervention. Nevertheless, a more coherent implementation of monitoring and actionable instruments needs to be promoted. This applies to the establishment of future IMO ECAs in coastal state EEZs where current risks have already been identified.

Meanwhile, at sea, maritime shipping will increase steadily and will be more diversified in technical and operational terms. Furthermore, on land, inter-modality will be the most likely option for coping with the evolving mix of on-going maritime and port activities. Consequently, the transformation process towards the uptake of alternative energy fuel resources in maritime activities becomes an essential element to support blue growth.

To this end, harmonization of development strategies within port-cities, maritime spatial planning, and integrated coastal zone management planning needs to be properly ensured, along with an acceptance by port-cities of the timeline tyranny required by climate change adaptation.

Due to their unique concentration of a significant number of specialized human resources, scientific and technological research centers, and the equipment and infrastructure required to project the blue economy, to respond to an increasingly broader range of major and related societal challenges, port-cities are emerging as major players in enabling transformation towards the sustainable and sustained development of the activities that the blue economy embraces.

As best practices recommend, a monitoring process must be put in place not just to increase understanding about how slow and complex such transformation has become for the different sectors, but also to mobilize for engagement and to enable a fast pace of action.

A future body of discussion, such as an Atlantic Basin Port-Cities Forum would be a valuable tool for materializing such capacities and capabilities, and for driving and implementing such a transformation.

The manner in which transformation of energy use and transportation affects the blue economy cannot be ignored further. Even some 2025-2030 sustainability target measures should be anticipated, since sea-based emissions will surpass the land-based emissions by 2020 without any more effective preemptive measures put into place.

Annex

Table 7. Port-City Transformation Monitoring Card

Country	aaa...	Atlantic Basin Region	bbb...
Port	ccc...	Regional Economic Communities	ddd...
		Other Regional Organizations	eee...
Geographical Position		**Other Services**	
Latitude	dd°mm's'ss" N/S	Ship Repairs	Major
Longitude	dd°mm's'ss" E/W		Moderate
Position in relation to ECAs	Inside/Outside		Limited
Major Characteristics		Dirty Ballast	Yes/No
Port Type	Seaport	Local renewable energy production	Yes/No
	River Port	Main LNG Terminal	Yes/No
Port Size	Very Large	**Integration of Port-City Plans and Projects**	
	Large	Integration of the Port in the City Climate Change Adaptation Plan	Yes/No
	Medium	Integration of Urban Mobility Projects in the Port	Yes/No
	Small	**Intermodal Integration**	
Max Draft	In meters	Transshipment	Yes/No
Harbor Size	Large	Railway	Yes/No
	Medium	Motorway	Yes/No
	Small	Inland waterway	Yes/No
Maximum Vessel Size	Over 500 feet in length	Airway	Yes/No
	Less than 500 feet in length		
Harbor Type	Coastal Breakwater		
	River Tide Gate		
	Lake or Canal		
Provisions			
Fuel Oil	Yes/No		
Diesel Oil	Yes/No		
LNG	Yes/No		
CNG	Yes/No		
Hydrogen	Yes/No		
Electricity at shore-side	Yes/No		

Source: Own elaboration.

Table 8. Atlantic Basin Coastal Countries

Atlantic's Africa	RECs ROs	Atlantic's Europe	RECs ROs	Atlantic's North and Central America	RECs ROs	Atlantic's South America and Caribbean	RECs ROs
Angola	AU ECCAS SADC GGC	Belgium	EU EEA	Belize	OAS Caricom SICA LAES CELAC	Antigua and Barbuda	OAS Caricom OECS CELAC
Benin	AU ECOWAS WAEMU CEN-SAD	Bulgaria	EU EEA	Canada	OAS NAFTA	Argentina	OAS Mercosur SICA (observer) LAES CELAC UNASUR
Cameroon	AU ECCAS CEMAC GGC	Croatia	EU EEA	Costa Rica	OAS SICA CACM LAES CELAC	Bahamas	OAS Caricom LAES CELAC
Cape Verde	AU ECOWAS	Cyprus	EU EEA	Greenland	EU EEA NC	Barbados	OAS Caricom LAES CELAC
Democratic Republic of the Congo	AU ECCAS SADC GGC	Denmark	EU EEA CBSS NC	Guatemala	OAS CACM SICA LAES CELAC	Bermuda	Caricom (associated)
Equatorial Guinea	AU ECCAS CEMAC GGC	Estonia	EU EEA CBSS NC (observer)	Honduras	OAS CACM SICA LAES CELAC	Brazil	OAS Mercosur BRICS SICA (observer) LAES CELAC UNASUR
Gabon	AU ECCAS CEMAC GGC	Finland	EU EEA CBSS NC	Mexico	OAS NAFTA Mercosur (observer) SICA (observer) LAES CELAC UNASUR (observer)	Colombia	OAS Mercosur (associated) Caricom (observer) SICA (observer) LAES CELAC UNASUR
Gambia	AU ECOWAS WAMZ CEN-SAD	France	EU EEA CBSS (observer)	Nicaragua	OAS CACM SICA LAES CELAC	Cuba	OAS (suspended) LAES CELAC
Ghana	AU ECOWAS WAMZ CEN-SAD	Germany	EU EEA CBSS	Panama	OAS SICA LAES CELAC UNASUR (observer)	Dominica	OAS Caricom OECS
Guinea	AU ECOWAS WAMZ CEN-SAD	Greece	EU EEA	United States	OAS NAFTA CBSS (observer)	Dominican Republic	OAS Caricom (observer) SICA LAES
Guinea-Bissau	AU ECOWAS WAEMU CEN-SAD	Iceland	EFTA EEA CBSS NC			French Guyana	EU EEA
Ivory Coast	AU ECOWAS WAEMU CEN-SAD	Ireland	EU EEA			Grenada	OAS Caricom LAES OECS CELAC

Liberia	AU ECOWAS CEN-SAD	Italy	EU EEA CBSS (observer)	Guyana	OAS Mercosur Caricom LAES CELAC UNASUR
Mauritania	AU CEN-SAD AMU	Latvia	EU EEA CBSS NC (observer)	Haiti	OAS Caricom LAES CELAC
Morocco	AU CEN-SAD AMU	Lithuania	EU EEA CBSS NC (observer)	Jamaica	OAS Caricom LAES CELAC
Namibia	AU SADC SACU	Malta	EU EEA	St. Kitts and Nevis	OAS Caricom OECS CELAC
Nigeria	AU ECOWAS WAMZ CEN-SAD GGC	Netherlands	EU EEA CBSS (observer)	St. Lucia	OAS Caricom OECS CELAC
Republic of Congo	AU ECCAS CEMAC GGC	Norway	EFTA EEA CBSS NC	St. Vincent and the Grenadines	OAS Caricom OECS CELAC
São Tomé and Principe	AU ECCAS CEN-SAD GGC	Poland	EU EEA CBSS	Surinam	OAS Mercosur (associated Caricom LAES CELAC UNASUR
Senegal	AU ECOWAS WAEMU	Portugal	EU EEA	Trinidad and Tobago	OAS Caricom LAES CELAC
Sierra Leone	AU ECOWAS WAMZ CEN-SAD	Romania	EU EEA CBSS (observer)	Uruguay	OAS Mercosur LAES CELAC UNASUR
South Africa	AU SADC SACU BRICS	Slovenia	EU EEA	Venezuela	OAS Mercosur (suspended Caricom (observer) LAES CELAC UNASUR
Togo	AU ECOWAS WAEMU CEN-SAD	Spain	EU EEA CBSS (observer)		
		Sweden	EU EEA CBSS NC		
		United Kingdom	EU EEA CBSS (observer)		

Conclusion

Paul Isbell and Eloy Álvarez Pelegry

The conclusions and recommendations offered below are presented as *broad* and *general* (to be relatively synthetic and brief), *provisional* (based as they are on an initial and still incomplete analytical Atlantic map of the energy and transportation nexus) and *partial* (given that they are framed by the editors — if based on the analysis and conclusions of the authors). Nevertheless, they are suggestive and substantive enough to provide a worthy foundation for future research and policy explorations by the members of the Jean Monnet Network on Atlantic Studies, and by others, whether working within the budding epistemic community of the New Atlantic and pan-Atlanticism or beyond it in the more traditional national, regional or global frameworks.

General Conclusions and Broad Findings

Decarbonization of the transportation sector is an essential, indispensable component of any possible global defense of the 2-degree guardrail, as marked off by the Paris Agreement. This is true in the Northern Atlantic, but it is particularly true in the Southern Atlantic, where it also poses a greater underlying challenge.

Although both transportation energy demand and emissions have significantly slowed in the Northern Atlantic, they are growing rapidly in the Southern Atlantic. Under current projections transportation is poised to overtake the electric power and AFOLU (agriculture, forestry and land-use) sectors to become the largest greenhouse gas (GHG) emitting sector in the coming decades.

Maritime transport demand and emissions are on also the rise across the Atlantic Basin. As with the Southern Atlantic, current and expected future economic growth is one of the principal drivers. However, another important factor in the maritime realm is the relative lack of effective regulation, mainly because it remains beyond the effective and easy reach of land-based, national jurisdictions.

The energy and transportation sectors of the wider Atlantic world are increasingly subject to co-transformation. Put another way, increasingly the two sectors are beginning to change in ways that are mutually dependent on one another, as innovations and developments in energy open new possibilities for transportation infrastructure, and as innovation in transportation creates new horizons for energy. This creates synergies where the pathways of opportunity overlap.

Given the market and technological features of the current energy and transportation nexus in the Atlantic Basin, and in the face of the decarbonization imperative, co-transformation is understood as a self-reinforcing, synergistic process in which renewable energy rollout, battery storage deployment, electric vehicle (EV) penetration, dynamic grid modernization, distributed energy and prosumer participation[1] in the grid, all feed each other in the direction of wider and deeper electrification of the energy and transportation economy. Furthermore, ongoing development of information and communications technology (ICT) applications, together with innovative policy, business, market and regulatory models, could rapidly accelerate the energy and transportation co-transformations.

The energy and transportation co-transformations are most likely to accelerate first in the Northern Atlantic and on land. However, the potential exists for much of the Southern Atlantic to leapfrog over early phases of co-transformation, and for the land-based energy and transportation co-transformations to catalyze change in the maritime realm.

The energy and transportation co-transformations engage each of the strategic approaches of the EASI framework presented in the Introduction: to *enable* energy and transportation policy (e.g., the dynamic grid) to *avoid* future transportation demand and vehicle fleet growth (e.g., integrated urban policy, land-use, energy and transportation planning, along with new platform and sharing models for urban transportation), to *shift* such demand to higher occupancy transport modes (e.g., public transportation and mass mobility), and to *improve* the quality of the vehicle fleets in terms of fuel economy and emissions (e.g., vehicle fuel efficiency and emissions standards, and alternative vehicles and fuels).

---

1. A "prosumer" is defined by the U.S. Department of Energy, as someone who both produces and consumes energy—a shift made possible, in part, due to the rise of new connected technologies and the steady increase of more renewable power like solar and wind onto our electric grid. https://energy.gov/eere/articles/consumer-vs-prosumer-whats-difference.

If the co-transformations accelerate, the energy-transportation nexus of the Atlantic will begin to move toward: (1) progressive electrification of land-based passenger transportation; (2) a passenger modal shift from private light-duty vehicles to public transportation and mass transit, particularly in urban areas; (3) a fuel switch to liquified natural gas (LNG) for freight and cargo transportation on both land (in heavy-duty road vehicles) and at sea (in tanker and container vessels); and, over the longer run, (4) the partial electrification of land freight transport (through modal shift from road to rail); along with (5) partial electrification of maritime transportation (in smaller vessels and in ports at shoreside).

The factors and trends shaping the energy and transportation nexus and driving its co-transformation are diverse, but the most influential include:

1. the global policy imperatives to: (a) reduce GHG and air pollutant emissions; and (b) eliminate energy poverty and foster sustainable development and growth, particularly in the Southern Atlantic;

2. continued globalizing economic growth, deepening global value chains (GVCs), and ongoing expansion of maritime trade and transport;

3. the ongoing technological advances in renewable energy, battery storage, and electric vehicles, and the resulting and continuing drop in costs in all three interrelated markets;

4. the emerging potentials for dynamic grid modernization and transformation;

5. the catalytic impact on the energy-transportation nexus of a series of other potentially interlocking co-transformations in the ICT and related sectors, including manufacturing and trade, maritime affairs and regional governance.

The Land-Based Nexus of Energy and Transportation in the Wider Atlantic

The decarbonizing potentials for co-transformation of *land-based* energy and transportation are strongest, in the short to middle run, in the transportation markets that are the most mature, the most easily electrifiable, and where ICT and energy model innovations can rapidly transform grids that are dense and complex.

As such, the potentials for more rapid and deeper co-transformation—at least in the short and middle run—are more visible and immediate in the Northern Atlantic than in the Southern. In Europe and North America, nascent electrification of transportation, increasingly powered by renewable energy (both central grid-based and distributed), is already underway and gathering momentum, and it is currently poised for major infrastructural expansion. The total cost of ownership (TCO) of alternative-fuel vehicles is projected to equalize with those of conventional vehicles around 2025 (based on a recent study of the Basque country in Spain)—and this date is likely to be brought forward, if recent experience with renewable energy and battery cost reductions is any indication. The major unknown, influenced by future technological development, policy and political economy, is how intense this co-transformation will ultimately be, and how rapid (or slow) and how far-reaching (or limited) the resulting electrification of transportation.

In Africa and Latin America and the Caribbean (LAC)—where such electrifying co-transformation might appear farther off along the development horizon—there are, however, some other approaches with significant potential to stimulate the initial phases of the decarbonization of transportation in the short to middle run, and to lay the foundation for deeper electrification over the longer run. These include, for example, transport modal shifts and smart motorization management policies. In addition, by facilitating the modernizing process of dynamic grid transformation, ICT developments increasingly allow less mature markets in the Southern Atlantic to leapfrog over stages and configurations already passed through by the mature markets. As a result, it might be possible for LAC and Africa to engage the electrifying energy and transportation co-transformations more rapidly than would otherwise be the case. However, the pattern of electrification is likely be very different (and more distributed than in the Northern Atlantic), given that the central-grid-utility model of electric energy has limited reach in the Southern Atlantic, and given that energy poverty invites and favors off grid and micro-grid development.

The Northern Atlantic

The Northern Atlantic transportation sectors are mature, the average fleet is fairly young, and the private vehicle markets, under their current fossil fuel configurations, are relatively saturated. Broad anti-emissions efforts, underway for some time, have improved vehicle and fuel efficiency and quality, while fuel demand has levelled off and projected business as usual demand for transportation is also relatively flat. Because the opportunities for avoiding future increases in GHG-producing transportation demand have largely passed, the most pressing need is to improve the large vehicle fleet, from an economic and environmental standpoint. Therefore, vehicle and fuel standards, along with policy facilitation or promotion of alternative vehicles and fuels (and their accompanying infrastructures and market and regulatory models) remain at the forefront of academic research, policy debates and private sector innovation.

Nevertheless, some opportunities for emissions-cutting transportation modal shifts in the Northern Atlantic could also still be taken advantage of—for example, at least a partial modal shift of land-based freight transport from road to rail. This potential exists because LNG—increasingly considered the lower carbon bridge fuel substitute for diesel in truck freight transport—is still a fossil fuel. Natural gas emits about 75 percent of the CO_2 emissions of diesel, per million British thermal units (Btu) of energy. On the other hand, rail transport can be electrified more easily than heavy-duty road trucks (and more or less completely decarbonized if renewable energies eventually dominate the generation mix).

The Southern Atlantic

In the Southern Atlantic, the highest transportation policy imperative would be, at least in theory, to avoid future transportation emissions by eliminating future passenger transport demand, along with the attendant rise in the motorization rates and in passenger VKT (vehicle-kilometers-traveled). However, the most efficient way to do this—by developing dense, compact, multifunctional and economically aggregating cities which structurally eliminate the demand for motorization by providing for the possibilities of cycling, walking and more use of efficient two-wheel vehicles, in addition to public transport and mass transit—is less viable in the Southern Atlantic (particularly in Africa, if to a lesser extent in LAC).

The many imperfections in local land, property and other markets, together with a relative lack of effective urban policy planning, land-use management and adequate regulation, have led African cities, in particular, to sprawl in ways which reduce density. Nevertheless, with ongoing improvements in municipal, land-use and regulatory governance across an increasingly large and still growing cohort of large cities in the Southern Atlantic—whose continents have the highest and fastest urbanization rates in the world as well as the world's fastest growing cities—the potential for municipal and urban policy to avoid transport demand and emissions will increase—particularly if Atlantic Basin cities cooperate in these areas.

In the short to middle run, however, much of the potential to reduce transportation emissions in the Southern Atlantic is found in the possibility of provoking modal shifts from higher to lower-emitting transportation modes (or by improving or refining currently ongoing modal shifts, as in the continued development of public transportation and mass mobility programs in LAC). This would involve shifting passenger and freight traffic—both existing and that projected in the future—from (higher-emitting) road to (lower-emitting) rail, in general; and from (low-occupancy) private passenger vehicles to different forms of (higher-occupancy) public transportation and mass transit, both road- (BRT, or bus rapid transit) and rail-based (metro and light rail), in particular. Such public transportation-related modal shifts could be supported as well, particularly in LAC, by low carbon generated electrification of high use/high occupancy vehicles. Nevertheless, some modal shift options in the Southern Atlantic face entrenched barriers, including many of the same obstacles that complicate an avoid approach to transportation decarbonization.

It would seem obviously useful as well to attempt to improve the efficiency and emissions quality of vehicles and fuels in the Southern Atlantic, and to reduce the age profile of the fleet and related infrastructure. But this approach is partially undermined by the existence of international market and regulatory failures which are abetted by policy planning, regulatory and governance weaknesses in the Southern Atlantic. The combination of these failures and weaknesses leads to a form of emissions dumping or leakage.

Operating in both halves of the wider Atlantic, these market and regulatory failures combine to generate carbon externalities which are exported from the Northern Atlantic (and industrialized Asia) and dumped or leaked into the Southern Atlantic (and particularly into Africa) in the form of older, less-efficient, dirtier, higher-emitting secondhand vehicles. A global supply of such vehicles is continually created as increasingly stringent vehicle and fuel efficiency and emissions standards in the Northern Atlantic provoke their retirement from advanced economy fleets. Globally, at least 15 million—but as many as 35 million—light duty vehicles are estimated to be traded internationally as secondhand vehicles every year. They are easily (and principally) imported into LAC and Africa, where regulation and governance are relatively weak, tax income is still partly dependent on import tariffs, and a burgeoning, aspiring, would-be urban middle class provides strong structural upward demand for relatively cheap secondhand vehicles—along with a short term political motive to facilitate them.

However, another policy distortion relatively widespread in the Southern Atlantic provides yet additional support for secondhand vehicle demand: transportation fuel subsidies—which in LAC alone account for a quarter of the global total—push down the per kilometer cost of driving, increasing demand for private over public transport and slowing even further the development of alternative vehicles markets in the Southern Atlantic. As a result, by 2030 it is estimated that the secondhand vehicle trade will equal new car sales in the EU and China combined, unless new policy or cooperation intervenes.

Some Southern Atlantic countries prohibit secondhand imports, but many do not. In the absence of secondhand vehicle trade restrictions, this set of circumstances undermines the obvious improve approach open to the Southern Atlantic — that is, to establish and enforce progressively more stringent vehicle and fuel efficiency and emissions standards. Any such standards — which currently are largely and conspicuously absent from both continents — would be broadly circumvented by the steady flow of secondhand imports — which increasingly dominate private vehicle fleets (both light- and heavy-duty) in the Southern Atlantic (and particularly in Africa) — at least while they remain insufficiently regulated at the national, regional and international/transnational levels.

Grid Modernization as a Catalyst of Co-transformation at the Nexus of Energy and Transportation

Actions to *enhance the quality of the electricity grid* through modernization and dynamic transformation could constitute an essential contribution to the decarbonization of transportation in both the Northern and the Southern Atlantic. The dynamic grid and the distributed energy services model technologically *enable*, even catalyze, other avoid, shift and improve policies and actions impacting on the energy-transportation nexus and its co-transformation — much like the quality of governance and regulation institutionally enable these other policy approaches within the EASI framework.

The interlocking intersection — precisely at the energy-transportation nexus — of all the previously mentioned co-transformations (incorporating energy, transportation, ICT, manufacturing and trade) increasingly facilitates grid modernization and transformation. These overlapping co-transformations structurally favor the emergence of a dynamic grid in which central-station-based utilities, involved in generation and distribution under centralized grid management, increasingly co-exist with distributed energy and microgrids, interactive grid and demand side management, prosumer participation in energy generation and in provision of ancillary grid services, including significantly increased storage capacity as a result of the growing aggregate of plugged-in appliances (e.g., home batteries, hot water heaters and electric vehicles, among others). A dynamic grid transformation would reinforce the economic and scale logics of the electrification of both passenger and freight transportation, which in turn would feed further decarbonizing modal shifts from road to rail.

New organizational (market, business and regulatory) models, including sharing platforms, energy services companies (ESCOs), and energy (and related) cooperatives, could help stimulate a leapfrogging of the fossil-fuel-based central-grid model by contributing to the modernization and transformation of the dynamic grid in the Southern Atlantic, particularly in Africa. Dynamic grid transformation, in turn, would further stimulate renewable energy generation, EV penetration, and the electrification of transportation and the broader economy.

The Maritime Energy-Transportation Nexus in the Wider Atlantic

While the emergence of the dynamic grid has the potential to intensify the land-based energy and transportation co-transformations and to provide opportunities for technological leapfrogging, the maritime realm continues to represent a potential sink for the leakage of carbon and air pollutant externalities into the sea.

Deepening globalization—driven by containerization, declining shipping costs and proliferating global value chains (GVCs)—has created and absorbed significant new trade and transportation demand. But the transport sector has been allowed to externalize within the maritime realm the cost of ever greater shipping emissions (GHGs but also air pollutants). Maritime emissions are poised to continue growing over the next two decades and are projected to expand to over 5 percent of all GHG emissions (from under 4 percent as of recently). This is happening even as land-based transport emissions are beginning to slow under the regulatory effects of the global climate efforts represented in the Paris Agreement. This is in part because maritime emissions remain beyond the United Nations Framework Convention on Climate Change (UNFCCC) framework and are negotiated instead within the International Maritime Organization (IMO). The growing lure of the emerging blue economy[2] will only intensify the maritime leakage of these emissions externalities—unless action is taken to strengthen maritime governance, in general, and emissions control, in particular, across the Atlantic Basin.

---

2. Broadly defined, "blue economy" means ocean or marine economy; more tightly defined it has come to mean sustainable ocean economy, analogous to green economy within the land-based, continental contexts. For a discussion on the various competing definitions of the blue economy, see "What a blue economy really is—WWF's perspective," July 10, 2015 http://wwf.panda.org/homepage.cfm?249111/What-a-blue-economy-really-is.

Maritime transportation is a key element in the Atlantic (and global) emissions profile; but its true significance remains obscured if it is not considered in integral fashion within the more encompassing context of multi-model transportation networks which incorporate both terrestrial and maritime transportation infrastructures and flow routes (along with links to complementary and growing air transport).

Multi-modal transportation has been part and parcel of both the post-War and post-Wall phases of globalization. But during the most recent phase of the post-Wall period, characterized by the constantly shifting fragmentation patterns of global production and the intensifying development of global value chains, the notion of multi-modal transportation has been a particularly salient aspect of the energy-transportation nexus. Deepening global integration and intensifying global value chains not only stimulate increased trade volumes, but they also provoke ongoing shifts in trade routes and patterns. This in turn results in an expansion of multi-modal transportation journeys which incorporate both land-based and maritime transportation.

As the inter-modal interfaces of the global energy-transportation nexus, port-cities have an increasingly important role to play in this energy and transportation co-transformation. While maritime transport can facilitate, even catalyze, the blue economy, port-cities can bind, energize and direct it. Port-cities are the natural, if still potential, economic, technological and governance gateways and platforms for the co-transformations of the land-based energy-transportation nexus, empowered by dynamic grid transformation across the continental landmasses, to reach into and integrate with the maritime realm.

As the fulcrum of maritime and trade operations, hinterland transportation, and regulatory governance of overlapping land and maritime jurisdictions and policy areas, port-cities can strategically enable the related land-based co-transformations to catalyze their counterparts in the maritime realm. With the ongoing development of the nascent blue economy in the Atlantic, the energy, transportation and ICT co-transformations in the maritime realm are also poised to intensify, if port-cities can renovate their strategic operation and policy interfaces.

Recommendations

Recommendations for Energy and Transportation Policy

A number of broad policy recommendations for particular continents and transport modes are made by the authors. These include:

For Latin America and the Caribbean:

- More (and increasingly stringent) vehicle and fuel standards.
- More active motorization and fleet management policies (including feebates and vehicle registration tax emissions adjustments).
- Progressive elimination of transportation fuel subsidies.
- A broadening and deepening of modal shift to public transportation, urban mass transit and mobility.
- Electrification of high use/high occupancy vehicles such as taxis, buses, metros, light rail.
- A partial mode shift for freight from road to rail.

For Africa:

- Informal (paratransit) bus sector reform
- Policies to improve last-mile connectivity (supported by ICT and sharing platforms)
- Motorization and fleet management policy (including feebates for retiring secondhand vehicles)
- Freight logistics consolidation and partial freight modal shift to rail

For the North Atlantic:

- Establishment of specific targets for electric vehicle penetration
- Provision of more EV incentives and supports
- Grid modernization and dynamic grid transformation
- Incorporation of maritime emissions into the ETS and other emerging regional emissions markets

Recommendations for Pan-Atlantic Cooperation

The following are recommended areas and modes of pan-Atlantic cooperation in energy and transportation:

Pan-Atlantic Cooperation on Maritime Emissions Reduction

This could involve transnational cooperation (see below) between Atlantic coastal countries, regional economic communities, port-cities and the private sector, and the creation of an *Atlantic Forum on Maritime Emissions*. Specific agenda items could include the extension of IMO Emissions Control Areas to the broader Atlantic, and the inclusion of maritime emissions in the EU's ETS. Such cooperation would enhance the approach to improving the maritime transportation fleet in terms of vessel and fuels, efficiency and emissions of both GHG and air pollutants. It would also help close the carbon externality leakage from land to maritime jurisdictions, as a result of, among other factors, the development of global value chains—which have contributed to a reduction in maritime transport costs but also to a highly elastic response in terms of maritime transport demand and traffic volumes which have more than compensated for the high levels of carbon efficiency achieved by maritime shipping.

Pan-Atlantic Cooperation for the Greening of Maritime Energy, Transportation, and Climate Infrastructure

Compatible with the pan-Atlantic cooperation on maritime emissions just proposed (either in parallel with or as an integral part thereof), this could involve specific cooperation among Atlantic cities, but particularly port-cities, and the establishment of an *Atlantic Port Cities Forum*. The agenda could include data sharing and coordinated strategy planning, and policy and best practice development and exchange. The multiple synergies generated by effective city/port-city modernization and transformation would strengthen the enable approach to transportation decarbonization—grounded upon quality institutions, effective policy and land-use planning, and smart regulation and governance. This would in turn also support shift and improve approaches, both in the terrestrial and maritime transportation realms.

In shipping and other maritime vessels, such collaboration would facilitate both the fuel switch to LNG and the increasing provision of green energy in ports —produced both onshore and offshore, through the central-grid and from distributed sources—to ships at shore and during their approaches to and departures from port. Pan-Atlantic cooperation among Atlantic cities could also stimulate appropriate modal shifts for the land-based transport between port terminals and hinterland production sources and/or consumption destinations.

Pan-Atlantic Cooperation for Effective International Regulation of
Secondhand Vehicles Trade

This could involve cooperation among Atlantic Basin regulators, regional
economic communities and relevant private sector associations — in an
Atlantic Forum on Motorization Policy and Fleet Management — to seek
efficient and effective collaborative methods for reducing secondhand vehicle trade and promoting smart motorization management. The agenda could
be structured upon a *quid pro quo* of regulatory commitments on behalf of
both exporters and importers — possibly recycling of retired vehicles in the
Northern Atlantic and fiscally-neutral feebates (pioneered in France and
Chile) in the Southern Atlantic to encourage and support the displacement
of secondhand imports by newer, more efficient and lower-emitting vehicles.

Such pan-Atlantic transnational cooperation could improve regional/inter-
national policy planning, regulation and governance which in turn would
increasingly enable emissions-cutting improvements in the vehicle fleets by
overcoming international market and regulatory failures which continue to
delay the decarbonization of passenger (and freight) transportation in the
Southern Atlantic. This would help to stem the other carbon externality
leakage of retired higher-emitting vehicles imported from the Northern
Atlantic (and Asian) economies into the exploding Southern Atlantic transportation markets.

Pan-Atlantic Cooperation on Grid Modernization and Transformation

This could involve pan-Atlantic cooperation among a transnational range
of grid-relevant actors and grid-interested stakeholders in an *Atlantic Forum
on the Dynamic Grid*. The agenda might embrace the evolving role of utilities, new generation, distribution and business models, and best practices
for dynamic grid transformation.

There is enormous multiplying and amplifying potential of the dynamic
grid in both the Northern and Southern Atlantic, even if such potential would
follow geographically specific patterns in the different continents. Therefore,
there is long term value to pan-Atlantic collaboration that tests and accelerates
a new energy and transportation future, and the co-transformation at their
nexus, focused on local control and grid-optimization, enabling and enabled
by electrification.

As part of this pan-Atlantic grid cooperation, or independent of it, pan-
Atlantic cooperation could also take place directly among energy coopera-
tives and cooperative associations in North America, Europe, Africa and
Latin America: An *Atlantic Energy Cooperatives Forum*. Energy coopera-

tives already cooperate trans-Atlantically and globally; their operating methods, goals and objectives, and areas of action and potential overlay neatly with the possibilities of a more distributed and dynamic grid. Pan-Atlantic cooperation among energy cooperatives could facilitate dynamic grid transformation by serving as a most effective conduit and catalyst for Latin American and African leapfrogging of much of the Northern Atlantic's energy and transportation development phase, defined by the central-utility-grid model in energy and fossil fuels in transportation.

Implications for the European Union and Other Atlantic Actors

The implications for Europe, of both the conclusions and the recommendations, are large. The ongoing story of the Atlantic energy renaissance and the recent intersection of the energy, transportation and ICT co-transformations call out for EU pan-Atlantic initiative, if not outright leadership. Many characteristics which Europe (in general and the EU in particular) has acquired over time now overlap in a synergistic way such as to recommend a concerted effort to exercise leadership in the creation of a tangible, useful pan-Atlantic transnational space in energy, transportation, and broad maritime affairs.

Europe is not only one of the original sources of the pan-Atlantic idea; it is also one of the world's regional leaders—if not the leader—in the nascent energy, transportation and related co-transformations already underway. Europe is also the global regional leader in the interdisciplinary integration of strategic and policy planning and execution, in the crafting of related domestic and international EU strategies and policies in ways that are consistent with—and reinforcing of—each other's objectives and dynamics. In the international governance realm, the EU has also long been a pioneer of transnational cooperation. This is evident in the EU's approach to climate change and maritime governance.

Not only is Europe experienced and innovative enough to take the catalytic lead in the construction of pan-Atlantic, transnational cooperation, it is also big enough to have an effect. The specific weight and gravity of the EU and broader Europe within the energy, transportation, climate and trade sectors of the Atlantic Basin is large enough to overcome, and perhaps even to fill, the relative vacuum created by the retreat of the U.S. from the global climate regime embodied in the Paris Agreement and from the most recent cyclical cresting of the quest for effective global governance.

Europe has the international credibility and weight to catalyze cooperation across the Atlantic Basin. The EU's regional integration, its integrated strategic policy planning capacities, and its strategic global posture with respect to governance (with its transnational map of relevant actors), all serve at least as inspirational models in the Southern Atlantic. However, Europe's leadership role in the pan-Atlantic space should focus primarily on providing initiative to such pan-Atlantic cooperation projects and initial support to galvanize their activities—as opposed to directly managing the agenda or imposing EU models upon the Atlantic.

This is because both the challenges and the opportunities of the energy and transportation co-transformations in the pan-Atlantic context exhibit strong transnational features: (a) they have a regional, international or global reach (and are therefore beyond the capacity of any single country to decisively influence) and (b) they involve and affect a broad cross-section of actor and stakeholder agents. Therefore, the EU will need a range of different kinds of Atlantic partners in this endeavor, each contributing their own unique capacities.

Transnational cooperation is not just multinational, whether regional, transregional or interregional; it is also, crucially, multi-actor and multi-agent. It is based on, and comprised of, not just formal national representations or relations between states (and sometimes not even), but also other geographical and spatial levels of governance—both from scales larger than the state (i.e., regional organizations and regional economic communities, or RECs, to which nation-states belong), and from smaller scales (i.e., sub-state regions and cities)—along with non-state actors, including civil society groupings, academic and strategic studies communities, non-governmental organizations and the private sector.

This means that, in addition to the EU, the Atlantic Basin's other regional economic communities (or RECs) also have an important strategic role to play in pan-Atlantic transnational cooperation on energy, transportation and the related maritime realm. Among other capacities, RECs are essential cooperative agents for the integration, coordination and tracking of strategies.

Atlantic Basin cities—both in the Northern and Southern Atlantic—and particularly the Atlantic port-cities, also have a special and transformative role to play in any pan-Atlantic energy and transportation future. Atlantic port-cities should become the central nodes in a pan-Atlantic network of multiple types of transnational actors collaborating and cooperating on a series of overlapping pan-Atlantic maritime issues linked to energy-transportation nexus.

The private sector is a key source of information, finance and infrastructure, and an underlying driver of the energy, transportation and blue economy activity that gives rise to the need for pan-Atlantic transnational cooperation. Civil society groups, including NGOs, are also key actors in transnational cooperation, in their role as essential stakeholders for providing balance and input to the private sector. In a similar way, academic and strategic studies provide a third-party-assessed analytical support to the public sectors of multi-level-state governance.

A series of transnational Atlantic Basin cooperation platforms—the *Pan-Atlantic Forums*—could embrace energy, transportation, maritime and related realms, and could be supported and engaged by Atlantic governments, Atlantic regional economic communities (including the EU, in a key leadership and catalytic role), Atlantic port-cities, cities and regional-subnational governments, the relevant and interested Atlantic private sector, along with Atlantic civil society organizations and strategic studies centers.

The proposed *Pan-Atlantic Forums* could be developed under the auspices of the Jean Monnet Network on Atlantic Studies (directed by the Fundação Getulio Vargas), the Atlantic Basin Initiative (of the Center for Transatlantic Relations at Johns Hopkins University SAIS), the Atlantic Dialogues (of the OCP Foundation and OCP Policy Center), the Wider Atlantic Program (of the German Marshall Fund of the U.S.), or the legacy network of the EU's FP7 Atlantic Future project (formerly directed, and still stewarded, by CIDOB)—or under any combination of partnership or consortium involving of any or all of the above institutions.

Limitations, Gaps and Future Research

Admittedly, this book has limitations—many of them imposed by the typical constraints of resources and time which almost inevitably force the editor to triage certain potential areas of coverage. As a result, there are some gaps in the initial, analytical Atlantic map of energy and transportation surveyed by this book. We explicitly identify some of them here, providing some attempt at justification, along with some additional comment on their potential significance and place within an ongoing agenda for future research and treatment.

The nearly complete absence of *air transportation* from the book's discussion clearly constitutes a gap. The reason is found in the justification given by Viscidi and O'Connor in Chapter Four when explaining their focus on passenger and urban public transportation in LAC, and their exclusion of maritime and air transport from their analysis: priority of coverage was given to the modes with the largest current and future projected market and emissions shares. Beyond land-based transportation, the book gave priority of coverage to maritime transport. Nevertheless, air transport remains an important element to eventually incorporate, particularly as ICT and the cybereconomy enable the freighting of small, light consumer goods by air.

Biofuels, the first major substitute for oil in transportation, are also only lightly touched upon. Although biofuels are key in Brazil, and could contribute eventually to some of the fuel mix in parts of Africa, they remain in partial competition with electrification, and as liquid fuels they are at least partially dependent on the fate of the traditional fossil-liquids based transportation system. While it is difficult to see Brazil reversing its path on biofuels and bioenergy, the fact that LAC's largest country will likely remain with a mixed transportation system—based on some balance between the traditional liquids-based transportation infrastructure (if increasingly supplied with biofuels as opposed to gasoline and diesel) and electrified transport (perhaps concentrated in urban public transportation, mass transit and mobility)—means that land-use competition could intensify, as biofuel production places greater agricultural land-use demand upon Brazil's tropically-sensitive AFOLU sectors. This, in turn, will increase the premium not just on land-use planning, forest protection and restoration of degraded lands, but also on the *strategic coordination and integration of energy, transportation agricultural, land-use and forestry policies*. A continued strategic bet by Brazil on biofuels would require it to more effectively integrate the energy and land components of climate strategy. The potentials and limits of such strategic coordination of climate policy, particularly in Brazil, remains as an important future research agenda item.

The United States—usually an obligatory, and privileged, vantage point in any transatlantic or pan-Atlantic discussions and framings, if not the leading focus—has also not be treated independently or at length. However, developments in the U.S., and their evolving contexts, are touched upon in a comparative way by at least half of the authors. Furthermore, there is also a widespread and intensifying Atlantic perception of U.S. retreat from climate (and even global) leadership, and at least a temporary return to a nationalist, fossil fuel privileged energy policy. This perception, in turn, has fostered a sense of prudence among those accustomed to headlining U.S. reality and perspectives precisely because of that long-established leadership role, given that this retreat and reversal were relatively unexpected and very large in their potential consequences, like Black Swans. Furthermore, the recent U.S. retreat from the Paris Agreement, in addition to its continued absence from the UN Law of the Sea Treaty, is one of the underlying motivations for this book's recommendation that Europe take the initiative on pan-Atlantic cooperation in energy, transportation and maritime affairs, collaborating with the full range of US actors, but placing the priority of stimulating transnational cooperation which embraces the Southern Atlantic.

The future potential of *ocean energy*, including offshore wind, has also not been incorporated; however, this too remains a research agenda item for the future. Important research and analysis also remains to be undertaken on the impacts of energy and transportation decarbonization on the *future patterns of maritime trade (particularly international energy trade)* and on shipping and port infrastructure, as well as on *the future evolution of what we know as the geopolitics of energy,* and the *wider implications for geopolitics* in general. While such themes are very relevant to energy and transportation, they are also integral to a discussion of Atlantic trade and security, the next items on the Jean Monnet Network research project agenda, and can therefore be undertaken and incorporated with time.

About the Authors

Eloy Álvarez Pelegry is the Director of the Energy Chair at Orkestra, the Basque Institute of Competitiveness, located at Deusto University in Bilbao, Spain. Dr. Álvarez received his PhD in Mining from the Higher Technical School for Mining of Madrid (ETSIMM). He holds a bachelor's Degree in Economics and Business from the Complutense University of Madrid, and a Diploma in Business Studies from the London School of Economics. His career has been devoted to the field of energy. He has had a long executive career at Union Fenosa in Spain. He has had a parallel career in the academic field as an Associate Professor at the Higher Technical School for Mining of Madrid (ETSIMM), the Complutense University of Madrid, the Spanish Energy Club (where he was an Academic Director), and Deusto University. He is a member of the World Energy Resources Study Group Meeting of the World Energy Council (WEC). He has published more than 35 articles, various books and has given more than 100 public presentations. He is a member of the Energy Group of the Elcano Royal Institute and of the Energy Group of the Engineering Institute. In 2012 he was named to the Real Academy of Engineering.

Jordi Bacaria is the Director of CIDOB, the Barcelona Centre for International Affairs, the lead institution in the recent ATLANTIC FUTURE project of the European Union. He holds a degree in Economics (1975) and a PhD in Economics (1981) from the Autonomous University of Barcelona (UAB). From 2000 he has been co-director of the Institute for European Integration Studies in Mexico, an institution that is funded by the European Commission and the Autonomous Technological Institute of Mexico. He is also director since February 2009 of the journal *Foreign Affairs Latinoamérica* published in Mexico. He is a member of FEMISE (Euro-Mediterranean Forum of Economic Science Institutes) and evaluator of ANECA (National Agency for Quality Assessment and Accreditation of Spain). He has also been Dean of the Faculty of Economics at the UAB (1986–1988) and director of the Institute for European Studies (1988–1992, 1994–2000). From 2000 to 2009, he coordinated the Doctoral Program in International Relations and European Integration of the UAB. He is the author of publications on economic integration, Latin America, Mediterranean economy, monetary institutions and public choice.

João Fonseca Ribeiro is a Portuguese Navy officer with 25 years of service, most of which has been dedicated to naval operations, in deployed combined forces, communications and information systems, and international and interdepartmental cooperation and collaboration. He has participated in live operations in the Balkans, the Eastern Mediterranean and Africa. On land, he was the Portuguese national representative to the Allied Command for Transformation, as well as to the Command of the Joint Forces of the U.S., both in Norfolk, VA. He has held many high level posts within the Portuguese Navy and government, including as Division Chief for Operations and External Relations of the Navy and as Secretary of State for the Sea in the Portuguese Ministry of Agriculture, the Sea, Environment and Territorial Order. He has also been a key figure in the design of Portugal's national maritime strategy and a national representative at many organizations and governance bodies dedicated to the sea and the Atlantic, in particular. Currently, he is the CEO of Blue Geo Lighthouse, a firm dedicated to the maritime infrastructures of the Atlantic.

Roger Gorham is a transport economist and urban development specialist with the World Bank, with over 20 years of experience in urban transport, land-use, air quality, and climate change. He currently focuses on Latin America and the Caribbean, with projects in Ecuador and Haiti, but until recently, he worked extensively in Africa, with work on urban transport projects in Lagos, Addis Ababa, and Nairobi, among other cities. He also worked extensively with the Africa Transport Policy Program (SSATP), on urban transport and sustainability policy. He led efforts on behalf of the Bank and SSATP, in concert with the United Nations Environment Program and others, to support the establishment of an Africa Sustainable Transport Forum, whose inaugural meeting in October 2014 was sponsored by the Kenyan government. Prior to joining the World Bank, Mr. Gorham worked as a transport, climate change, and air quality specialist with the U.S. Environmental Protection Agency, and has also been a consultant for a range of international and private sector organizations, including the International Energy Agency, the International Transport Forum, and the Inter-American Development Bank, among others. He is the author of a number of publications and reports, including *Air Pollution from Ground Transportation* (United Nations 2002) and *Flexing the Link between Transport and Greenhouse Gas Emissions* (International Energy Agency 2000). Mr. Gorham holds a Master's of City Planning and Master's of Transportation from the University of California at Berkeley.

Paul Isbell is a Senior Fellow at the Center for Transatlantic Relations (CTR), Johns Hopkins University SAIS in Washington DC and a Senior Research Associate at the Elcano Royal Institute for International and Strategic Studies in Madrid. He has been a leading researching in CTR's Atlantic Basin Initiative and the research director of its Atlantic Energy Forum. He has taught energy and geopolitics, international economics and global affairs at many leading universities across the Atlantic Basin (George Washington University, Syracuse University, ICADE-Pontificia Comillas, University of Alcala de Henares, and the Technological Institute of Buenos Aires-ITBA, among others). He has worked as an emerging market economist for Banco Santander, and as a private consultant for regional development banks, international NGOs and research institutions, and private companies in the fields of energy, land-use, climate change and geopolitics. Currently he is the leader of the energy component of the Jean Monnet Network Project on Atlantic Studies, on behalf of the Center for Transatlantic Relations, Johns Hopkins University SAIS.

R. Andreas Kraemer is Founder and Director Emeritus of Ecologic Institute in Berlin, Germany and Founding Chairman (pro bono) of Ecologic Institute US in Washington DC. He is currently Senior Fellow at the Institute for Advanced Sustainability Studies (IASS) in Potsdam (Germany) and the Centre for International Governance Innovation (CIGI) in Waterloo (Ontario), Director (non-executive) of the Fundação Oceano Azul in Lisboa (Portugal), and Visiting Assistant Professor of Political Science and Adjunct Professor of German Studies at Duke University. His research focuses on the role and functions of science-based policy institutes in theory and practice in different political systems, the interactions among policy domains and international relations, and global governance on environment, resources, climate, and energy.

Macarena Larrea Basterra is a senior researcher at Orkestra (the Basque Institute for Competitiveness) at Deusto University in Bilbao, Spain. She holds a Ph.D. in Business Advertising and Development from the University of the Basque Country. Her research is centered mainly on energy and climate issues, such as the energy sector, and energy, climate and industrial policies, especially within Europe and Spain. She has a Master's Degree in Management of Port and Maritime Businesses run by the University of Deusto in conjunction with the Basque Country School of Maritime Administration, and has a Degree in Business Administration and Management, specializing in Logistics and Technology. She was awarded a Professional Qualification grant in the areas of European Matters and Inter-Regional

Cooperation from the Basque Country General Secretariat of External Action.

Martin Lowery is Executive Vice President, Member and Association Relations of the National Rural Electric Cooperative Association (NRECA) with overall responsibility to ensure that NRECA excels in meeting the needs of its 1,000 member cooperatives. His career at NRECA began in 1982 and includes managing NRECA's Consulting, Training and Market Research Division, providing essential management services to the NRECA membership. Martin serves on the National Cooperative Business Association (NCBA) board and is a past Chair. He also serves on the board of the National Cooperative Bank (NCB), the Ralph K. Morris Foundation board and is the U.S. representative to the International Cooperative Alliance (ICA) board. He has spoken extensively in the U.S. and around the world on behalf of cooperatives, was instrumental in the creation of the Touchstone Energy Cooperatives brand used today by most electric cooperatives and provided leadership in the creation of the first electric cooperative in the state of Hawaii, Kauai Island Utility Cooperative. Martin was recognized at the annual Cooperative Hall of Fame Dinner and Induction Ceremony at the National Press Club in Washington, DC, on Wednesday, May 7, 2014.

Jaime Menéndez Sánchez is Mining Engineer and Major in Energy from the University of Oviedo. He works as research assistant in the Energy Chair of Orkestra (the Basque Institute for Competitiveness, University of Deusto), where he has participated on research projects focused on energy transitions and sustainable transport. Part of his studies were carried out in the Technical University of Ostrava (Czech Republic) through an Erasmus grant. This was followed by a grant by EDP for an internship in that company (in the Department of Environment, Sustainability, Innovation and Quality, where he participated in the development of the Lean Programme and other activities). In 2015 he was awarded with the CEPSA Prize for the best Degree Final Project on Exploitation and Exploration of Hydrocarbons

Rebecca O'Connor is a program associate in the Energy, Climate Change and Extractive Industries Program. She has contributed to the program's research on topics including U.S. energy policy and its effects on Latin America, clean energy innovation, electric transportation, and the commodity price decline's effects on the region. Her articles have been published in the *New York Times*, *Foreign Affairs*, *Mexico Energy and Business Magazine* and *Instituto per gli studi di politica internazionale* (ISPI).

Natalia Soler-Huici, is a member of the CIDOB research group at Jean Monnet/ Network on Atlantic Studies. Her research focuses on International Regulation of Emissions from the Maritime Industry. She graduated in Law from the Autonomous University of Barcelona (2011). She holds a Master's Degree in Enterprise Law from the Autonomous University of Barcelona (2012) and a Master's Degree in Environmental Law (LLM) from the University of Iceland (2016). Natalia has worked on the field of personal data protection (Barcelona) and enterprise law (Luxembourg). Based in Iceland since 2013, she has worked as a representative in Iceland of the Network for European Studies (Canada) and as a translator.

Lisa Viscidi is the director of the Energy, Climate Change, and Extractive Industries Program at the Inter-American Dialogue. A specialist in Latin American energy, Viscidi has written numerous reports and articles on energy policy and regulations, oil and gas markets, climate change, social and environmental impacts of natural resources development, and the geopolitics of energy. Previously, she was New York Bureau Chief and Latin America Team Leader for Energy Intelligence Group and a manager for Deloitte's energy practice.